Hidden In A Book

~~Forty Acres & Mule~~
$40 Trillion——Keep the Mule

Larry Kenneth Alexander

Copyright © 2019 by Larry Kenneth Alexander.

All rights reserved. No part of this publication may be reproduced, distributed, or transmitted in any form or by any electronic or mechanical means, without the prior written permission of the publisher, except in the case of brief quotations embodied in critical reviews and certain other noncommercial uses permitted by copyright law.

Printed in the United States of America

ISBN: 9781691082919

Contact author at lalexander@metroworksusa.com

Table of Contents

Forward i

Preface vi

Britannia and the Southern Colonies Timeline xi

Chapter 1 Slavery in the American Colonies 1

Chapter 2 Dunmore the Emancipator 30

Chapter 3 Declaration of Independence 59

Chapter 4 Tenth Generational Dodge 84

Chapter 5 America's Slave Imagined 114

Chapter 6 America's Original Sin 142

Chapter 7 America's True Legacy 174

Chapter 8 Below The Rule of Law 204

Chapter 9 Commander to Commander 231

Chapter 10 Restitution Opposed to Reparations ... 260

Chapter 11 The Legal Right to Restitution 283

Conclusion 312

Acknowledgments 338

Bibliography 339

End Notes 353

Forward

How would our view of reparations, restitution, restorative justice (or whatever other term one might prefer) be affected if history confirmed that slavery in England's colonies had been declared illegal well before the American Revolution? What if, before the founding of our Nation, everyone held in bondage had actually been confirmed by Great Britain's highest court to possess the full rights of English citizenship? In our view, that's exactly what happened.

In the beginning, way back in 1619, the first nineteen Africans arriving on the shores of Virginia were understood to have had the status of indentured servants, in accordance with English common law. In short, they possessed the same "rights of Englishmen" as all other Virginians. For this reason the subsequent "legalization" of slavery by colonial legislatures was anything but that. Instead, as English common law decreed, those enslaved by white colonists throughout the 17th and 18th centuries actually retained their rights as citizens even as they were treated as "chattel property." With respect to English legal precedent, they were, by common law definition, as free as those who bought and sold them.

This truth received powerful reaffirmation in the 1772 *Somerset vs. Stewart* case, when England's highest court declared that slavery was "not allowed or approved by the laws of this Kingdom" and could only be enacted through the application of "positive law." None of the colonial slave codes qualified as "positive law" as they had not been *officially* approved by the British parliament, in which the King participated directly. Moreover, in the aftermath of the Stamp Act Crisis (1765-67) Parliament anticipated this point very directly when passing the Declaratory Act making it clear that it, with the King included, should "legislate over the colonies in all cases whatsoever." English law alone was to prevail within the colonies. According to the *Somerset* Decision and the Parliament mandated to enforcing it, the enslaved held every right in British citizenship, that is, freedom from chattel bondage, but not, we must hasten to add, the expectation of political or social justice.

Not that this made a whit of difference to the profit-hungry English slavers who delivered an estimated 310,000 shackled West Africans to the Colonies between 1660 and 1776. In this vital respect, Somerset was truly a dead letter decision and also a Decision that left colonists uncertain as to whether or not Mansfield had intended his decision to apply outside England proper.

But such issues are not germane when thinking historically about reparations, restitution, or restorative justice. What counts is that while *Somerset* had ruled for freedom as binding jurisprudence, the enslaved behaved as if it had force by behaving like profoundly rights-deprived people. They fled, resisted and rebelled. When they did so during the Revolution, British imperialists and rebellious colonists well-versed in Somerset assumed that the "rights of Englishmen" pertained to these black rebels and acted accordingly.

None was more sensitive to this situation than slaveholding Thomas Jefferson, whose indictment of the King as an emancipator of the enslaved was edited out of the Declaration of Independence at the last minute by zealously proslavery colleagues. After blaming the King (not himself and fellow slaveholders) for fastening black bondage upon the unwilling white colonists. Jefferson concluded by accusing the King of:

> "...exciting those very people to rise in arms among us, and to purchase that liberty of which he has deprived them, by murdering the people on whom he has obtruded them; thus paying of former crimes committed against the Liberties of one people, with crimes which he urges them to commit against the lives of another."

Along with its gross-deception Jefferson's indictment persuasively documents his fearful concerns over Somerset's applicability on his own Virginia plantation. Though once dead in this beloved

Monticello, Somerset had come into force in 1775 when its Governor Lord John Murray Dunmore issued a Proclamation promising freedom to those enslaved who took up arms in opposition to the Patriot cause. As Dunmore saw it, all the colonists, not just the white ones, held English citizenship and the Patriots who now rejected it were nothing more than traitors while slaves who picked up arms were doing their duty as English citizens. In short, his view and Lord Mansfield's *Somerset* decision lined up perfectly. English law made slavery illegal in its colonies.

Leaping ahead to the end of the Revolution, in 1783, and to the aftermath of the Treaty of Paris that confirmed British defeat we find George Washington struggling to deny this truth during negotiations with British General Guy Carleton. Carleton insisted that black as well as white loyalists who had been captured by the Americans were in point of legal fact English citizens and always had been. They must therefore be fully included when the two exchange prisoners. Claiming that black loyalists had been declared by Colonial statute to be human property long before the Revolution, Washington refused and the stalemate was broken only after the two negotiators had agreed that each should compile registries listing the captured black loyalists by name in American and English versions of what became known as *The Book of Negroes*. These listing, it was agreed, would serve as the basis for further negotiations that led to still further disagreements.

Though Carleton had capitulated he did manage to secure the liberty for a fraction of the captured

American black loyalists (3,000 or so). In his eyes, as English law required they had reclaimed their citizenship. In the end, for them, the *Somerset* Decision restored their "rights as Englishmen," which confirms once more that after 1772, enslavement within the colonies had been patently illegal.

Dr. James Brewer Stewart
James Wallace Professor of History Emeritus
Macalester College, St. Paul, Minnesota
Founder, *Historians Against Slavery*

Preface

Often, I'm asked how did you get interested in the topic? What's the meaning of the term, "America's native son" and why write this book?

My DNA history report establishes that I am of African ancestry, mixed with Cameroon/Congo, Benin/Togo, and British. The report highlights that my ancestors settled in colonial Virginia, and "migrated" to varied southern states, and were sharecroppers. A tenth generation American, born in Memphis, Tennessee—though my family left the segregated south during my infancy, and I was raised on the west-side of Chicago. As a young son of the South, I was active, enthusiastic, and curious about everything, and while most people come to history late in life... I did not. I bought my first history book at ten... titled *Great Negroes Past and Present*.

This book introduced me to so many lesser known historical facts causing an epiphany—there's countless, historically consequential black people, and relevant, empowering events not mentioned in America's history books.

It was boundless curiosity, an unrequited thirst for knowledge that led me to discover the noted Lord Chief Justice Mansfield who delivered the *Somersett* decision in June, 1772—the Court of the King' Bench's unanimous declaration that slavery was not allowed and approved throughout Great Britain; then Lord Dunmore, the Royal

Governor of Virginia who emancipated slaves before the Declaration of Independence in November, 1775. And my favorite, England's Queen Charlotte—the black wife of King George the Third... whose son George IV became England's first black King under America's "one drop of black blood" rule.

These blue-blooded Englishmen were marginalized in revolutionary writings, and U. S. history books, but all had important roles in the resulting American Revolutionary War of 1776. Though regretfully, their historical relevancy was purposefully, painstakingly airbrushed out of America's historiography. Such being the case, America's emergence is memorialized as fables, fabricated lies, and propaganda—not history, causing the miseducation of an entire nation.

Hereditary slavery's illicit origins, the *Somersett* decision and Lord Dunmore's executive emancipation of black Englishmen pushed Thomas Jefferson to bring a bill to adopt Roman law. However, Jefferson's bill failed, and the First Congress then adopted English law in 1776. Afterwards, all the States followed Congress' lead, by adopting English law and during the resulting civil war called the American Revolution—England reaffirmed its executive proclamation of liberty for black people, suffering as slaves. Then having endured five years of war and on the verge of financial collapse—the U. S. sued for peace. England negotiated for a status *quo antebellum* peace and the Americans agreed. However, the founding generation reneged and then they institutionalized the disfranchisement and enslavement of 500,000 black people—who were legally-free

Englishmen. This was a crass violation of international and Anglo-American law.

Years later, as a child I returned to Memphis, a truly sad occasion——the death of my grandfather. And one of my earliest memories about my family was formed at the cemetery when an elderly cousin remarked that my grandmother's father had been born a slave in Haywood County, Tennessee in 1862. She pointed to his marker——George Washington Peete, and with pride she said that his ancestors were slaves in colonial Virginia to George Washington and she beamed. I have never questioned the veracity or accuracy of my cousin's claim. During colonial times, and early America——slaves were given or adopted the names of their slave masters. In many parts of Europe, Africa and colonial America too——the surname is placed before a person's given name. And notwithstanding my ancestor's surname possibly being George Washington, my grandfather by two was named after his American-born slave father, and throughout his life called Pete. And I vividly remember thinking then——what if anything made "Poppa Pete"... George Washington's slave?

America's claim of fealty to the rule of law disappeared, as millions of black people disappeared behind a firewall of institutionalized inequality. Wealthy Americans, whose wealth and power was based directly or indirectly upon slavery were inaugurated to expect and receive superior treatment by the U. S. legal system, while others much less. It has proven to be the case. It is a legal system——not a justice system and spanning ten generations, my ancestors have called the U. S. home, yet I was the first in my family to attend and graduate a four-year college. The descendants of the enslaved black Englishmen and women were institutionally denied education——it was illegal to teach them to read or write. Thus, the racist anecdote developed that "if you want to hide something from a 'nigger'——put it in a book."

Purposefully, education was denied to blacks here in the U. S. and as a descendant of slaves I am grateful for the ruling in the 1954 case of *Brown v. Board of Education*. The Supreme Court declared state laws establishing separate public schools for black and white students to be unconstitutional. Affirmative action, a progeny of the historic ruling afforded me a first-rate liberal arts education at Macalester College in St. Paul, Minnesota, where I majored in history, and then the University of Iowa Law School.

In honing my critical thinking skills——at Macalester, there I openly questioned America's narrative, and it was hearing then former Vice-President Hubert H. Humphrey's insight, perspective who was then a professor at Macalester that opened my mind to the question I'd long puzzled. Having never been in the presence of anyone famous, I remember still how I gushed when he responded to my question: what is the test a country must use to claim itself to be a moral nation? He said:

> "The moral test of government is how that government treats those who are in the dawn of life, the children; those who are in the twilight of life, the elderly, and those who are in the shadows of life, the sick, the needy and the handicapped."

The profundities of Humphrey's words resonated, soared and would later roar——after I heard a first generation Lithuanian American; first——shaming a black community activist for his speech and then marginalizing his complaints about social issues. The man claimed America was a moral country, bound by the rule of law and immigrants made it culturally superior and he marked the late 1960s as the line for when America's cultural superiority began to decline. He also claimed the U. S. was a nation built by white people for white people. This was a false statement, as black slave labor built much of America's infrastructure from 1776 until 1865. Their uncompensated labor according to big data econometricians hovers between twenty-nine to forty trillion dollars——yet no one mention this fact, nor challenged him. That event, as well as in coming to terms with my slavery roots and obligations to my marginalized ancestors and America——I became purposeful, as my first youthful curiosity had already piqued me to answer the question: what made my great grandfather a slave——not too many years ago, this descendant of a slave began to write.

Britannia and the Southern Colonies Timeline

100,000 years ago Nigritic Africans migrated to the Americas——by way of Bering Strait.

10,000 years ago Cheddar Man thrived in England. He's a hunter gatherer who had dark brown skin, blue eyes, and Negroid features.

7,000 years ago Aboriginal black Native Americans migrated to the Mississippi Valley region of the southern United States.

43 AD The Roman Empire conquered England.

410 AD Roman rule ended in England.

1215 King John signed Magna Carta. The Magna Carta prohibited slavery in England and guaranteed justice for all under the rule of law throughout the British Empire.

1328 King Edward the Third married a woman of Moorish descent... Queen Phillipa. She's England's first black Queen consort.

1526 Enslaved Africans were part of a Spanish expedition to establish an outpost on the

	North American coast in present-day South Carolina.
1586	Scores of Africans plundered from the Spanish were aboard a fleet under the command of Sir Francis Drake when he arrived at Roanoke Island, Virginia.
1606	King James the First granted the first charter to the colony of Virginia and it memorialized that the colony will be bound by England's rule of law and the Magna Carta. Born in Virginia conferred British subjecthood per charter and all legal rights of being an Englishman.
1616	Africans in the West Indies were at work in Bermuda providing expert knowledge about the cultivation of tobacco.
1619	The first nineteen Africans are brought to Point Comfort, Virginia in British America. The rule of law officials made Africans indentured servants and after a proscribed period each was granted freedom and British subjecthood. Their children were born Englishmen.
1632	The colony of Maryland was granted a charter and it memorialized that the colony was bound by England's rule of

	law and the Magna Carta. Born in Maryland conferred British subjecthood.
1638	The New England slave trade begins in Boston.
1640	The legislative assembly of Virginia enacted a law that excluded blacks from the requirement of possessing arms.
1662	The legislative assembly of Virginia enacted a law of *partus sequitur ventrem*: chattel slavery. Any child born to an enslaved woman will also be a slave. It changed English law of *partus sequitur patrem* without the King's Assent.
1663	In Gloucester County, Virginia, the first documented slave rebellion in the American colonies took place.
1663	The colony of Maryland legalized slavery without the King's Assent.
1664	The legislative assemblies of Virginia, Maryland, New York, New Jersey and the Carolinas each passed a law that mandated lifelong servitude for black slaves without the King's Assent.

1676	The British created the "white race" in response to Bacon's Rebellion in Virginia where all classes within colony rebelled against British rule.
1667	The legislative assembly of Virginia enacted a law that baptism does not bring freedom to blacks.
1668	The legislative assembly of Virginia enacted a law that free black women, like enslaved females over the age of 16 are taxable. White women remained non-taxable.
1669	The legislative assembly of Virginia enacted a "casual killing of slave" law that if a slave dies while resisting his master, the act will not be presumed to have occurred with "prepensed malice."
1672	The legislative assembly of Virginia enacted a law that it is legal to wound or kill an enslaved person who resisted arrest. Owners of any slave killed as he resisted arrest would receive financial compensation for the loss of an enslaved laborer.
1680	The legislative assembly of Virginia enacted a law that it now legal for a

white person to kill an escaped slave who resisted capture. Slaves are forbidden to:
- arm themselves for either offensive or defensive purposes. Punishment: 20 lashes on one's bare back:
- to leave the plantation without the written permission of one's master, mistress, or overseer:
- "[to]... lift up his hand against any Christian." Punishment: 20 lashes on one's bare back.

1682　　The legislative assembly of Virginia enacted a law that made imported Africans—slaves for life without the King's Assent.

1689　　England's Parliament enacted Bill of Rights. The bill codified the liberty rights of all Englishmen. No Englishman can be born a slave.

1691　　The legislative assembly of Virginia enacted a law that any white person married to a black or mulatto is banished and could not stay in colony for more than three months after they are married.

- A mulatto child born to a white indentured servant would serve a 30-year term of indenture.
- A fine of 15 pounds sterling was levied against white women who gave birth to mulatto children. And if a woman could not pay the fine, she was condemned to serve five years as an indentured servant.

1692   The legislative assembly of Virginia enacted a law that slaves are denied the right to a jury trial for capital offenses. They also legislate that enslaved individuals are not permitted to own horses, cattle and hogs after December 31 of that year.

1702   England's Court of the King's Bench ruled in *Smith v. Browne & Cooper* that "as soon as a negro comes to England, he is free; one may be a villein [serf] in England, but not a slave."

1705   The legislative assembly of Virginia enacted a law that declared all non-Christian servants entering the colony to be slaves. It defined all slaves as real estate; acquitted masters who killed slaves during punishment; forbade slaves and free colored people from

physically assaulting white persons and denied slaves the right to bear arms or to move abroad without written permission.
- Determined that if a white man or white woman married a black partner, the white individual would be sentenced to jail for six months and fined 10 pounds current money of Virginia.
- Determined that any minister who married an interracial couple would be assessed a fine of 10,000 pounds of tobacco.
- Determined that any escaped slave who was unwilling or unable to name his or her owner would be sent to a public jail.

1708 The Southern colonies required militia captains to enlist and train one slave for every white soldier.

1708 Blacks outnumbered whites in South Carolina.

1712 The New York Slave Revolt of 1712. The American colonies restricted the importation of Africans into their colonies and encouraged domestic slave practices.

1729 The colonies of South and North Carolina were granted charters and each memorialized that the colony would be bound by England's rule of law and the Magna Carta. Born in either colony conferred British subjecthood per charter and all legal rights of being an Englishman.

1732   The colony of Georgia was granted a charter and it memorialized that the colony as bound by England's rule of law and the Magna Carta. Born in Georgia conferred British subjecthood and all legal rights of being an Englishman.

1735   Georgia's Assembly enacted slavery laws within the colony without the King's Assent.

1739   Slaves in Stono, South Carolina rebelled, sacked and burned an armory and killed whites. The militia put an end to the rebellion.

1751   King George II specially repealed Virginia's Slave Code of 1705.

1761   King George the Third married Sophia Charlotte, daughter of Duke Charles Louis Frederick of Mecklenburg-Strelitz——Queen Charlotte. She's a direct descendant of the black branch of the Portuguese Royal House. Under

	America's Black Codes—she's black and due to their interracial marriage Virginia's 1691 law outlawed the King and Queen.
1762	Queen Charlotte gave birth to George the Fourth, who upon birth was named the Prince of Wales; the heir apparent to the British throne. Under America's Black Codes—he's black.
1766	The Parliament enacts the American Colonies Act, commonly known as the Declaratory Act that operated as the formal end of Britain's unwritten policy of salutary neglect.
1770	Crispus Attacks, a black Englishman was the first person to die in Boston Massacre.
1772	A unanimous ruling in *James Somerset v. Charles Stewart*, Lofft I, 18-19, 98 Eng. Rep. 499, 509-510 (King's Bench, June 1772) by England's Twelve Judges that slavery was not "allowed and approved by the laws of this Kingdom" and can only be lawful by way of "positive law." Slavery was deemed unconstitutional throughout the British Empire and 15,000 native sons are immediately

	released from bondage in England and Wales.
1774	The First Continental Congress convened in Philadelphia to organize colonial resistance to Parliament's Intolerable Acts passed in May of the same year and vowed to discontinue the slave trade after the first of December.
1775	Lord Dunmore, the governor of Virginia declared martial law and granted freedom for all slaves held in bondage by colonial patriots. However, per English law, all slaves in American colonies are liberated.
1776	England's thirteen colonies declared themselves an independent nation and issued its Declaration of Independence in July. The first three grievances against King George III related to his failure to freely give his "Assent" to laws proposed by colonial assemblies. The First Congress of the U.S. conferred citizenship unto all free Englishmen and formally adopted English rule of law.
1779	England's General Henry Clinton issued The *Phillipsburg Proclamation* that declared freedom to all Revolutionary

War-era slaves and conferred British subjecthood unto Africans suffering as slaves in the American colonies.

1782   The United States sued for peace and preliminary articles of peace are finally agreed to and signed by the parties. England required that all its citizens be "set at liberty" and the United States agreed, as a condition for peace. All hostilities ceased.

1783   Abuses were rampant. Black Englishmen were terrorized by slave catchers, and England filed a formal complaint with the U. S. delegation which included George Washington. The delegation was informed that England took the position that former slaves, those born in colonial America were Englishmen under his Majesty's protection and that its practices of assaults and kidnappings had to cease.

1783   General Guy Carleton transported 3,000 black citizens out of the United States. Carleton and the U. S. both in respective registries called *Book of Negroes* journaled their names and other supporting information.

1784	Congress ratified the Treaty of Paris of 1783—but failed to release 500,000 black citizens, relegated them to slavery claiming black people are legal property of white Americans. The United States violated its first international treaty.
1787	Delegates convened a constitutional convention to draft a new federal United States Constitution.
1787	Congress reached a compromise to have an Electoral College and to count black Englishmen as three-fifths of the number of white inhabitants of that state for legislative and taxing purposes.
1788	Congress ratified the United States Constitution.
1790	Congress denied naturalization to a anyone who is not a free white.

To all the Sons and Daughters of the Enslaved, supporters and activists who have fought and continue to fight

"Slaves cannot breathe in England; if their lungs receive our air, that moment they are free... they touch our country and their shackles fall". William Cowper

Chapter 1
Slavery in the American Colonies

First principles require a study of colonial slave laws, and community from the beginning of the 17th century to the eve of the ratification of the U. S. federal constitution in 1789. In furtherance, I have tried to accomplish two tasks. Firstly, identify the beginning of colonial American slavery and the ways people used the colonial legislative system to create the extrajudicial institution called hereditary slavery; *partus sequitur ventrem*. Secondly—explain the legal consequence in the context of other, often related, England's declaration in 1772 that colonial slavery had not been legally instituted; emergence of the United States of America and then cooperative federalism. During the federal constitutional convention, the federal, state and local governments worked cooperatively and collectively to disfranchise and enslave black Englishmen. They, although British subjects and being under the protection of the Treaty of Paris of 1783 were made the bedrock of America's slave-based economy and slavery was institutionalized. To these ends, it melds legal with social history and offers a rethinking of the practice of hereditary slavery and the founding generation's kidnapping, disfranchisement and enslavement of 500,000 black people *after* the American Revolution.

The ethnic group Afro-Briton or commonly called black Englishmen—born in England's North American colonies predates the rise of the U. S. by over one-hundred and twenty-five years. However, this ethnic group of Englishmen were institutionally attacked and suffered under a species of tyranny called hereditary slavery beginning in 1662 when Virginia's legislative assembly purported to enact a law called *partus sequitur ventrem*. Virginia's colonial slave laws were never lawfully enacted since it was bound by colonial charter to English common law and suffered under a bicameral legislative system that required the assent of the British monarch on such laws. Virginia's legislative assembly failed to secure the British monarch's assent. Nonetheless, hereditary slavery became endemic throughout the American colonies due to graft, corruption and a culture of hooliganism. The practice of hereditary slavery became an extrajudicial institution and black Englishmen suffered during colonial times.

The long arc toward justice for black Englishmen began in 1749 or so, when the Englishman Charles Stewart, a customs officer purchased a Virginia-born slave named James Somersett—as his manservant in the colony of Massachusetts. [1] He spelled his surname with two "T's". [2] Then in the spring of 1769 James Somersett was taken to London, England—but by the fall of 1771 he'd surreptitiously left Stewart's service, abandoning involuntary servitude in search of freedom. But when he's recaptured in late November, 1771—he realized... freedom wasn't free. James was assaulted, beaten, and then imprisoned upon the slave ship—*Ann & Mary* that would be heading to Jamaica, along with captive Africans. And now James would be heading to a Jamaican sugar plantation—where few survived.

Stewart felt betrayal and as a punitive measure had engaged Captain John Knowles to sell James in Jamaica, as a sugar plantation laborer. But James' godparents, Elizabeth Cade, John Marlow, and Thomas Walkin became aware of his plight, and they petitioned the Court of King's Bench, and were granted a writ of habeas corpus. The habeas writ caused a hearing before Lord Chief Justice William Mansfield on December 9, 1771. [3]

During colonial times, legal cases decided by England's Court of King's Bench were not officially reported, [4] but there are five reports of the *Somersett* decision, although it was delivered orally by Mansfield on June 22, 1772.

1. An account in 34 *Scots Magazine* 297 (June 1772). [5]
2. Lofft I, 18-19, 98 Eng. Rep. 499, 509-510 (King's Bench, June 1772).
3. An account in the London *Gentleman's Magazine* 293-94 (June 1772).
4. An unsigned handwritten document in the Granville Sharp transcripts, New York Historical Society, captioned "Trinity Term 1772 On Monday 22 June 1772 In Banco Regis.
5. An account in the *General Evening Post* of June 21-23.

At the resulting habeas hearing on January 21, 1772, Charles Stewart claimed lawful ownership of James Somersett based upon Virginia's slave law. James' lawyer disagreed and asked Mansfield to be allowed to prepare a legal response to this claim and the request was granted. The case was heard on February 7, 1772. James' lawyers argued that slavery was a legal fiction in the Kingdom of Great Britain and by extension—colonial America. England's Parliament had never enacted a law allowing and approving slavery and while Virginia's colonial assembly might have enacted a law permitting slavery, any such "law" was extrajudicial in the

Kingdom, and a nullity under English law on English soil. Somersett's lawyers focused on legal issues, rather than humanitarian principles.

Stewart's ownership claim was a conflict of laws defense. He claimed—colonial enacted slave laws defined Somersett as property, with all the consequences of transmission and alienation and wanted England's Court of King's Bench to give full faith and respect to this colonial enacted slave law. However, slavery on British soil violated every colonial charter. Parliament had also enacted the Declaratory Act that had divested colonial legislatures of putative authority to enact colonial laws. Colonial slavery was created extralegally and thrived extrajudicially, as the colonial legislatures were never granted legal authority to enact a law repugnant to English common law, such as hereditary slavery. But England's unofficial policy of salutary neglect toward the American colonies had caused many to see slavery as being a lawful institution. Stewart's lawyers attempted to exploit this sentiment, by arguing it would be dangerous to free Somersett. He argued that there were thousands of blacks in England, and in Wales who'd be immediately liberated by a Court of King's Bench ruling—if Somersett prevailed.

Routinely, historians and legal scholars have misapprehended the legal issue raised and determined by the Twelve Judges in the *Somersett* case. Core has been the mistaken belief that colonial slave laws were not the legal underpinning of Stewart's slave ownership claim and that the ruling did not address the lawfulness of such laws. This is totally false, as colonial slave laws were front and center since Stewart's ownership claim was based purely upon Virginia and Massachusetts' slave laws. The record supports that Stewart bought this Virginia-born person named Somersett in Massachusetts in 1749 and John Dunning—Stewart's lawyer pressed the high court of England to confer full faith and respect upon Virginia's slave laws. He argued "… the law of the land of that country disposed of him as property, with all the consequences of transmission and alienation". This was purely a conflict of laws issue and William Davy—Somersett's lawyer focused upon this issue according to press accounts, when he stated, "With regard to the laws of Virginia"… "do they bind here? Have the laws of Virginia any more influence, power, or authority in this country, than the laws of Japan?" "Either all the laws of Virginia are to attach upon" people "here, or none, for where will they draw the line?" [6] Davy's summation to the panel of judges established that 1) the justiciable issue in the

Somersett case was Virginia's slave laws and 2) whether such laws were to be accorded full faith and respect within the Kingdom. These dispositive issues were centrally litigated and conclusively resolved in the *Somersett* case.

The imperial political implications of the *Somersett* case were fresh in Mansfield's mind, who'd presided over a criminal assault case *R. v. Stapylton* (K.B. 1771, unreported) the prior year, where a criminal defendant proffered a slave ownership defense. This was a problematic defense under English law and Mansfield had subtly nudged the defendant Robert Stapylton to settle with the black victim, Thomas Lewis, as he explained the exacting standard of proof he faced: that "being black will not prove the property". However, Stapylton was unpersuaded and he did not voluntarily release Lewis, nor did he sustain his burden of proving legal ownership of Lewis. Stapylton was found guilty of the crime. The ruling in the *Stapylton* case was controlling legal precedent for resolving the *Somersett* case and Mansfield's comments to the jurors that "I think you have done very right. I should have found the same verdict... for he was not the property" were instructive of his views and sentiments.

Mansfield was settled on the law, but was cautious, in part, based upon his family situation. He was caring for a bi-racial niece, he called Belle, who was born a slave under Jamaica's hereditary slave law. She was the out of wedlock daughter of his nephew John Lindsay and lived at his family's home—Kenwood House. Mansfield was certain that this aspect of his life would be politicized and exploited, if he declared James Somersett to be free. There would be vast economic consequences throughout the Kingdom of Great Britain. Such were motivating factors as to why he first urged Stewart to voluntarily free James, but—Stewart like Stapylton was adamant: he wanted to keep his slave. Then on May 14, 1772, Mansfield said "...Let justice be done, though the heavens may fall..." and reserved the question: is slavery a lawful institution in the Kingdom of Great Britain to the Twelve Judges Procedure—more than a month out. This also gave Stewart additional time to reconsider. [7] This off-the-record procedure had been followed by judges for centuries and it was the Mansfieldian Moment. [8]

Stewart did not change his mind concerning freeing James in the interim, nor did he otherwise abandon his objections to his petition for freedom and on June 22, 1772 additional arguments were heard and then a recess was ordered. Afterwards,

Mansfield reconvened the court to publicly announce the unanimous decision of the Twelve Judges, although some twelve-judge decisions were altogether unreported and at times were not even entered in the notebooks kept by the Chief Justice of the Court of King's Bench. [9]

The public flocked to the *Somersett* trial that began in February 1772. There were hearings on May 4, then another hearing on the 14th of May when Mansfield urged Stewart to settle with Somersett, stating that if "he shall insist on demanding judgment, we shall not fail to give it faithfully, however irksome and inconvenient". [10] And then the case was postponed until June 22, 1772 and additional arguments was heard and the tribunal took a recess to deliberate. Mansfield then reappeared on behalf of a panel of judges delivering their verdict; yet scholarly writings have always attributed the decision solely to Mansfield. [11] This is a particularly disturbing note, as it boasts such a large historiographical resume of academic writings, about such an important historical event and while each variant report of the *Somersett* decision have indicated multiple judges rendered the seminal decision, everyone claims it to be Mansfield's alone. However, scholar Matthew Mason have made the illuminating observations that Mansfield "after hearing more arguments and then deliberating over a recess he ruled on behalf of the four-judge court... that Somerset should go free," and that he——Mansfield had "explicitly expressed reluctance to decide such a weighty matter involving such fiercely competing interests and with such potential to disrupt property rights". [12]

As an initial matter, reflecting upon Mansfield's tenure as Lord Chief Justice he had never exhibited judicial reluctancy and the *Somerset* case was no exception. Rather, Mansfield was seeking to resolve the substance of this important case in the most propitious manner and in being England's chief justice he was thoughtful, deliberative and deferential to competing imperial interests. Also, if Mansfield was indeed reluctant to decide the weighty issues raised in the *Somersett* case——he could have merely denied Somersett's godparents' writ of *habeas corpus* petition that initiated the case. Mason have misconstrued exactitude for tentativeness.

Further, although I disagree with the number of judges Mason states was on the *Somersett* panel——his scholarly writing supports my core claim that the *Somersett* decision was rendered by a panel of judges and in fact, the Twelve Judges procedure was used to address and to resolve the case. There were four members on England's Court of King's Bench, but the procedure called for the other eight judges on the Court of Common Pleas and Exchequer to be temporarily elevated to address the Court of the King's Bench. Thus, Mason's conclusion that the Court of King's Bench presided *en banc* with only four judges was reasonable but wrong.

In the article *Informal Law-Making in England by the Twelve Judges in the Late 18th and Early 19th Centuries,* [13] scholar James Oldham observes that "When a legal question arose about which the trial judges were doubtful, the most sensible course was to reserve the question for discussion with brother judges at the next opportunity, perhaps at the gathering of all of the judges on the first day of the following term." He observed further, that judges would also gather intermittently in the chambers of one of the Chief Justices, in the Exchequer Chamber, or even in the home of one of the judges. It is significant that he states also that "the deliberations of the twelve judges made substantial contributions to the growth of the law by establishing controlling precedents, interpreting statutes, fixing rule of evidence, and resolving differences of views among the judges and the three common law courts… In many ways, the twelve judges had become a *de facto* court of appeals."

Prior to the late 18th century, there were no regular printed records of the Twelve Judges cases, but, history supports, Mansfield was one of a panel of judges who decided the *Somersett* case. Such decisions took on the force of precedent, even though the deliberations often survived only in unpublished notes or the memories of the judges. Certainly, the panel consisted of Mansfield in combination with three other judges of the King's Bench, plus the four judges of the Court of Exchequer, and the four judges of the Court of Common Pleas, as was the practice. [14] Mansfield was acquainted with earlier applications of the Twelve Judges procedure like the *Calvin's Case*, [15] that established Scotsmen born after James VI became King in 1603 were Englishmen by birth. Another example was the 1762 common law copyright case of *Tonson v. Collins*, where Mansfield refused to "make a case". [16] Instead, he reserved the question for the Court of King's Bench, stating because, "I was determined it should be argued and judged in the most solemn manner," and anticipating that the parties might acquiesce under the decision of the Court of King's Bench, he was "desirous to have it argued before all the judges". Thus, the case stood over to be argued before the judges, but as Justice Willes explained in the latter case of *Millar v. Taylor*, the judges suspected that the action in *Tonson* had been collusive to set up a nominal defendant in order to get a judgment that might serve as a precedent, and for this reason, the Twelve Judges procedure was not used, as they refused to proceed in the cause. [17]

The case of *R. v. Bulkley*, or Buckley is instructive and is fully reported in the Old Bailey Sessions Papers (OBSP) for June 28, 1780, recounting the defendant's role in a riot. Buckley was found guilty and sentenced to death, although he was recommended by the jury to His Majesty's mercy. Nothing is indicated in the OBSP report to show that a question arose that was forwarded to the twelve judges, and the case is otherwise unreported. However, Justice Lawrence's manuscripts contain full notes of the deliberations by the twelve judges in the case, notes taken by Justice Ashhurst. Then you have the case of *R. v. Dempsey*. The OBSP contain a full account of Dempsey's trial by a London jury before Baron Thompson in April 1807, concluding with an entry of "Guilty, Death, aged 28." However, no record appears in the OBSP of the post-trial deliberations by the twelve-judges in May and June 1807 or of the judges' recommendation of a conditional pardon. Such things are mentioned to illustrate that vagaries associated with twelve-judge cases were commonplace.

Mansfield delivered the *Somersett* opinion.

"Trinity Term, June 22, 1772... The cause returned is: the slave absented himself and departed from his master's service and refused to return and serve him during his stay in England. Whereupon, by his master's orders, he was put on board a ship by force and there detained in secure custody to be carried out of England and sold. So high an act of dominion is this that it must derive its authority, if such it has, from the law of the kingdom where executed. Even a foreigner cannot be imprisoned here on the authority of any law existing in his own country. The power of a master over his servant is different in all countries; therefore, it must always be regulated by the laws of the place where exercised.

We pay due attention to the opinion of Sir Philip York and Mr. Talbot in the year 1729. By which, they pledged themselves to the British planters for the legal consequences of bringing slaves into this kingdom, or their being baptized; which opinion was repeated and recognized by Lord Hardwicke, sitting as Chancellor on October 19, 1749, to the following effect: he said that trover would lay for a negro slave; that a notion prevailed, that if a slave came into England or became a Christian, he thereby became emancipated; but there was no foundation in law for such a notion; that when he and Lord Talbot were Attorney and Solicitor General, this notion of a slave becoming free by being baptized prevailed so strongly, that the planters industriously prevented their becoming Christians; upon which, their best consideration they were both clearly of opinion, that a slave did not in the least alter his situation or state toward his master or owner, either by being christened, or coming to England; that though the statute of Charles II had abolished tenure so far, that no man could be a villain regerdane [sic], yet if he would acknowledge himself a villain engrossed in any Court of Record, he knew of no way by which he could be entitled to his freedom without the consent of his master.

We feel the force of the inconveniences and consequences that will follow the decision of this question. Yet all of us are so clearly of one opinion upon the only question before us, that we think we

ought to give judgment, without adjourning the matter to be argued before all the Judges, as usual in the Habeas Corpus, and as we at First intimated an intention of doing in this case. The only question then, is the cause returned sufficient for remanding him? If not, he must be discharged. *emphasis added.*

The state of slavery is of such a nature, that it is incapable of now being introduced by Courts of Justice upon mere reasoning or inferences from any principles, natural or political; **it must take its rise from positive law**; the origin of it can in no country or age be traced back to any other source: immemorial usage preserves the memory of positive law long after all traces of the occasion; reason, authority, and time of its introduction are lost; and in a case so odious as the condition of slaves must be taken strictly, the power claimed by this return was never in use here; no master ever was allowed here to take a slave by force to be sold abroad because he had deserted from his service, or for any other reason whatever; we cannot say the cause set forth by this return is **allowed and approved of by the laws of this**

Kingdom, therefore the man must be discharged." *emphasis added*.

Uniquely, all transcribed *Somersett* opinions supports that a panel of judges under the aegis of the King's Bench made the rulings in 1772 that slavery was not "allowed and approved by the laws of this Kingdom" and can only be lawful by way of "positive law". Thus, the *Somersett* decision being historically attributed to Mansfield when he was only one of a panel of judges during colonial times was conscientious maneuvering by the British government to manage the verdict's reception throughout the Kingdom. Such was understandable, as the *Somersett* decision being a unanimous verdict of England's Twelve Judges would have been a blunt rebuke of slavery. However, the present-day scholars acceptance of this narrative that the *Somersett* decision was Mansfield's alone is an inexcusable misapprehension of a material fact—when one takes into account scholar Mason's admission that "[H]istorians and legal scholars have probed the significance of this [*Somersett*] decision ever since" [18] and especially, given legal scholars Leonard W. Levy and Kenneth L. Karst conclusions in the *Encyclopedia of the American Constitution* that the *Somersett* decision was English law and is part of America's common law. Thus, scholars attributing the *Somersett* decision to Mansfield—with no mention of the eleven other judges who concurrently deliberated and determined the seminal case is problematic and harbors only one conclusion.

The *Somersett* decision was an expression of British imperial politics directed at the American colonies that impacted the Kingdom. [19] Mansfield was truly an "avatar of the existing order in Britain," who played his role masterfully. The underpinning of this conclusion is bridged to Mansfield's statement in the *Stapylton* case where he stated that "he would have all Masters believe their Negroes free; and the Negroes think themselves Slaves for the sake of good behavior on both sides". He then stated after the verdict was announced that all might "find more in the question than you see at present... There are a great many opinions given on it." The *Somersett* decision accomplished that as nearly 15,000 slaves were immediately freed in England and Wales and as Mason observed "that American slaveholders saw *Somerset* as a fundamental denial of their property rights and their political control over their slaves within an increasingly hostile, antislavery empire". [20] Substantively, Britain and the slaveholding Americans knew the importance of this decision and the decision only would have obliqueness to those whom were not initiated, or not inclined to entertain and engage the first principle—that colonial slave laws violated English common law and were not the product of lawfully promulgated colonial laws since the monarch had not conferred his assent. [21]

The positioning of the *Somersett* decision as being Mansfield's alone and its endurance speaks to misdirection and purpose. In broad strokes, the *Somersett* decision was an implement of British imperial control—targeted at American colonies and it had sweeping significance because it was a unanimous ruling of the Twelve Judges, and England was "a nation of laws, not of men". The unanimous ruling of the Twelve Judges, or four if one prefers Mason's claim became the law of the land and colonial slavery ceased being "allowed and approved" throughout His Majesty's Kingdom as of June 22, 1772, by virtue of English law. This message was received loudly and clearly by the pragmatic American slave masters. They knew slavery was now a criminal institution since the colonial leadership did not establish slavery by virtue of positive law. England's monarch had never been consulted, least of all had he given his assent to colonial America's practice of slavery. And while Lord North directed colonial governors to disregard the precedential effect of the *Somersett* decision, placing blame upon Mansfield, the slave holding Americans were not convinced.

The *Somersett* decision created consternation, and dissonance within the American colonies. The political machinations of the British government caused northern patriots, such as John and Samuel Adams of Massachusetts to clamor loudly that this evidenced England's blithe disregard for the rule of law——proving tyranny. In Massachusetts, several slaves had filed freedom suits based upon the *Somersett* decision and two successive colonial governors vetoed legislative actions of the Massachusetts' General Court to liberate slaves in 1773 and 1774. And although slave-owning Englishmen in the colony of Virginia, such as George Washington, Thomas Jefferson, John Marshall, and others were pleased with England's imperial policy in the aftermath of the *Somersett* decision——they were still convinced that the legal ruling foretold of a nefarious plot to deprive them of their wealth... and power created from slavery, including their value as capital, and the value of what slaves produced. Oddly, this British imperial policy regarding the *Somersett* decision had the unintended consequence of unifying and galvanizing the American colonies.

The Twelve Judges' preamble to the *Somersett* decision repeatedly used the pronouns "we" and "us" and the plural term "judges" when they apologized for not adjourning the case to allow the parties to argue their position "before all Judges".

> **"We feel the force of the inconveniences and consequences that will follow the decision of this question.** Yet **all** of **us** are so clearly of one opinion upon the **only question before us**, that **we think we ought to give judgment**, without adjourning the matter to be argued before **all the Judges**, as usual in the Habeas Corpus, and as **we at First intimated an intention of doing in this case**. The only question then, is the cause returned sufficient for remanding him? If not, he must be discharged." *emphasis added.*

Under English law, the Twelve Judges procedure as it was called was used to address major points of law, such as conflict of laws questions surrounding colonial slave laws and to interpret statutory words. Such decisions made by the Twelve Judges had kingdom-wide effect and established precedents and procedures that would govern like cases. The twelve-judge decisions constituted law-making in two additional ways; (1) they settled the meaning and limits of statutory language as applied to fact situations and (2) they established controlling rules of procedure and evidence. [22]

Lord Mansfield offered Stewart the chance to abandon his slave ownership defense, as he did in the case *R. v. Stapylton (1771, unreported)*. But Stewart held fast, refusing to compromise.

> "Easter Term, May 14, 1772... **Mr. Stewart advances no claim on contract; he rests his whole demand on a right to the Negro as slave** and mentions the purpose of detainure to be the sending of him over to be sold in Jamaica. If the parties will have judgment, *fiat Justitia, ruat coelom*, **let justice be done though the heavens fall.** 50ℓ. A head may not be a high price; then a loss follows to the proprietors of above 70,000ℓ. Sterling. How would the law stand with respect to their settlement; their wages? How many actions for any slight coercion by the master? We cannot in any of these points direct the law; the law must rule us. In these particulars, it may be matter of weighty consideration, what provisions are made or set by law. **Mr. Stewart may end the question, by discharging or giving freedom to the Negro.**" *emphasis added.*

Similarly, Matthew Mason posits that "since 1756 when Mansfield began his term as Chief Justice of King's Bench, he had expanded especially the appellate powers of this court that sat atop England's complex legal system"... and that he was "the very avatar of the existing order in Britain, [but he had] explicitly expressed reluctance to decide such a weighty matter involving such fiercely competing interests"... although he had "played a major political role advocating the centralizing position on empire in the House of Lords". [23] Local legitimacy of colonial laws was premised upon an abiding deference to the power of the monarchy over his dominions and as the lawfulness of colonial slave laws was a kingdom-wide issue—that implicated conflict of laws this made sense. This case had kingdom-wide significant since colonial legislative assemblies had all failed to secure the monarch's assent on slave laws. These laws were abjectly "repugnant" to England's common law and had evolved during the period of Britain's unwritten policy of salutary neglect. However, salutary neglect was over due to Parliament's American Colonies Act of 1766, commonly known as the Declaratory Act.

Mistakenly, historians suggest that the *Somersett* decision did not address the conflict of laws issue... did not impact any colony in colonial America and all too many openly questions the notion that slavery was abolished within the American colonies. Firstly, the substance of Stewart's case was that Virginia's slave laws were lawful and thus entitled to full faith and respect by England's highest court; Court of King's Bench. Stewart's sole claim of ownership of Somersett was based upon Virginia and Massachusetts' slave laws. Stewart was unsuccessful in proving the lawfulness of colonial slave laws to the Court of King's Bench. The high court refused to confer any lawfulness upon Virginia's slave laws by ruling such laws were not "allowed and approved by laws in this Kingdom".

Substantively, colonial slave laws violated the common law, did not have the King's assent and evidenced disdain for a sovereign's prerogative. The ruling that slavery was not "allowed and approved by the laws of this Kingdom" determined that colonial slave laws were not lawfully enacted. And then, as the Twelve Judges went on to establish standards and procedures to be applied when habeas corpus actions concerning putative slaves implicate the substantive laws of a different British colony and did extrapolate a slave's rights, as against his putative master by ruling slavery was not "allowed and approved by the laws in this Kingdom" and that slavery is only legally recognized in the Kingdom if it is the result of "positive law"——colonial slavery was abolished. The Twelve Judges had addressed and resolved the important, novel, and difficult question of whether slavery had been lawfully authorized during the period of Britain's salutary neglect and whether such slave laws should be accorded the force of law throughout the Kingdom. Thereby, the conflict of laws and abolishment of colonial slavery questions were squarely addressed by the *Somersett* decision. Thus, the *Somersett* decision addressed the conflict of laws question.

Secondly, all colonies in North America used and emulated Virginia's legislative assembly, House of Burgesses' procedures and practices to enact their hereditary slave laws and all were bound by colonial charter to adhere to English law. Thus, the Twelve Judges' determination of legal insufficiency of Virginia's slave laws in the *Somersett* case resolved the same outstanding questions concerning other American colonies' slave laws pursuant to English jurisprudence.

Thirdly, the colonial legislative systems within the American colonies were bicameral: legislative assembly and the monarchy. The *Somersett* decision ruled slavery must be enacted by virtue of "positive law". Mansfield using the Twelve Judges procedure was a masterful maneuver—the Mansfieldian Moment as it abolished colonial slavery since none of the colonial slave laws were the product of "positive municipal law". [24] Thus, it was unnecessary to specify or expound upon that such jurisdiction resides exclusively with the Parliament as the Kingdom was a unitary government.

The *Somersett* decision repudiated the notion that Virginia's colonial slave laws were entitled to full faith and respect. The decision rendered all colonial slave laws inert because the high court declared slavery could only be lawful in the Kingdom by virtue of "positive law"... and [slavery was not] "allowed and approved by the laws of this Kingdom". This ruling zeroed out all slave laws within the Kingdom. The American colonies had nowhere to retreat to on these points since slavery was not the product of lawfully promulgated municipal laws either. The Kingdom of Great Britain included the American colonies and West Indian Islands—a unitary State and based upon this structure, only Parliament held power to pass "positive law".[25] The textbook analysis of the British State and the doctrine of parliamentary sovereignty is set-forth in A. V. Dicey's book *Introduction to the Law of the Constitution 1885*: "Unitarianism, in short, means the concentration of the strength of the State in the hands of one visible sovereign power, be that Parliament or Czar." None of the American colonies had such authority. *Somersett* abolished the slave and transmuted British slave masters into criminals under English law and started the journey for restorative justice for the victims and nation.

On this point, the *Somersett* decision was a manifestation of British imperial power and sought to discretely communicate a reality to America's slave owners and to do so bluntly would not have served the British government as effectively, in the way an oblique decision did. Also, it would have been provocative for the Twelve Judges in the *Somersett* decision to explicitly declare slavery was abolished, although respective rights and powers of colonial legislatures were front and center in British imperial politics. The British government was cautious, especially in the aftermath of the Stamp Act in the years 1765 through 1767, as Parliament had anticipated this point very directly when it passed the Declaratory Act, that made it clear that it and with the King included, Parliament should "legislate over the colonies in all cases whatsoever." Arguably, Parliament's enactment of the Declaratory Act had already rendered colonial slave laws void—but during this time some were openly questioning Parliament's authority over the American colonies, and even believed taxes violated the British constitution. Under the British constitution, northern patriots claimed, the government could not place a tax on the people without their consent. This approval came through the representatives elected to Parliament by voters. But the colonists did not have any representatives there. However, they had representatives involved in colonial governments and it was their own representatives in the colony who failed to secure the monarch's assent on its laws and thereby had not enacted positive municipal law. These laws violated the British constitution, as well as each colonial charter. The British determined that this was a less confrontational way to proceed. The belief was that people in the colonies who needed to understand the legal consequence of the *Somersett* rulings would understand and they did.

Decidedly, be it four or twelve judges... Mansfield was a member of a panel who decided the *Somersett* case—yet he has emerged as being the sole judge. Certainly, the British government knew that in publicizing the *Somersett* ruling as a Twelve-Judges decision it would have robustly advanced an anti-slavery precedent and would have settled the malingering legal questions throughout the Kingdom. Yet, Mansfield was anointed as the standard-bearer and he dutifully allowed himself to receive total credit. This material fact has been all too durable and it was not hubris on Mansfield's part to take responsibility for the *Somersett* decision and a careful student of history would realize that since he and no other judge who was a member of the *Somersett* panel ever disabused the public of this material misapprehension, larger forces were at work and it had to have been a manifestation of imperial policy. This could not have occurred any other way. Thus, it is reasonable to conclude that the *Somersett* decision was an overt British imperial policy initiative that addressed colonial slave laws within the American colonies and it also resolved the broader social question of institutional denial of rights and privileges to certain British citizens living in the American colonies. To this end, the unanimous decision of the Twelve Judges was analogous to the civil rights case of *Brown v. Board of Education* where the U. S. Supreme Court unanimously rejected the state of Kansas enacted laws of "separate but equal" within public school systems. By failing to recognize *Somersett* as an Afro-Briton civil rights victory during colonial times its historic significance has been diluted and totally misapprehended by all. The underlying colonial slave laws, that gave legal existence to the misanthrope institution of hereditary slavery were struck down as being unconstitutional in 1772. Thus, abolishing colonial slavery was not necessary and would have been duplicitous since objectively, all colonial slave laws that did not meet the legal standard of being "positive law" were void *ab initio*.

"As soon as a Negro comes to England... he is free; one may be a villein in England... but not a slave". Lord Chief Justice John Holt (*circa* 1702)

Chapter 2
Dunmore the Emancipator

The *Somersett* decision ruled in 1772 that slavery had not been lawfully enacted within the American colonies and as the entire Kingdom of Great Britain was bound by the Twelve Judges' decision—colonial slavery was exposed as being a criminal practice. [26] The British did not criminally prosecute violators—but this habeas case did render colonial slave laws void *ab initio* and it also decisively established and affirmed the liberty rights of black Englishmen and established conflict of laws standards and procedural rules; the Twelve Judges ruled unanimously slavery was not "allowed and approved by the laws in this Kingdom" and "that it is incapable of being introduced on any reason, moral or political" except by means of "positive law". Thus, it has always been an errant interpretation of the *Somersett* decision to even suggest that it was an abolishment of slavery, as slavery was already classified as being the crime of manstealing and the practice was extralegal.

The *Somersett* decision had addressed and resolved the important, novel, and difficult question of whether colonial slave laws had been lawfully promulgated and whether such laws should be accorded the force of law throughout the Kingdom. It was a full-throated repudiation of slavery, as William Wiecek observed, "Mansfield's utterance had a plangent quality, suggesting that slavery was of dubious legitimacy everywhere." [27] Given this as well as the fact that all twelve judges had agreed unanimously, people suffering as slaves had reason to celebrate; and they did.

Local legitimacy of colonial slave laws was based upon an abiding deference to the power of the monarchy over his dominions; slave laws enacted without the King's assent did not evidence sovereign prerogative and as a matter of law, were nugatory. The American colonies were bound by colonial charter to English law and was a defined realm within His Majesty's King George III's Kingdom in 1772. The formal adoption of English law by the First Congress *after* the Declaration of Independence continued to bind the U. S. to English law and the *Somersett* decision… that declared slavery was not lawfully authorized. This was a dispositive legislative enactment, as the U. S.

legislature bound this country to English law. There's no legal support for the argument, endorsed by too many historians that the *Somersett* ruling did not resolve the slavery question within the American colonies during colonial times and if it did not——why not?

In his book, *Black History in the White House,* [28] Clarence Lusane stated that a ruling in a 1772 habeas case freeing a Virginia born slave named James Somersett caused anxiety within the American colonies, as slaveholding Founding Fathers "drew the sobering conclusion that the day was likely near when the *Somerset* decision would also apply to them". Point in fact, that day was already upon them since the American colonies were already bound by colonial charter to English law and England's highest tribunal——the Twelve Judges ruled slavery could only be legal by "positive law" and it was not "allowed and approved by the laws of this Kingdom". The *Somersett* decision was self-executing, as the jurisdiction of a Twelve Judges decision was comprehensive and spanned throughout the Kingdom. The extrajudicial practice of colonial slavery became criminal since kidnapping, rape, assault, and trespass were already crimes under English law. The Founding Fathers were facing their day of reckoning.

History supports, from very early times through the end of colonial times—England's informal Twelve Judges procedure allowed a judge before whom any case of difficulty arose to postpone judgement and report the matter to other judges. From the judge's viewpoint, the twelve-judge procedure allowed him to address a perplexing question with which he might have little or no experience. Some of these cases were in print, even though the reports of a few of the cases in the twelve judges' notebooks were much more extensive than the printed reports. The typical procedure for twelve-judge cases was to withhold the judgment of the trial court until the twelve judges had conferred, then report the decision of the judges. Such was the legal process used by Mansfield in resolving defendant Charles Stewart's claim of legal ownership of James Somersett.

The Twelve Judges declared slavery was not "allowed and approved by the laws in this Kingdom" in 1772 and all badges of legality were withdrawn from the practice. Slavery within the American colonies became void *ab initio,* [29] and the *Somersett* decision did not need to specially abolish slavery, as it automatically reverted to its criminal character and nature, as it was not authorized by positive law. [30] And having established that property in man was illegitimate throughout the Kingdom under English law, the *Somersett* decision did not need to go any further.

The unanimous ruling of the Twelve Judges delivered by Mansfield was a reaffirmation of a core British ideal—slavery was disallowed and prohibited on British soil. This was the common perspective and the public interpretation saw it as an ideological rebuke to slavery. Although no one went to jail, or faced criminal charges, there was no way to put the genie back in the bottle, as colonial slave laws were not lawfully promulgated. Colonial legislative systems were bicameral, and by way of graft, corruption, and tyranny, slavery existed extrajudicially. Clearly, slavery did not exist by virtue of positive law. Colonial assemblies failed to secure the King's assent.

Kidnapping was a crime in early America. The State of Pennsylvania on March 1, 1780 enacted a kidnapping law: "[N]o negro or mulatto slave… shall be removed out of this state, with the design and intention that the place of abode or residence of such slave or servant shall be thereby altered or changed." Then on March 25, 1826 the State of Pennsylvania passed further legislation:

"[I]f any person or persons shall, from and after the passing of this act, by force and violence, take and carry away, or cause to be taken or carried away, and shall, by fraud or false pretense, seduce, or cause to be seduced, or shall attempt so to take, carry away or seduce, any negro or mulatto, from any part or parts of this commonwealth, to any other place or places whatsoever, out of this commonwealth, with a design and intention of selling and disposing of, or of causing to be sold, or of keeping and detaining, or of causing to be kept and detained, such negro or mulatto, as a slave or servant for life, or for any term whatsoever, every such person or persons, his or their aiders or abettors, shall on conviction thereof, in any court of this commonwealth having competent jurisdiction, be deemed guilty of a felony."

These Pennsylvania laws bridge back to the ancient Roman concept attributed to Roman Byzantine Emperor Justinian in 565 C. E.: "captivity and servitude are both contrary to the laws of nature; for by that law all men are born free." That in turn followed Christian doctrine——all men are free by nature, which became a maxim of the common law of England. Then in 1102, a council held in London, England "Let no one hereafter presume to engage in that nefarious trade in which hitherto in England men were usually sold like brute animals." For centuries, there were no records of noncompliance.[31]

Then in 1569, an enslaving incident was attempted in England. The slave master attempted to beat the slave. The violence was deemed an assault and battery. The resulting case, *Matter of Cartwright*, [32] ruled slavery was unconstitutional on British soil, observing, "England was too pure an air for slaves to breathe in." This precedent was applied in *Shanley v. Hervey*, [33] and three years later in *Smith v. Brown and Cooper*, [34] where Chief Justice Holt ruled "that as soon as a negro comes into England, he becomes free: one may be a villein [serf] in England, but not a slave."

Kidnapping and slavery were prohibited on colonial America's soil, as although disembarking the Dutch privateer ship *White Lion* in chains, the "legal" status of the first kidnapped nineteen Africans brought to the colony of Virginia, at Point Comfort in August 1619 were indentured servants—not slaves. This was not serendipitous fortune—rather—it was because of English law. They were conferred indentured servant status—even though these Africans arrived in chains, without papers of indenture.

History supports—under English common law, there were no legal defense, excuse or exception for the organized, widespread kidnappings of black loyalists by Americans after signing the Treaty of Paris of 1783. Carleton's attestation of treaty violations was proffered to Washington as rebuttable presumptions. The failure of the U. S. to substantively address Carleton's claim that black loyalists were legally entitled to liberty based upon British "Proclamation and promises"—per the treaty was not a mere oversight. The then six century old prohibition against slavery under English common law; each legislative assembly within the American colonies failure to promulgate colonial slave laws in accordance with the bicameral legislative system and the Twelve Judge's ruling that slavery was not "allowed and approved by the laws of this Kingdom" in the *Somersett* decision made the bare claim feckless. [35]

In May 1774, England forced the hands of slave masters throughout colonial America by closing the Port of Boston, sending in troops of occupation, and appointing a military governor for the colony of Massachusetts. These British policies, called the "Intolerable Acts" radicalized northern colonies, dispelling any lingering illusions about colonial Americans' status, and their rights as Englishmen. And later that year in 1774—friendly relations between slave masters in the southern colonies, and Lord North's government were shattered when

England found out they were providing money and assistance to rebellious elements in the colony of Massachusetts. They had been instrumental in the formation of a shadow revolutionary government, and a militia— to prepare for armed conflict against the British troops occupying Boston.

Lord North felt such conduct by England's partners in crime—slave owners as being an act of utter betrayal... causing him to direct Lord Dunmore to dissolve Virginia's legislative assembly, and all colonial governors to abandon the status-quo protecting narrative... that the *Somersett* decision only meant "a person, regardless of being a slave could not be forcibly removed from England against his will and carried him abroad." Then early in the rebellion—rumors of a British plan to liberate colonial America's slave population and to draft former slaves into the military began circulating to such an extent that a group of slaves presented themselves to Lord Dunmore to volunteer their services in April 1775. And although Dunmore turned them away—suspicions were not allayed, as rumors swirled that an emancipation bill was set to reach the floor of the Parliament any day, but it was something that did not materialize until the 1807 Slave Trade Act.

Afterwards, tensions between England, and the American colonies increased, causing Lord North to order colonial governors to secure all gunpowder, depriving potential rebels of this crucial military supply.

Virginia's Lord Dunmore complied on April 20, 1775—ordering Royal Marines to load gunpowder from the public magazine in Williamsburg—removing fifteen half-barrels and transported it to a British warship.

The American colonists in Virginia protested... believing Lord Dunmore's actions exposed them to slave insurrections, and Native Americans. Dunmore mishandled the situation by repeatedly threatening to free and arm slaves to defend the cause of the Royal Government. He believed the thought of armed black people running throughout Virginia made the concession of a few barrels of gunpowder much less upsetting to the colonists—but he was wrong.

On May 3, 1775, the Hanover militia led by Patrick Henry arrived outside of Williamsburg. This caused Lord Dunmore to flee the Governor's Palace for his hunting lodge in Porto Bello, in nearby York County. His lordship then issued a proclamation on the sixth of May against "a certain Patrick Henry... and a Number of deluded Followers" who had organized "an Independent Company... and put themselves in a Posture of War." Afterward, members of Virginia's militia laid siege to Lord

Dunmore's hunting lodge, and he was wounded in the leg—forcing him to flee and to take refuge aboard the man-of-war Fowey at Yorktown. Once aboard, Dunmore issued a proclamation declaring:

> "My declaration that I would arm and set free such slaves as should assist me if attacked has stirred up fears in them which cannot easily subside as they know how vulnerable they are in that particular, and therefore they have cause in this complaint of which their others are totally unsupported."

On November 7, 1775, Lord Dunmore made good on his threat to liberate slaves, and he did so before the thirteen colonies declared themselves independent, the following July. He declared Virginia's patriots as traitors to the Crown and having declared martial law, he proclaimed "all indented servants, Negroes, or others... free that are able and willing to bear arms", exercising *executive* power of His Royal Majesty, King George III.

A PROCLAMATION

> As I have entertained Hopes, that an Accommodation might have taken place between GREAT BRITAIN, and this Colony, without being compelled by my Duty to this most disagreeable but now absolutely necessary Step,

rendered so by a Body of armed Men unlawfully assembled, firing on His MAJESTY'S Tenders, and the formation of an Army, and that Army now on their March to attack his MAJESTY'S Troops and destroy the well-disposed subjects of the Colony. To defeat such treasonable Purposes, and that all such Traitors, and their Abettors, may be brought to Justice, and that the Peace, and good order of this Colony may be again restored, which the ordinary Course of the Civil Law is it Proclamation, hereby declaring, that until the aforesaid good Purpose can be obtained, I do in Virtue of the Power and Authority to ME given, by His MAJESTY determine to execute Martial Law, and cause the same to be executed throughout this Colony and to end that the Peace and good Order may the sooner be restored. I do require every person capable of bearing Arms, to resort to His MAJESTY'S STANDARD, or be looked upon as Traitors to His MAJESTY'S Crown and Government, and thereby become liable to the Penalty the Law inflicts upon such Offenses; such as Forfeiture of Life, confiscation of Lands, &, &. And I do hereby further declare all indentured Servants, Negroes, or others (appertaining to Rebels) free that are able and willing to bear Arms, they joining His MAJESTY'S Troops as soon as may be, for the more speedily reducing this Colony to a proper Sense of their Duty, to His MAJESTY'S Crown and Dignity. I do further order, and require, as His MAJESTY'S Liege Subjects, to retain their Quitrents, or any other Taxes due or that may become due, in their Custody, till such a Time as Peace may be again restored to this at present most unhappy Country, or demanded of them for their former salutary Purposes, by Officer properly authorized to receive the same. GIVEN under my Hand on Board the Ship WILLIAM BY Norfolk, the 7th Day of November in the SIXTEENTH Year of His MAJESTY'S Reign. DUNMORE (GOD save the KING)

Dunmore's executive proclamation confirmed and had the legal effect of being a writ of habeas corpus that validated subjecthood and liberated all "black people" suffering as slaves in derogation of English law. It entreated "every person..." "to resort to His Majesty's standard." And given the fact that all colonial-born slaves were "free negroes" due to the self-executing nature of the Twelve Judges' *Somersett* decision of 1772, and as there were no positive municipal laws authorizing the condition known as "slave" in any colony in colonial America... there has never been a factual basis to claim native-born blacks or an African suffering as a "slave" in any of the American colonies were excluded from Dunmore's "free negroes" reference. The condition known as slave was a legal fiction per *Somersett*.

Under the common law, born in colonial America conferred British subjecthood under the British tradition of *jus soli*. Pursuant to the common law, a child's legal condition was based upon his father's legal condition—*partus sequitur patrem*. Born in colonial America conferred British nationality and a liberty right. Thus, it arose to the level of being an oxymoron to even suggest that there could ever be "African slaves born in English colonies" under English common law.

The legal rights associated with birthright English subjecthood was addressed in the Elizabeth Key case. This ruling concerning a mixed-race woman born in Virginia, litigated in the colony of Virginia in 1655 was controlling precedent. Key's father was a white Englishman and she prevailed in her lawsuit. [36] Key relied upon England's common law of *partus sequitur patrem* to substantiate her legal status as a freeborn English citizen.

History supports, the ruling in the *Key* case caused Virginia's House of Burgesses to enact a colonial law in 1662—that introduced the principle of *partus sequitur ventrem*. Virginia's colonial law purported to absolve white Englishmen of responsibility of financial support. The law allowed white Englishmen to sell their children of African ancestry, or to put them to work as slaves. It purported to establish a matrilineal descent system in the colony of Virginia. However, at no time was Virginia's colonial law of *partus sequitur ventrem* lawful because it conflicted with the English common law tradition of *partus sequitur patrem*. Virginia, like each other colony in America had a repugnancy proviso in the colonial charter, that withheld, defined, and limited the legislative authority of the colonial assembly. They had no lawful authority to enact any colonial or municipal law that was "repugnant" to English law. This 1662 law was in obvious conflict. Then, even if the legislature could pass such a law, Virginia's assembly did not secure the King's assent, and in failing to do so—Virginia's slave law was extrajudicial and nugatory throughout the American colonies.

England's constitution, and laws are designed to survive, and remain in force, in extraordinary times and a careful review of common laws and the Constitution—beginning in the year 1606, and spanning forward reveals that none of the colonial assemblies in the American colonies ever lawfully enacted "positive municipal law" to authorize slavery. The colonial assemblies all failed to overturn *partus sequitur patrem*: a patrilineal descent system. The legislative failure of the assemblies within the American colonies foreclosed the lawfulness of hereditary slavery since *partus sequitur ventrem* was repugnant to established English law of *partus sequitur patrem*. Ninety-five percent of all "slaves" were native-born when the U. S. declared itself a new nation in 1776. Clearly, *partus sequitur patrem* remained the law of the land.

Thus, the Twelve Judges' determinations in the *Somersett* case that "the state of slavery is of such a nature, that it is incapable of now being introduced by Courts of Justice upon mere reasoning or inferences from any principles, natural or political; it must take its rise from positive law"…and that slavery was not "allowed and approved by the laws of this Kingdom" was a conclusive judicial construction of colonial slavery's lawfulness. This was decidedly so, as Stewart pressed his slave ownership claim based upon Virginia's slave laws.

Slavery was not based upon law—but upon force. Then as now, kidnapping people during colonial times was illegal and as the Supreme Court, in the case of *The Antelope*, [37] ruled "That it [slavery] is contrary to the law of nature will scarcely be denied. That every-man has a natural right to the fruits of his own labor, as generally admitted; and that no other person can rightfully deprive him of those fruits, and appropriate them against his will, seems to be the necessary result of this admission... Slavery, then, has its origins in force..." As one of Somersett's lawyers claimed during the trial, slavery was a "new species of tyranny...created entirely by Colony government".

The colonial newspapers published Lord Dunmore's proclamation in full. *The Virginia Gazette* warned slaves to "Be not then... ye Negroes, tempted by this proclamation to ruin yourselves... Whether we suffer or not, if you desert us, you must certainly will." In addition, the newspaper urged blacks to "cling to their kind masters"—claiming Lord Dunmore's proclamation was only a ploy—but it did not work, as black people from all colonies were leaving their colonial slave masters in pursuit of freedom.

Then colonial slave masters attempted to discredit Dunmore's executive proclamation by calling it "conditional." But it was not conditional... rather; the slave masters' ownership claims, and interests in black people were nullified by Dunmore's *executive* proclamation of liberation under English law, as his proclamation was not reversed by higher authority.

Then with respect to African slaves, Dunmore's proclamation promised British subjecthood and freedom if these people took arms against their patriot slave masters during the rebellion. He addressed the legal plights of "black native sons", and African slaves in colonial America, separately and it encouraged thousands of black slaves to escape plantation life and to fight for the British. But on November 12, 1775, General George Washington issued a directive that barred black people from joining the Continental Army. However, what this meant militarily was soon spelled out at an encounter at Kemp's Landing in Virginia in December 1775 and it later caused a reversal of policy in January 1776. The patriots feared... that if the British militarization of blacks was not addressed——it alone could topple the fledgling rebellion.

The enthusiasm of black people was self-evident, and by late November 1775, countless "slaves" had enlisted for military service. Lord Dunmore's proclamation was a measured *pre*-Declaration of Independence liberation of the American colonies' slave population—England's *Southern Strategy*. For example, Lord Dunmore formed an all-black regiment with former slaves called Dunmore's Ethiopian Regiment in November 1775—*before* America's patriots declared themselves independent.

The formation of Dunmore's Ethiopian Regiment marked a significant turn in both British and American race relations. England's recruitment efforts led to 12,000 black Englishmen serving with the British forces during the Revolutionary War—America's first Civil War and forced the American colonists to change its decision that banned blacks from serving in the Continental Army. By December 1775, Dunmore's Ethiopian Regiment had nearly three-hundred recruits. Their regimental uniforms had sashes inscribed with the words "Liberty to Slaves".

The former slaves saw action in Virginia at the battle of Kemp's Landing where former slaves proved their mettle by defeating a detail of Virginia militiamen. And when the white colonists broke rank and retreated into the swamps, Dunmore's Ethiopians gave chase. There then occurred one of those little vignettes that illuminated a whole era as

Lerone Bennett, Jr. explained in his seminal book, *Before the Mayflower*.

"One Colonel Hutchings, a proper Virginian, was cornered by a black man he recognized as one of his escaped slaves. The indignant colonel fired at the former slave, but the bullet missed. The black rebel closed in and whacked his former master across the face with a saber. Then, in the greatest humiliation of all, Colonel Hutchings was led into the British lines by his own slave."

Then in May 1776—the Black Company of Pioneers, also known as the Black Pioneers was established out of Lord Dunmore's disbanded Ethiopian Regiment. The Black Pioneers retained Dunmore's Ethiopian regimental slogan "Liberty to Slaves." And while it was not a fighting unit, the Black Pioneers built both huts and accommodations, and dug fortifications while under consistent heavy fire, and in the most dangerous conditions.

The Black Pioneers served under British General George Clinton in a support capacity in North Carolina, New York, Rhode Island and Pennsylvania.

Alongside the British, these black regiments fought in the North and in the Battle of Monmouth in 1778 in occupied New York until war's end. Black people also commonly served in the Royal navy and as musicians in nearly all units. Also, the Jersey Shore Volunteers, the King's American Dragons, the Jamaica Rangers, the Mosquito Shore Volunteers and the Black Brigade were all combat regiments.

Patriot James Madison thought England's militarization of black Englishmen was the kind of "tampering with the slaves," that he had most feared. "To say the truth," he'd later confided in a friend, "that is the only part in which this colony is vulnerable... we shall fall like Achilles by the hand of one that knows that secret." But, in having been their partner-in-crime—the British knew the colony of Virginia's "secret" all too well, and it was because of this knowledge that England liberated and then militarized America's native sons—all to splinter the colonial coalition, and quell rebellion in the southern colonies.

Lord Dunmore's emancipation of slaves had caused Washington to concede in a letter to Colonel Henry Lee III in December 1775 that success in the rebellion would come to whatever side that could arm "negroes" the fastest. Congress reversed Washington's ban on black recruitment within the ranks of its military in January 1776 by permitting the enlistment of free blacks in the Continental Army, who had fought in the early battles and by

1778, the New England states and eventually all northern states enlisted blacks. Ultimately, some 5,000 black citizens bore arms for the U. S. and it was approximately five percent of the total number of men who served in the Continental Army.

The U. S. advanced the baseless narrative that Lord Dunmore relinquished authority when Patrick Henry forced him to flee from the governor's mansion in May of 1775—but it was not supported by English law. And in fact, this narrative would be negated by expressed terms, and acknowledgements in the Treaty of Paris of 1783, as the U. S. Congress conceded continued British rule over the American States. However, it does queue up the question of the lawful authority of Virginia's delegates to the Continental Congress to represent the colony of Virginia that voted for independence in July 1776 and the federal constitution in 1787. The legal implications to the federal constitution are that Virginia's assembly was in suspense and putative members only had lawful authority once Virginia's Royal governor called the assembly into session.

History supports—for a full year starting in 1772 Dunmore governed the colony of Virginia without convening Virginia's House of Burgesses. The suspense of Virginia's legislature pre-dates *Somersett* and in March 1773—needing funds to finance his campaigns against Native Americans known as Lord Dunmore's War—Dunmore finally convened Virginia's legislature. However, instead of dealing with the funding issue, Virginia's assemblymen resolved to form a committee of correspondence to communicate their continued concerns about the Townshend Acts and Gaspee Affair to Great Britain. Lord Dunmore immediately placed Virginia's assembly in recess, divesting them of any legislative power, per colonial charter.

However, in the spring of 1774 Dunmore did reconvene Virginia's assembly, but he quickly dissolved the assembly when Virginia's assemblymen passed a resolution declaring June 1, 1774... a day of fasting and prayer in Virginia. Afterwards, Dunmore declared martial law, and yet, without facial legal right, authority, or privilege the assemblymen purported to reconvene, as the Second Virginia Convention on March 20, 1775 and elected delegates to the Continental Congress. The act of reconvening Virginia's Assembly was done without legal authority. Dunmore's suspense of the legislature terminated Virginia's assemblymen's legal authority. They only had lawful authority when the assembly—House of Burgesses was lawfully convened by His Majesty's Royal governor.

Afterwards, Dunmore then issued a proclamation that excoriated and challenged the credentials of these putative Virginian assemblymen. However, these people took seats in the Continental Congress anyway and all voted for the Declaration of Independence. They blamed King George III for "taking away our Charters, abolishing our most valuable Laws and altering fundamentally the Forms of our Governments: For suspending our own Legislatures, and declaring themselves invested with power to legislate for us in all cases whatsoever."

Doubtlessly, Virginia's delegation to the Continental Congress had no lawful authority to represent the colony of Virginia at the Continental Congress. Bound by colonial charter to English law that granted the governor sole power to assemble Virginia's legislature, coupled with Dunmore's *executive* proclamation of martial law reveals that Virginia's assemblymen did not have the color of legislative power and authority. And despite Dunmore's challenging the credentials of Virginia's delegates to the Continental Congress they were seated and became instrumental in drafting the Declaration of Independence and ultimately, the federal constitution of 1787. Dunmore's challenge of the Virginia's delegates credentials framed the threshold question: did these Virginia's delegates have lawful authority to represent Virginia in the Continental Congress?

Dunmore's proclamation of liberation in November 1775 was the exercise of *executive* authority. The proclamation granted freedom to all people suffering as slaves based upon the *Somersett* decision and as the First Congress adopted English law after the declaration, all former slaves were free Englishman. Black people were not and could not be legally owned by Americans, as slavery was not "allowed and approved by the laws in this Kingdom" and consequently, each black person was duly entitled to be "set at liberty," pursuant to the Treaty of Paris of 1783. Washington knew court precedent had found slavery on British soil was illegal, and all colonial slave laws were nugatory—having not been approved by both chambers of the colonial bicameral legislative system.

The colonial legislative systems throughout the American colonies were bicameral. Two chambers: the King and the colonial legislative assembly. The bicameral legislative nature of the American colonies required both chambers of the colonial legislature system to approve a proposed law, to be deemed properly promulgated "positive municipal law." And pursuant to colonial charter, the colonial legislative assemblies could not upon its own accord enact a law that decriminalized kidnappings or authorize the practice of slavery. This was the reason that the first nineteen Africans in Virginia in 1619 could not be slaves. The rule of law officials abided by English law when they made the Africans indentured servants. This directs a careful historian to look to inspect each colonial assembly's legislative history and to analyze their slave laws to discern whether the King gave his required assent to laws that gave rise to hereditary slavery.

It is significant that none of the colonies promulgated positive municipal laws that legalized slavery in the first instance. Kidnapping was not decriminalized, and no legislative assembly could on its own change the colonial descent system that gave rise to *partum sequitur ventrem*: hereditary slavery in the 1660s. The enactment and enforcement of slave laws in the American colonies was the product of British tyranny. The practice was extralegal—a criminal scheme that was totally beholding to British tyranny, corruption of the colonial judiciary and hooliganism. Slave laws were nugatory: lacking legal force since none of the American colonies had the requisite legal authority to enact "positive municipal law" to enact slave laws, based solely upon the legislative assembly's authority.

The House of Burgesses, Virginia's legislative assembly first acknowledged slavery in its laws in 1661. The colony of Virginia was bound by its bicameral legislative structure. Virginia's legislative assembly did not have the authority in 1661 to pass a slave law that decriminalized the kidnapping of Africans, as the practice was "repugnant" to English common law. Also, Virginia's legislative assembly did not secure the assent of England's King Charles II, to make this 1661 colonial bill "positive municipal law". Then, the next year, while the Royal governor was in England, Virginia's assembly enacted a law of hereditary slavery called *partus sequitur ventrem*. Virginia's municipal law purported to make a child born to an enslaved mother—a slave at birth. *But t*his 1662 slave law required the assent of King Charles II, as it was "repugnant" to the patrilineal descent system of *partus sequitur patrem*. The failure of Virginia's legislative assembly to secure the King's assent was fatal to the lawful institution of hereditary slavery, yet the practice and legislative model became endemic within the American colonies due to British corruption.

Virginia's colonial governor should have vetoed the decriminalizing of kidnappings and changing the patrilineal descent system—but due to corruption; Virginia's Governor Berkeley and all subsequent governors protected these misanthrope slave laws. The colonial governors foreclosed judicial and legislative review of colonial laws. But ultimately, the practice of colonial slavery found itself before the Twelve Judges of His Majesty's King's Bench in the *Somerset v. Stewart* case in early 1770s. This case ignited chaos, and dissonance, once the court declared slavery was not "allowed and approved by the laws of this Kingdom". This decision rendered all putative municipal slave laws unconstitutional (for failing to be positive law) and criminal throughout the American colonies in 1772. This was the legal consequence of *Somersett* because assault, rape, trespass, misprision, and kidnapping associated with slavery were already crimes under English law.

Abolishing slavery in the *Somersett* decision would have promoted judicial economy and resolved the slavery issue——but it took a rear seat to British imperial politics. There was no legal reason to specially declare its abolishment for those people in doubt and the Twelve Judges withheld doing so and slave masters seized upon this fact to further slavery by attacking the decision on this point. Collectively, colonial leadership saw the *Somersett* decision as being an imperial political tool and that knowledge both strengthened and galvanized them that included the suppression pro-*Somersett* newspapers accounts and pamphlets.

Scholarly analysis of colonial newspapers in 1772 supports this conclusion. Patricia Bradley posited that the Somerset story did not play a large role in any of the newspapers when compared to other stories of the day, and that the lack of panic was due to the fact that they believed themselves to be living under a clearly separate legal regime from that over which Mansfield presided. [38] However, this was pure wishful thinking, as Mansfield sat atop the British complex legal structure and colonial charters bound each American colony to English law, and the King's Bench's judicial construction of English law was final and controlling and the supreme law of the land in 1772. English law did not grant any class of colonist immunity from the rule of law. And while the scholar David Waldstreicher points out that there that "no public meeting denounced Lord Mansfield; his effigy did not hang in Charleston or Boston. Yet the Mansfield decision in the *Somerset* case demonstrated that slaveholders had at least as much to fear from parliamentary sovereignty as did merchants". [39] The founding generation were pragmatic men and all that which was driving this restrained behavior was the fact that colonial leadership was under no delusion as towards the lawfulness of slavery in the aftermath of the *Somersett* decision and for them the litmus test for colonial slave masters were criminal charges.

"We have abolished the slave, but the master remains". Wendell Phillips (*circa* 1865)

Chapter 3
Declaration of Independence

The ethos, culture within the American colonies was hooliganism, and corruption that turned chaotic after England's highest court… the Twelve Judges determined in the *Somersett* case that slavery could only be authorized by "positive law" and that it was not "allowed and approved by the laws of this Kingdom" as of June 1772—during colonial times. The assault upon the rule of law in the American colonies corrupted England's colonialization initiative. Hidden in myth is the fact that America's slave owning patriots were in criminal league with the British during colonial times. They reigned over a "new species of tyranny…created entirely by Colony government" as it was stated by one of Somersett's lawyers. They became committed to the rebellion and creation of a slavocracy, *after* Mansfield issued the Twelve Judges' decision that slavery was not "allowed and approved by the laws of the Kingdom" and could only be lawfully established by "positive law" in 1772. The colonial government assaulted the rule of law by placing black people *below* the rule of law. Their vision for America was an anathema to the core democratic ideal of the Declaration of Independence that "all men are created equal". The First Congress soon delivered a devastating blow to their vision of a slavocracy during the summer of 1776, when it rejected Thomas Jefferson's bill to adopt Roman jurisprudence, and once it formally adopted English law, Congress could not change U. S. citizenship requirements, or otherwise disfranchise black people since slave laws were rendered null and void, by operation of law. This meant *inter alia*—all black people held English citizenship by the day that the Declaration of Independence was issued, they were U. S. citizens, as a matter of law.

However, there was a well-placed resistance within the First Congress—who were supremely dissatisfied, and by the time it came to draft and then ratifying a new federal constitution during the 1780s—they forced a capitulation out of the delegates. The enslavement, disfranchisement and enactment of repressive laws to effectuate and sustain slavery placed black people *below* the rule of law. Respecting the rule of law, proved itself to be an inadequate guardrail and it has enduringly framed the restorative justice debate here in the U. S.

The founding generation envisioned an Anglo-Republic with the president at the top, and conditioned being a "natural-born citizen" as an indelible requirement to gate those who might aspire and then hold the august office of president. The exaltation of U. S. nationality by birth is apparent, as it was not subject to a prospective matriculation and then as an accommodation to influential foreign-born citizens involved in the American Revolution, such as Alexander Hamilton and others of that generation, waived the requirement of being "natural-born citizen", as they were a "Citizen of the United States at the time of the Adoption of this Constitution"——as provided for in the Constitution. And although the founding generation did not define the term "natural-born citizen" in the Constitution, it was unnecessary, since England's common law defined the term to mean "born within the dominion of the crown of England". Further, white immigrants were not held in high regard by the founding generation——John Jay, who was president of the 1st and 3rd Congress——a signer of the Declaration of Independence wrote a letter to then President George Washington specially stating: "Permit me to hint, whether it would be wise and seasonable to provide a strong check to the admission of Foreigners into our national Government." Jay was troubled during the 1790s about "white" immigration, and President Washington did not rebuke or disabuse him of this stated concern.

The myth surrounding white immigration furthered an assault upon black loyalists, but the founding generation did not embrace the notion that white immigrants would have the same rights, privileges, and opportunities as its natural-born populace. They used peonage white European as tools of racial repression. The myth that America was a nation envisioned for immigrants was popularized in the late 19th century by immigrants arriving in America *via* Ellis Island. During such time, in the U. S., the prevailing sentiment was that non-Europeans, and to an extent, European Catholics, and certainly people of the Jewish faith were unfit for citizenship in the United States.

Science and nature have long confirmed that modern humanity from the famous 3.2 million years old Australopithecus female called Lucy, to Homo sapiens are from Africa. Humans left Africa and arrived in Europe about 45,000 years ago, having a mixture of light and dark variants of skin color. There's no such thing as a white race.

Scientists theorized populations living in Europe became lighter-skinned over time because pale skin absorbed more sunlight. As well, there's skeletal remains discovered in a cave in Britain——dating back 10,000 years ago... called Cheddar Man. And the genome of this early Englishmen reveals that he had blue eyes, dark brown skin, and dark curly hair——Negroid features.

The discovery of Cheddar Man and research disproves the notion of skin color as a classifier for defining an Englishman. Also, researchers now theorize that genes for lighter skin became widespread far later than originally thought, and that early immigrants to England had dark pigmentation for millennia after they left Africa.

Native Americans were here well before the British, and earlier people in the Americas were people of the Nigritic African race——who entered the Americas as early as 100, 000 years ago, by way of the Bering Strait. There is archeological, and cultural evidence that proves ancient Africans predates Native Americans.

The earliest trade, and commercial activities between prehistoric and ancient Africa included shipping, and travel across the Atlantic. This became part of the oral history of the Choctaw People. They are an aboriginal black Native American Nation, who were the original inhabitants of the Mississippi Valley region. This

Nation settled the former Louisiana Territories, and parts of the southern U. S., having crossed the Atlantic Ocean—perhaps earlier than 7,000 B. C.

Then in 1606, Virginia was Tsenacommacah—the name given by the Powhatan people to their homeland. The area encompassed all of Tidewater Virginia, and Englishmen were a hoard of immigrants on death's doorstep, and "but-for" the compassion, humanity of the Powhatans they would have perished. The system of indentured servitude had enabled these poor whites—paupers, ne'er-do-wells, religious dissenters, waifs, prisoners and prostitutes to sell their services for a stipulated number of years. And some were kidnapped off the streets of London and Bristol, as the first blacks were kidnapped in the villages of Africa. Many were sold, as the first blacks were sold, by the captains of ships. And with respect to black settlers—Africans were kidnapped from different countries and arrived at Virginia's shores in chains. They did not immigrate to the U. S. and by virtue of English law, their descendants were America's native sons—free-born Englishmen.

The legal effect of Dunmore's proclamation was that it was a habeas corpus decree that freed all other slaves within the American colonies. This also occurred with the *Somersett* decision—15,000 other slaves throughout London and Wales gained freedom. The colonists who continued to enslave black people *after Somersett* were criminals under English law. They did not become immunized by virtue of the Declaration of Independence, nor based upon any subsequent laws enacted by U. S. lawmakers and if so, how so... since the First Congress formally adopted English law in 1776, rooted in centuries of English jurisprudence, and each state followed suit the same year. Dunmore's proclamation liberated all slaves within the American colonies. [40] These facts have been ignored and they frame the threshold question—how could any founding father within the American colonies legally own black slaves when the Declaration issued in July 1776? It must be analyzed and viewed through the prism of English law during colonial times. The case of *R. v. Stapylton (1771,* unreported*)* remains controlling precedent. [41]

By spring 1776, as the vote on independence neared... Lord Dunmore's proclamation of liberation had caused unrest within the rebellion. The patriots' rhetoric about England's tyranny and their own violations of legal rights of black people was placing the rebellion on precarious footing. They were using repressive, lawless violence towards black people... who all knew were legally free under English law.

Under English common law... born in colonial America made the person an Englishman with an inalienable right of liberty under England's Bill of Rights and colonial charters. As Chief Justice Holt, Mansfield's predecessor, had declared nearly seventy years earlier, "the common law takes no notice of negroes being different from other men. By the common law no man can have a property [interest] in another..." [42] The British leadership knew that if its government recognized slavery in the Kingdom that it would have undermined or fundamentally altered English common law.

At the Fifth Virginia Convention—held in May and June of 1776 it was Patrick Henry who attacked Lord Dunmore's proclamation, declaring that he was encouraging insurrection among slaves who he had armed and Henry exclaimed that it reveals the King to be a "tyrant instead of the protector of his people." Henry was decrying equal protection under the rule of law for black people, as Virginia's colonial governor... its highest judicial official, Lord Dunmore was finally defending England's rule of law, and in training and arming black people, he was providing them the best assistance to protect their own liberty rights.

Lord Dunmore's actions were in consonance with the Crown's duty to provide protection for all citizens under each colonial charter, and as slavery had been declared not "allowed and approved by the laws of this Kingdom" by the Twelve Judges in the *Somersett* decision, his actions could not be the cause of insurrection. This was ahistorical since Henry was labelling legally free people—"slaves," when in fact they were freeborn Englishmen by virtue of the Twelve Judges' decision in the *Somersett* case.

Belatedly, the American colonists tried to inform King George III that they were only unhappy with ministerial policy—not his own, but their attempt to repair deteriorated relations was rebuffed. The King even refused to read their olive branch petition. Then Lord Dunmore liberated the black people being held as slaves on November 7, 1775 and although many colonists were against declaring independence—they came to believe it to be their only option once King George III stated to his Ministers:

> "Keep the rebel harassed, anxious and poor, until the day when, by a natural and inevitable process, discontent and disappointment were converted into penitence and remorse."

Everyone in the world saw American colonists as British subjects—rebelling against their King. The hardening of King George III's position was forcing each patriot to view the repression of black people, who were British citizens differently and to realize that they had only one course of action: independence. It was abundantly plain—His Majesty's ministers were acting with total royal approval and only by declaring independence, would the rest of the world see the American colonies as a separate country. And only then would foreign nations, such as France or Spain might possibly offer help.

Under English law, the legal condition of each colonist was established by the same protocol used for the first nineteen Africans, who'd arrived on Virginia's shores in August 1619. It was the same law that made the Founding Fathers Englishmen. No erstwhile Englishman—who later became an American in 1776 held a heighten status. They were not immunized from English law, nor was any class of British citizen granted the legal right, license or privilege to own fellow countrymen, or Africans. And as such—every black person living in colonial America was an English citizen.

These English settlers in the American colonies were split and were not singularly in favor of independence or republicanism during the mid-1770s. Although some believed the American colonies did not benefit from being part of the

British Empire——loyalists thought differently. But many English settlers were undecided, or totally indifferent when on the second of July 1776, the Second Continental Congress finally voted for independence.

Two days later, lawmakers from the thirteen American colonies approved a final version of the Declaration of Independence, written for the most part by Virginia's Thomas Jefferson. It was a clarion call, a compact by and between Englishmen in the American colonies that all of King George III's subjects would be equal in in this new nation called the United States. A bargain was struck by and between American colonists, and it was the formal beginning of another English civil war. [43]

The colonial legislative assemblies, being just one chamber of a bicameral legislative system could not, on its own... promulgate "positive law". The bicameral legislative system vexed America's colonial legislative assemblies, and the frustrations surrounding their inability to secure the King's assent with respect to enacting lawful colonial law was a shared grievance. And in furtherance of their commonality——the first three of twenty-seven complaints lodged against King George III in the Declaration of Independence were:

> "He [King George III] has refused his Assent to Laws, the most wholesome and necessary for the public good."
>
> "He has forbidden his Governors to pass Laws of immediate and pressing importance, unless suspended in their operation till his Assent should be obtained; and when so, has utterly neglected to attend to them."
>
> "He has refused to pass other Laws for the accommodation of large districts of people, unless those people would relinquish the right of Representation in the Legislature, a right inestimable to them and formidable to tyrants only."

The interplay, and necessity of each colonial assemblies to have the assent of the *executive* chamber of the bicameral colonial legislative system——the King was further high-lighted in the eighth, and ninth grievances alleged against King George III in the Declaration of Independence.

> "He [King George III] has obstructed the Administration of Justice, refusing his Assent to Laws establishing judiciary powers."
>
> "He has made judges dependent on his Will alone, for the tenure of their offices, and the amount and payment of their salaries."

The Declaration is illustrative of the fact that the King's "Assent" upon colonial laws was required to promulgate positive municipal laws, and that the founding generation knew it. These grievances in the Declaration would lead a careful historian to review colonial slave laws that decriminalized kidnappings, legalized slavery, and changed the patrilineal descent system to the matrilineal based system of *partus sequitur ventrem* that gave rise to hereditary slavery, within the colonies during the seventeenth century to see if the King gave his assent. This would be the threshold inquiry.

Soon the compact was put to the test and Congress appeared to be committed to honoring its contract with all erstwhile Englishmen, now American citizens, when they rejected Jefferson's bill to supplant English law with Roman law. If Congress had done so, it could have allowed for the legalization of slavery on U. S. soil, and the lawful elevation of slaveholding Americans *above* the rule of law, and to place black Englishmen *below* the rule of law. Roman law recognized slavery at birth. The notion that the public is deemed to both own and is presumed to know the law and court precedents are basic principles of constitutional law. [44]

Congress formally adopted English law in 1776 and went on to ratify the Treaty of Paris in 1784—promising to "set at liberty" all Englishmen.

These congressional actions bound the United States—but black Englishmen was not freed.

The Congress placed black people, who held U. S. citizenship pursuant to the Declaration of Independence *below* the rule of law and put the young nation at odds with the rule of law that culminated into the U. S. Civil War in 1861. It was disfranchisement and by acceding to the urgings of slaveholding Americans, in furtherance of the enslavement of black citizens in derogation of the Treaty of Paris of 1783, the rule of law was assaulted.

Late in the Revolutionary War, Royal authority had been restored in Georgia and South Carolina was occupied by the British. And among others, George Washington and Thomas Jefferson had lost "slaves" to England's *Southern Strategy* as British commanders, such as General Charles Cornwallis were zealously liberating slaves. [45] Well into England's *Southern Strategy*... the codename the King's ministers used to refer to resolve the conflict in the American colonies—England was close to reclaiming substantial territory within its once-vast American Empire.

England's *Southern Strategy* created an egalitarian society in the southern states, as it made all slaves "free negroes," socially equal to white Englishmen, like Washington and Jefferson... before the Declaration of Independence. And while the Royal Government's *Southern Strategy* was not altruistic in nature and was economic warfare... done militarily to financially ruin the founding generation's leadership, whose wealth was based upon slavery and being used to finance rebellion in colonial America——it was still legal and conclusive.

England freed all slaves by way of the *Southern Strategy*. The British Commander-in-chief General Henry Clinton issued *The Phillipsburg Proclamation* on June 30, 1779. It was the final iteration of England's *Southern Strategy* of 1775. Exercising executive power, Clinton declared liberty and subjecthood to all black people suffering as slaves in colonial America. England's rationale for this proclamation was to stimulate a mass desertion, by encouraging blacks to come over to the British. Clinton was positive that an unconditional liberation of all slaves in colonial America would turn the lagging war around. Clinton thought an additional proclamation of liberation for slaves would strike a devastating blow at the plantation economy, as it would force southern slave masters to use their men for guarding slaves, instead of fighting them. It was estimated that 100,000 black people left captivity in search of freedom.

Under the rubric of patents of subjecthood and habeas relief——all 500,000-black people throughout the American states became legally free. The British proclamation applied to males and females, including their children.

The war proceeded and the United States won an important battle in October 1781. British General Lord Cornwallis had stationed his troops in Yorktown, Virginia, overlooking the York River, which flowed into Chesapeake Bay. French naval ships took control of the bay, preventing a British escape to the open sea. Then, French and American ground forces closed in on the British camp. Cornwallis was forced to surrender, rather than risk the lives of thousands of British soldiers.

But by 1782——France had all but withdrawn its vast military, and financial support for the United States. America's national government had no money to pay the war debts owed to France, estimated at twelve-million dollars——no money to pay private banks estimated at forty-million dollars, or money to pay U. S. citizens who were given promissory notes, estimated to be forty-million dollars for military services, merchants, and supplies during the war. Additionally, state governments owed nearly one hundred and fourteen million dollars to Americans who had sold food; horses and supplies to the revolutionary forces and in finding it teetering on the verge of financial collapse and with anarchy looming, the U. S. sued for peace in late 1781 and early 1782. America's treasury was empty, France was withdrawing her army and navy and it had patriots' problems. The value of Continental paper dollars had plummeted... which served to pay colonial soldiers, causing a large-scale mutiny. This pay-inspired uprising framed the patriots' principal wartime mobilization challenge during the late stage of the American Revolution: economics and the crumbling supply system.

Benjamin Franklin, John Jay, John Adams, Thomas Jefferson and Henry Laurens negotiated peace terms on behalf of the U. S. For Britain, protecting loyalists and freedom for black citizens who'd suffered as slaves under colonial rule were central to negotiations. The preliminary articles of peace provided for these concerns. The resulting armistice was signed by Franklin, Jay, Adams, and Lauren along with Richard Oswald, for England on November 30, 1782. The two nations agreed upon ten articles for peace.

1. Acknowledge the United States (viz. the Colonies) to be free, sovereign and independent states, and the British Crown, along with all heirs and successors, will relinquish claims to the government,

property, and territorial rights of the same, and every part thereof;
2. Establish the boundaries between the United States and British North America;
3. Grant fishing rights to United States fishermen in the Grand Banks, off the coast of Newfoundland and in the Gulf of Saint Lawrence;
4. Recognize the lawful contracted debts to be paid to creditors on either side;
5. The Congress of the Confederation will "earnestly recommend" state legislatures to recognize the rightful owners of all confiscated lands "provide for the restitution of all estates, rights, and properties, which have been confiscated belonging to real British subjects [Loyalists]";
6. United States will prevent future confiscations of the property of loyalists;
7. Prisoners of war on both sides are to be released, and all property left by the British army in the United States will remain unmolested;
8. Great Britain and the United States are each to be given perpetual access to the Mississippi River;

9. Territories captured by Americans subsequent to treaty will be returned without compensation;
10. Ratification of the treaty will occur within six months of the signing by contracted parties.

In this preliminary treaty, the U. S. agreed to cease all "hostilities," against British citizens, and upon ratification of the final treaty, promised to release all British prisoners in their care, custody, or detention. Africans and even sedentary black citizens who'd slave masters had continued to treat as slaves met the legal definition of being a "prisoner": a person who is confined in prison or kept in custody, especially as the result of legal process.

Centrally, as the treaty required release of each other's countrymen, this condition created major problems for the U. S. since everyone in the American colonies were Englishmen under the rule of law adopted by the U. S. The U. S. delegation fought hard to place extraneous wording "slave" in the treaty—but as slavery was never legal within the American colonies and slave laws had been rendered null and void by the Twelve Judge' ruling in the *Somersett* case in 1772 and all black people suffering as slaves had been liberated per the exercise of executive authority during colonial times, it was deemed superfluous wording since any treaty dispute would be resolved by way of English law.

Under colonial rule—the founding generation knew slavery was extrajudicial on British soil. The *Somersett* decision extinguished all putative ownership interests in other human beings; yet it criminally continued. America's founding generation who self-described themselves as slave masters could never substantiate an ownership claim of a black citizen as all people in the American colonies were King George III's subjects. They had the same legal rights and recourse under English rule of law.

The American Revolutionary War was a civil war about slavery. The enslavement of black people during colonial times was extrajudicial and as the term "prisoner" was defined as any person, whether a combatant or non-combatant who is held in custody by a belligerent power during or immediately after an armed conflict all black people should have been "set at liberty" in accordance to the rule of law. Liberty for black Englishmen was even more compellingly since colonial slavery was never authorized by positive law; the Twelve Judges ruled slavery was not "allowed and approved by the laws of this Kingdom" in the 1772 *Somersett* case and Lord Dunmore liberated all slaves during colonial times. The First Congress and each state in the union adopted English law and the legal consequence of these legislative acts made enslaving black citizens, an unconstitutional and violative of English law.

The Treaty of Paris, Article 7 provided:

> There shall be a firm and perpetual peace between his Brittanic Majesty and the said states, and between the subjects of the one and the citizens of the other, wherefore all hostilities both by sea and land shall From henceforth cease. All prisoners on both sides SHALL BE SET AT LIBERTY, and his Brittanic Majesty shall with all convenient speed, and without causing any destruction, or carrying away any Negroes, or other property of the American inhabitants, withdraw all his armies, garrisons, and fleets from the said United States, and from every post, place, and harbor within the same, leaving in all fortifications, the American artillery that may be therein; and shall also order and cause all archive, records, deeds, and papers belonging to any of the states, or their citizens, which in the course of the war may have fallen into the hands of his officers, to be forthwith restored

and delivered to the proper states and persons to whom they belong.

History supports, once news of this preliminary peace treaty with England was known, the founding generation in the U. S. began assaulting, kidnapping and imprisoning black people with impunity. They were being kidnapped off public streets and even out of their homes and then being enslaved—many of whom had never been slaves. The kidnappings were widespread, organized, and it violated the cessation of hostility truce between England and the U. S. This caused General Guy Carleton to lodge an attestation of treaty dispute against the U. S. directly to General Washington on May 6, 1783. This put the U. S. on actual notice of this treaty violation and thus it became their legal duty to purge Carleton's pre-ratification claim of treaty violation—if the U. S. could; but it could not. Afterwards, Washington described the meeting as "diffuse and desultory" as he learned that Carleton had permitted black people to embark and sail away ten days earlier. Carleton justified his decision, stating that "he conceived it could not have been the Intention of the British Government…to reduce themselves to the Necessity of violating their Faith to the Negroes who came into the British Lines under the Proclamation of his Predecessors." [46] General Clinton's Phillipsburg Proclamation in June 1779 declared liberty and subjecthood to all black people suffering as slaves. This patent of subjecthood was in accordance with England's rule of law and reaffirmed by General Leslie's proclamation in June 1782. Dunmore's pre-Declaration of Independence abolished slavery throughout the American colonies because of the Twelve-Judges ruling in the *Somersett* case in 1772. Carleton claimed that Washington's interpretation of Article 7 of the treaty was a misapprehension of English law. He explained to Washington that all former slaves as being British subjects and entitled to his protection.

The U. S. did not become an independent nation until January 14, 1784, with the ratification of the Treaty of Paris of 1783. Carleton's attestation of Treaty of Paris violations and his claim that all black people were entitled to be unmolested per the treaty in May 1783 were rebuttable presumptions under common law. Under English law—*praesumptio juris tantum* is an assumption made by a factfinder that is taken to be true *unless* someone comes forward to contest it and proves otherwise. The *Somersett* decision that slavery had not been "allowed and approved by the laws of this Kingdom" in 1772 rendered all colonial slave laws void. Mansfield's ruling in *R. v. Stapylton* that "being black will not prove the property" supports the legal conclusion that the Americans had the burden to prove black people were their legal property. [47] Mansfield's *Stapylton* ruling was controlling precedent for the legal proposition that under English law the U. S. could not merely claim ownership of black people; they had to prove it and as slavery was unlawful under *Somersett*—this nation was required to prove slave ownership claims with "positive law". But Washington was certain of the law and the outcome as he wrote a letter to Virginia's governor Benjamin Harrison. He told Harrison, "I wrote to you from Newburgh and informed you of the meeting I have had…I have discovered enough however, in the course of conversation…to convince me that the slaves which have absconded from their masters will never be restored to them." [48] There was no conflict of laws issue between the two nations since the First Congress adopted English law in 1776.

The *Somersett* decision was dispositive precedent for Carleton's claim of a treaty violation by the Americans in the spring of 1783. But the greatest obstacle was that the *Somersett* decision had doubled as British imperialistic policy during colonial times. Mansfield caring for his bi-racial niece in his home had softened the seminal decision, as it allowed people to use his complex family situation as a shield to deflect. Mansfield's actions are illustrative of this point, as he did not seasonably disabuse, nor did he ever see fit to correct anyone as to the true extent of his role in the *Somersett* decision; during colonial times. He was only one of twelve judges——not the sole jurist. This was a material fact, as a ruling by the Twelve Judge was viewed as a law-making tribunal. Mansfield allowed himself to become the avatar of a metropolitan antislavery movement that stood for the proposition that slavery in the Kingdom was so "odious"… "that it is incapable of being introduced on any reason, moral or political" except by the means of "positive law". Then in 1785 in the *Thames Ditton* case——Mansfield saw fit to interrupt a lawyer to state: "The determination go no further than that the master cannot by force compel him to go out of the Kingdom." [49] However, the four corners of the *Somersett* decision strongly rebuffs Mansfield's position as it was a seminal announcement of conflict of laws and determined that slavery by virtue of Virginia's slave laws were not allowed and approved by the laws of this Kingdom… a Kingdom at the time that included the American colonies. Mansfield may have not been an antislavery hero, but the public and even the American slaveholders correctly understood the *Somersett* decision as being more than a mere ideological rebuke to slavery throughout the American colonies.

> "We hold these truths to be self-evident, that all men are created equal... that among these are Life, Liberty and the pursuit of Happiness". Thomas Jefferson (*circa* 1776)

Chapter 4
Tenth Generational Dodge

Early American republic constitutional scholars have avoided first principles, that is "by [English] common law, no man could have a property interest in another" on British soil. [50] English common law was the reason why the first nineteen Africans appearing unto Virginia's shores in 1619 were indentured servants—not slaves. The rule of law officials abided by English law when they made these Africans and all others indentured servants. Scholars appear to misapprehend, or have failed to recognize, or perhaps have chosen to ignore the fact that slavery was a crime under English common law on British soil and that the *Somersett* decision determined that colonial slave laws were not lawfully promulgated. The general estimate of this thesis is that colonial slavery was a homegrown species of tyranny, operating within the American colonies extrajudicially—due to colonial corruption. None of the legislative assemblies in colonial

America promulgated positive municipal law to legalize slavery. The misanthrope practice of slavery never had a true badge of lawfulness, and consequently, all who purported to own other people here in the U. S. were criminals—nothing more elegant than that.

Colonial legislatures had no authority to enact laws that violated English common law during colonial times. Slavery and changing the patrilineal descent system to *partus sequitur ventrem* in colonial America violated the repugnancy proviso in each colonial charter. Even assuming arguendo that these two laws were not jurisdictionally barred by colonial charter, the *Somersett* case was a matter that was properly *before* the Court of King's Bench. [51] Both Virginia and Massachusetts were Royal colonies and as Somerset was a Virginian-born slave, who Stewart claimed he owned based upon Virginia's slave laws—the dispositive issue turned upon a conflict of laws determination. [52] Historians and legal scholars refer to conflict of laws as private international law, as it implies a legal dispute that have a foreign element in them.

The Royal Assent by Commission Act became English law in 1541 and colonial America's slave laws required the King's assent. Colonial governments were formed with a bicameral legislative structure and the King's assent was the final step required for a bill to be deemed lawfully enacted and then a promulgated colonial law. Bicameralism divided the colonial legislative power between two chambers; an "upper chamber," England's monarchy, and a "lower chamber," the colonial legislative assemblies. And according to modern scholars, the Founding Fathers specially adopted the colonial bicameral legislative system for the U. S. Congress—endorsing the need for checks and balances in America's legislative system. [53] Critics of bicameralism claims it makes meaningful political reform more difficult and increase the risk of gridlock since both chambers must agree upon a law. While proponents of bicameralism tout the merits of having checks and balances. Colonial laws without the assent of England's king—the upper chamber of the bicameral colonial legislative system were legal nullities and slaveowners proceeded at their own peril with slave mastering practices.

The Twelve Judges in the *Somersett* case announced standards and procedures for resolving habeas disputes underpinned by colonial slave laws in 1772. The threshold inquiry was to establish characterization or classification of the dispute. English courts apply the law of *lex fori*: when the conflict in laws pertains to a procedural matter or *lex loci*: when the conflict in laws pertains to a substantive matter. And once the Twelve Judges declared in the *Somersett* case that slavery was not "allowed and approved by the laws of this Kingdom" and could only be lawful by virtue of "positive law" all colonial slave laws became invalid from the outset of this misanthrope practice. British imperial politics made the announcement of standards and procedures more urgent for slaveholding colonists since all were in violations of colonial charters and the bicameral colonial legislative structure.

Historians and legal scholars have probed the significance of the *Somersett* decision for almost 250 years and all too many have come to focus upon the strict limits of the ruling, which do prohibit the forcible removal of blacks from the Kingdom—but they claim not their servitude in the Kingdom. [54] However, this circumscribed interpretation of the opinion has led many to conclude that the *Somersett* case "found the law on slavery in a state of confusion and that is precisely where he [Mansfield] left it". [55] That's an inaccurate interpretation of the *Somersett* decision, and in fact, it is as David Brion Davis has concluded that the ruling "removed any legal basis for slavery in England," and that it made it "no longer possible to take for granted the universal legality of slave property" [56] as the Twelve Judges declared slavery was not "allowed and approved by the laws of this Kingdom" and could only be lawful by positive law. Legal scholars then must have known that as the slaver Stewart claimed ownership of Somersett based upon colonial slave laws they were the subject of the Twelve Judges' determinations of not being lawfully promulgated based upon the laws of the British Empire. These legal scholars must then have concluded that under any interpretation of the term "positive law" colonial slave laws had been adjudged as not being lawfully enacted and thus they became nullities.

The Founding Fathers signed a Declaration of Independence in 1776 on behalf of the thirteen American colonies acknowledging that the colonial legislative system was bicameral, and that the King's assent upon colonial bills were jurisdictional and his assent was being unduly withheld. The first three grievances in the Declaration framed the shortcomings of colonial bicameralism from their perspective:

(1) "He [King George III] has refused his Assent to Laws, the most wholesome and necessary for the public good..."

(2) "He has forbidden his Governors to pass Laws of immediate and pressing importance, unless suspended in their operation till his Assent

should be obtained; and when so suspended, he has utterly neglected to attend to them..."

(3) "He has refused to pass other Laws for the accommodation of large districts of people, unless those people would relinquish the right of Representation in the Legislature, a right inestimable to them and formidable to tyrants only."

The founding generation in the Declaration, by negative inference the objectionableness of a bicameral legislative structure. And although these grievances were attacks upon King George III's governance, they and other enumerated grievances serves as inculpatory proof that colonial America's leadership knew slave laws were nugatory.

King George III and his predecessors were codified check and balance to the power of each colonial assembly. And presently, a bicameral legislative system is the core constitutional safeguard of America's democracy. "A formidable sinister interest may always obtain the complete command of a dominant assembly by some chance, and for a moment, and it is therefore of great use to have a second chamber of an opposite sort, differently composed, in which that interest in all likelihood will not rule." [57] Slavery and its profitability was a "formidable sinister interest" that overwhelmed colonial assemblymen and all colonial

America. Additionally, there were no lawfully enacted slave laws—and even if laws had existed in a bicameral manner, they were overruled in June 1772 when the Twelve Judges ruled slavery in the Kingdom was unconstitutional, arguably because of the Magna Carta of 1215. Consequently, the *Somersett* decision abolished slavery. This remains an inescapable conclusion; as (1) each colonial legislative chamber was deemed to know the extent of their authority within their legislative system; (2) the colonial charter contemplated the monarchy and colonial legislature to agree upon a proposed colonial law—to promulgate "positive municipal law" and (3) the colonial charter does not contemplate a proposed law effectiveness in the absence of the monarch's assent. Judicial relief from the effects of an overreaching colonial assembly was a remedy available to an aggrieved party under English law. However, due to the nature of the corruption of colonial government, no earlier application for relief was applied for and granted. The Court of King's Bench held original jurisdiction over such matters as, the constitutionality of colonial laws, or disputes between colonial legislative chambers and that of the monarch.

The Declaration of Independence announced the creation of a new nation, and as a matter of English law, the resulting Treaty of Paris of 1783 extinguished any possible return to *status quo antebellum* because the U. S. agreed that the independence of the erstwhile American colonies would be deemed once the treaty was ratified. Thus, January 14, 1784 is America's true date of independence from England, not July 4, 1776 and it also materially implicates and terminates the legality of U. S. slave ownership claims. The term *status quo antebellum* has been shortened to form the phrase *status quo,* and *status quo ante*. An example of a war resolved *status quo antebellum* was the War of 1812, between the U. S. and England or *Mr. Madison's War*. The British negotiators suggested ending the war *uti possidetis*—that territory and other property remains with its possessor at the end of a conflict. However, the final treaty, due in large part to domestic pressure was a *status quo antebellum* peace. Such was the type of peace agreed to, by way of the Treaty of Paris of 1783 and thus America's claim of slave ownership had another legal hurdle to traverse; British *post* Declaration of Independence proclamations of liberation of black slaves; Clinton's Phillipsburg Proclamation in June 1779, as well as British General Alexander Leslie in May 1782 who liberated slaves from plantations in the countryside outside Charlestown, South Carolina renamed to Charleston after the treaty was ratified. [58]

Slavery was extrajudicial due to colonial corruption——colonial legislators ascribed lawfulness to slave laws that did not have the monarch's assent. Each chamber of the colonial legislative system was legally bound by colonial charter to jointly agree upon any promulgated colonial law, and to honor the limits of their legislative power. Laws passed without the King's assent were void *ab initio*. The *Somersett* decision overturned all colonial slave laws in 1772 and was a judicial construction of colonial slave laws within the Kingdom of Great Britain. The Court of King's Bench had original jurisdiction over colonial laws, and the ruling that such colonial slave laws were not "allowed and approved by the laws of this Kingdom" became the law of the land. Colonial slavery was abolished and this was supported by precedent, but too many historians misapprehend the material facts 1) slavery was prohibited on British soil; 2) colonies bound themselves to English law that prohibited slavery by colonial charters; 3) a colony had no lawful authority to pass a law that was "repugnant" to the common law and 4) colonial legislative systems were bicameral, and none of the slave laws had the assent of England's monarch. This was required to constitute a lawfully enacted "positive municipal law." The jurisdictional shortcomings, the lack of the monarch's assent on slave laws abolished colonial slavery and all such colonial slave laws became void *ab initio*.

The legal historian William Wiecek in his seminal article—*Somerset: Lord Mansfield and the Anglo-American World*, states that the *Somersett* decision "posed basic constitutional problems for the British imperial system, though these became irrelevant four years later with the declaration of American independence..." He concludes that the question of *Somersett's* force under the imperial constitution became academic with the Declaration of Independence. However, the threshold problem with Wiecek's claim is that the First Congress adopted English law in 1776 and effectively adopted the same constitutional problems faced by the British. The U. S. continued its legal ties to *Somersett*. Also, Parliament had anticipated this very point when it passed the Declaratory Act in 1766, making it clear that it should "legislate over the colonies in all cases whatsoever." Also, England's Court of King's Bench have always held original jurisdiction over the bicameral colonial legislative system and by virtue of the Twelve Judges procedure could indeed make policy for a putative American state, when it was under colonial rule and per the Treaty of Paris of 1783, colonial rule continued until Congress ratified the treaty in 1784.

Clearly, the Court of King's Bench had the legal authority to rule colonial slave laws violated colonial charters in 1772. Dunmore had the legal authority to liberate all black slaves in 1775. Further, the First Congress stated in the Declaration——resolves that "the respective colonies are entitled to the common law of England". Such makes it plain; the Founding Fathers were not endeavoring to distance themselves from English law. The adoption of English law, which did not carve out *Somersett*, is dipositive proof that the Twelve Judge' judicial construction was binding upon the U. S., even if the *Somersett* decision was subject to some prospective bar, or an affirmative defense. Also, the thirteen states in 1776 continued *Somersett's* binding authority, as one of the first legislative acts undertaken by each of the newly independent states was to adopt a reception statute that gave legal effect to the existing body of English law and *Somersett*. [59] Lastly, British General Henry Clinton issued an unambiguous emancipation proclamation that liberated all black slaves living within the American colonies.

The Treaty of Paris of 1783 conditioned a *status quo antebellum* peace, and it was ratified by Congress in January 1784. The two parties agreed that no side would gain from the conflict. The U. S. did not come through the American Revolution with greater rights over black people and could not *ex post facto* turn black people into slaves. They were free-born Englishmen when the U. S. declared itself an independent nation in 1776: they too were returned to *status quo antebellum* under English law. This was the legal consequence of the *status quo antebellum* treaty and the preliminary Treaty of Paris that ceased hostilities was signed November 1782 and it was not well-received in England, as it created political turmoil that forced the head of its imperial government Lord Shelburne to resign. Then a new government was formed under the Duke of Portland, who replaced England's treaty negotiator Richard Oswald with David Hartley. He sought to modify the treaty—but Hartley was unsuccessful. Thus, the preliminary treaty was pretty much static and unchanged when the Congress ratified the treaty on January 14, 1784.

The slave owners' partner-in-crimes were British government actors, and public confidence in English rule of law suffered. Personal liberty during colonial times had long been associated, first and foremost, with honest government. Demonstrably, it is quite telling, that while Parliament enacted the Petition of Right in 1628, which established certain liberties for all Englishmen, concurrently, history reports the genesis and explosion of race-based extrajudicial colonial laws that were squarely in conflict with the Petition of Right. But as contemplated, English law stood resolutely, as law was king. History supports, the Americans assaulted and recaptured black people immediately *after* the preliminary treaty was known. They were prisoners of American hostilities and each putative owner of a black person was saddled with the legal obligation of proving the claim under the precedent of *Stapylton*. Under the rule of law, all black loyalists were entitled to a due process hearing, but all were denied. The treaty violations raised by Carleton had to be viewed and analyzed through the prism of English law. The formal adoption of English law by the First Congress, and by each state legislature in 1776 bound the Americans to the Twelve Judges' rulings in the *Somersett* case that rendered colonial slave laws void *ab initio* in June 1772. Lord Dunmore, exercising executive authority on behalf of King George III liberated black people suffering as slaves in November 1775 and thus the Declaration of Independence applied to all black colonists who were suffering as slaves of white Englishmen, loyalists and patriots alike. England's constitution and common law continued uninterrupted through the war for American independence, and the American Revolution ended in January 1784 by ratification of the treaty and all black people had lawful rights under the rule of law.

During colonial times, British citizenship inured to black people born within the American colonies, in the same manner as it did for white colonists. The British government provided no coherent imperial oversight of the American colonies during the 17th century and an unwritten policy of salutary neglect created a culture of hooliganism and race-based slavery—a species of colony tyranny. The colonial Americans did not hold fealty to England's rule of law. Under English law, colonial slave laws were nugatory since colonial assemblies did not have the designated authority or power to authorize a slavery institution in the manner that they all proceeded. Pursuant to each colonial charter, the colonial legislative system was bicameral and white colonial legislators had no legal power, or right to change, or to interfere with a British grant of citizenship to colonial black people. The *Somersett* decision during 18th century colonial America was a civil rights ruling tantamount to the 1955 U. S. Supreme Court's unanimous ruling in *Brown v. Board of Education*. The 1772 unanimous ruling by England's Twelve Judges in the *Somersett* case rendered colonial slave laws unconstitutional throughout the Kingdom and declared that slavery within the Kingdom could only be lawful if enacted by "positive law". Under English law, only Parliament had the lawful authority to enact "positive law" and it had not done so, thus rendering all colonial slave laws void *ab initio*. This was the legal consequence as Mansfield's tribunal analyzed colonial slave laws and then specially ruled on June 22, 1772 that Somersett's condition of being treated as a slave based upon colonial America's slave laws were not "allowed and approved by the laws of this Kingdom". Lord Dunmore, exercising executive power liberated all blacks suffering as slaves in November 1775 and when the founding generation declared independence for colonial Englishmen on July 4, 1776, colonial blacks who'd suffered, or were then suffering as slaves under colonial tyranny were already legally free under English law.

The First Congress adopted English-law *post*-Declaration in 1776 and black Englishmen were not carved out nor somehow exempted. Without regard, independence and American citizenship inured to black people in colonial America, in the same manner as it did for white Englishmen. It is ahistorical to claim differently. Under English law, white colonists had no greater legal powers, or rights or status of British citizenship than black British citizens. Black citizens as Englishmen had a legal right to leave the U. S. *per* the Treaty of Paris and America's claim that Carleton violated the treaty by relocating 3,000 legally free black Englishmen to Canada is totally unsupportable. It was a demonstrable treaty violation by the U. S., who *after* Carleton indicated in the spring of 1783 his country's commitment to transport black loyalists away from U. S. soil—without legal justification or right the U. S. prevented their departure.

The British should have been allowed to transport all black people living within the American states to British soil since Congress adopted English law that rejected slavery, embraced due process and then conceded British imperial control of the U. S. states until ratification of the treaty—which occurred January 14, 1784. The legal consequence of these congressional acts purged all indices of black servitude based upon erstwhile colonial slave laws and inured U. S. citizenship unto the disfranchised and enslaved 500,000 black Englishmen. Nonetheless, the Americans relied upon words in the treaty that "His Britannic Majesty shall with all convenient speed, and without causing any destruction, or carrying away any Negroes, or other property of the American inhabitants" to claim differently. This language was not conclusive nor dispositive language as erstwhile Englishmen now Americans did not legally "own" colonial blacks during colonial times—slavery operated extrajudicially and was declared unconstitutional on June 22, 1772. The First Congress bound each American to English law in 1776 and liberty was a personal right of all Englishmen, which the British had affirmed by emancipating all blacks suffering as slave during colonial times—exercising executive authority of King George III. Also, in the same sentence in the treaty the two nations, negates the Americans' interpretation by stating "All prisoners on both sides SHALL BE SET AT LIBERTY". Thus, if the sentence is to be construed as "all" British prisoners except Negro prisoners are to be "SET AT LIBERTY" this too is a classic treaty dispute, requiring resolution through the prism of English law, as the American Revolution was an English civil war and both nations were bound by English law that guaranteed due process to everyone. The conflicting interpretation of this sentence was a treaty dispute, framed by Carleton's relocation of 3,000 black loyalists in November 1783. And if one were to accept the Americans' bare claim of ownership of 500,000 black Englishmen—it would require a total negation of the spirit and language that "All prisoners on both sides SHALL BE SET AT LIBERTY". [60]

The abandonment of the unwritten policy of salutary neglect that quelled the ethos of hooliganism and then the *Somersett* ruling that slavery was not "allowed and approved by the laws of this Kingdom..." that in effect, abolished colonial slavery were consistent with each colonial charter. The rulings in the *Somersett* case reaffirmed that which each colonial charter provided for, 1) that English law was King and 2) that any change in colonial laws, that were inconsistent with English law required the monarch's assent. The abolishment of colonial slavery merely returned the colonies to status *quo ante*, since during the period of salutary neglect the colonial legislatures were legally obligated to English law and each colony conceded to in the Declaration that all colonial assemblies were subject to securing the King's assent to enact positive municipal law and its assemblymen were bound by it. The period of salutary neglect did not anoint colonial legislators with the jurisdiction to enact positive laws within the colonies. Colonial slavery operated extrajudicially and necessarily, in the absence of the monarch's assent on any laws inconsistent with English law, such laws operated extrajudicially, and with Congress' adoption of English law in 1776 it eviscerated Wiecek's quarrels about the applicability of the *Somersett* decision, as defective colonial and municipal slave laws are subject to the legal principle of *quod ab initio non valet in tractu temporis non convalescet*—that which is bad in its commencement improves not by lapse of time. They required and mandated adjudication by the British courts.

In *Smith v. Brown and Cooper*, [61] Chief Justice Holt ruled "that as soon as a negro comes into England, he becomes free; one may be a villein [serf] in England, but not a slave." Bound by the rule of law, the legislatures of each American colony on their own had no legal right, power or license to decriminalize kidnapping of people. And in being bound by colonial charter to English law, and its bicameral legislative system, the threshold hurdle of any colonial or municipal slave law was its legislature's authority to legalize the kidnappings of Africans in the first instance. Bound by English law, slavery was unlawful since "man stealing" or kidnapping were serious criminal acts under English law. The colonial legislature had no authority to pass any law which was repugnant to England's common law. Kidnapping was a very serious crime under English law—settlers were protected by English law that experienced resurgence in the 1640s when King Charles I continued to believe that he was *above* the law. He was arrested in 1649 and tried for high treason and found guilty—adjudged to be a "tyrant, traitor, murderer and public enemy". The King was then beheaded on January 30, 1649 because he did not want to abide by English rule of law. The principle of "the law being king" was discussed by Montesquieu in *The Spirit of the Laws* (1748) and was infused into colonial America by way of the rule of law.

The colonial charters had language that all American settlers or natives "shall have and enjoy all Liberties and Immunities of free and natural subjects within any Dominions of Us. . . as if they were born within this Our Realm of England." In numerous freedom lawsuits, this language was advanced using the claim that, under English law, "no man could be deprived of his liberty, but by the judgment of his peers." Likewise, as *partus sequitur patrem* made the person an Englishman by birth—no colonial legislature had lawful authority to condemn an Englishman to be a "slave" at birth or to change the patrilineal descent system to *partus sequitur ventrem* for enslaved women, in the manner that they did. Hereditary slavery was institutional kidnapping and it too was repugnant to England's common law.

The *Somersett* decision was not an infringement upon colonial rights. Slavery was an extrajudicial institution, as colonial legislatures did not (1) decriminalize the act of kidnapping; (2) did not change the patrilineal descent system to accommodate hereditary slavery and (3) did not change, and broaden the legislative power of colonial assemblies to enact positive municipal laws without the monarch's assent. And as the Twelve Judges in furtherance of their legal obligation ruled in the *Somersett* decision in June 1772 that slave practices were unconstitutional throughout the Kingdom, it became criminal since kidnapping was a criminal practice under English law. The colonial assembly was only a branch of a bicameral colonial legislative system. The Court of King's Bench had original jurisdiction over the question colonial slavery, as it infringed upon the presumptive authority of England's King. The *Somersett* decision declared slavery was not "allowed and approved by the laws in this Kingdom" and could only be lawful in the Kingdom by "positive law".

England's abandonment of its policy of salutary neglect [62] and now this rebuke of colonial slave practices by the twelve-judge panel in the *Somersett* case on June 22, 1772 was an unambiguous message to planters within the American colonies and it was received as such. They knew that the ruling slavery was not "allowed and approved by the laws of this Kingdom" included the North American colonies. They were clear-headed in their knowledge that colonial slavery within the American colonies operated extrajudicially and was never the product of a properly promulgated legislative process. The failures of colonial assemblies to secure the King's assent upon slave laws could not be cured—and colonial slave laws became null and void. The crimes of assault, battery, kidnapping and rape associated with slavery were all serious crimes under English law. The *Somersett* decision had exposed slave mastering as being criminal since such laws violated English common law and it had been declared unconstitutional and not approved by the laws of this Kingdom and all slave masters were supremely relieved that this decision of the Twelve Judges panel had obliquely addressed the issue of slavery's legality within colonial America. We have seen that in the very year that Jefferson drafted his Declaration of Independence he brought a bill to supplant English law, and indeed in Philadelphia in 1787, members of the federal constitutional convention struggled yet again with the question of asserting equal claims for fundamental natural rights without calling the legitimacy, (constitutionality) of slavery into doubt. Their solution was to change the constitutional text to suggest that African slaves had not entered civil society. It was as though a retroactive law could rescue them from the adoption of English law; the *Somersett* decision that abolished slavery and

Congress' concession in the Treaty of Paris of 1783 that English rule extended until ratification. Moreover, such constitutional text did not ameliorate and alter the fact that ninety-five percent of the 500,000 black people whom they relegated to toil as slaves were native-born Englishmen by law.

There is no question that the Framers of the Constitution, who many were philosophically opposed to slavery compromised in drafting the Constitution to accommodate the institution of slavery. As an initial matter, after the ratification of the Treaty of Paris, it was clearly a question for the British to address, as to whether Africans entered civil society during colonial times—not the Americans. Also, the bare claim in the 1780s that African slaves had not entered civil society was ahistorical and each one of the black people who they relegated to slavery was entitled to a due process hearing. From 1619 forward each African who reached colonial America's shores were indentured servants—not slaves under English law and after their term expired each became part of civil society. None of the American colonies enacted positive law authorizing a legal condition called slave. The children of Africans were free-born Englishmen and there were no temporary adjustments uniquely related to the revolution, or the decision to declare independence. As early as

1788, George Mason drafted a proposed federal Bill of Rights that omitted the most troublesome equal rights language and conditioned protection of specified rights to "freemen" only. Madison did not go quite this far but omitted from his draft Bill of Rights specific reference to natural rights. Although it has been suggested by Robert J. Reinstein in *Completing the Constitution: The Declaration of Independence, Bill of Rights and Fourteenth Amendment*, [63] that Madison's language reflected "scruples" against using the term "slave" or "freemen" in constitutional text and that it is no coincidence that Madison's proposal came to be a prefix to the Constitution, and omitted the "harder" language of command and prohibition that could create legal limits on government.

There are early American constitutional scholars such as Pauline Maier, who made the observation that "the same argument that denied kings an inherited right to rule denied the right of masters to own whose status was determined by birth, not consent" in the American colonies. [64] This was a call to begin at first principles and although logical, the mainstream perspective is embodied by scholar Paul D. Carrington's position that everyone should take comfort in the fact that the Declaration proclaimed that it is "the obligation of government to accord equal legal status to all individuals, to confer upon all the same rights, and to impose on all the same duties." [65] Destructive to Carrington's perspective and others was the fact that slavery was a criminal enterprise, as colonial America's legislative system was bicameral and rulings of the twelve-judges in the *Somersett* decision abolished colonial slavery and Dunmore liberated black slaves exercising executive power in November 1775. The founding generation exploited 500,000 legally free British subjects to create an economy and institutionalized racial repression to further this goal.

Slavery within the American colonies was an anathema to English law, and it created an ethos of hooliganism and a species of colony tyranny—hereditary slavery, and were chief considerations that drove Mansfield to have a Twelve-Judges' ruling on the legal question of the lawfulness and efficacy of colonial slave laws within the Kingdom in the *Somersett* case. This was a manifestation of England's imperialism and its abandonment of the unwritten policy of salutary neglect and America's founding generation understood the intent and legal consequence of the ruling. And a careful reading of Thomas Jefferson reveals that he set-forth the southern colonists' fear of setting loose on society a race of "inferiors" that would undermine all social institutions. Such was the reason that he concurrently advocated supplanting English law with Roman law while drafting the Declaration in the summer of 1776. The founding generation knew slavery was criminal on the eve of the Declaration and nothing was more illustrative of their guilty knowledge than Jefferson's accusation in the Declaration that the King was:

> "... exciting those very people to rise in arms among us, and to purchase that liberty of which he has deprived them, by murdering the people on whom he has obtruded them: thus paying off former crimes committed against the Liberties of one people, with crimes which he urges them to commit against the lives of another".

Although this language was edited out of the Declaration by Jefferson's seasoned colleagues, they then yoked black bondage upon unsuspecting and unwilling white colonists. The founding generation's social institutions were built upon the extrajudicial practice of hereditary slavery, and as each colonial assembly had failed to secure the King's "Assent" to "wholesome" promulgated colonial slave laws—the *Somersett* decision lawfully eviscerated all social institutions within colonial America. The bicameral nature of the colonial legislature system had mandated the King's Assent on all colonial laws. In failing to promulgate positive slave law, it follows that those enslaved by white colonists throughout the 17th and 18th centuries retained their rights as Englishmen, even as they were treated as "chattel property" during colonial rule by white English colonists.

The American colonies were not sovereign nations unto themselves, with a separate and distinct constitutional system. All the American colonies were bound by their colonial charter to English law, and none lawfully exercised the power of positive municipal law to create slave laws. The core misapprehension, or possible legerdemain of constitutional scholars and historians has been that of construction and refusal to begin at first principles. The rule of law officials made the first nineteen Africans indentured servants—not slaves in 1619. This status was consistent with English law. The colonial assemblies were legally bound by colonial charter to secure the King's "Assent" to create a legal condition called "slave". In failing to seek, or otherwise secure the King's "Assent" on colonial slave laws, they were not lawfully promulgated "positive laws." The colonies proceeded at their own peril when they acted, as if these facially defective colonial slave laws were lawful and built their social institution upon slavery.

The twelve-judges' ruling in the *Somersett* case addressed the constitutional question of the extent of the power of a sole chamber of a colonial bicameral legislature to enact slave laws and it changed the calculus for slave holding colonists, as the King's Bench declared slavery was not "allowed and approved by the laws of this Kingdom" and could only be legal by virtue of "positive law"—none were. Jefferson understood that if the legislature of the U. S. held fealty to English law—it would cause the immediate release of black people held in bondage; destroying all their social institutions. Committed to sustaining the institution of slavery, he was firm in his belief that Roman law was the best, most proper law for the new nation and he pushed for supplanting English law. Roman law did not require a bicameral legislative system, accommodated slavery within the borders of a sovereign nation and allowed for hereditary slavery.

The *Somersett* decision clearly declared slavery was not legal within the Kingdom in 1772, and as most slaves were natural-born Englishmen suffering under colonial tyranny—and possessed the same legal rights and status under English law as Jefferson, Madison or Washington—their enslavement in the U. S. was in derogation of Anglo-American law. Although at the constitutional convention in Philadelphia in 1787 James Wilson of Pennsylvania—who George Washington would later appoint to the Supreme Court said, "Laws may be unjust, may be unwise, may be dangerous, may be destructive; and yet not be so unconstitutional as to justify the Judges in refusing to give them effect." However, George Mason of Virginia agreed that judges "could declare an unconstitutional law void. But regarding every law, however unjust, oppressive or pernicious, which did not come plainly under this description, they would be under the necessity as judges to give it a free course." However, in having formally adopted English law—none of the states had legal authority to enact slave laws or pass a law to make any person born in colonial America under English rule a slave *after* the Declaration of Independence.

Even a careful review of controlling legal precedent, treatises, and colonial charters provides no legal support for even the inference that black people could be legally excluded from U. S. citizenship because slavery was a legal fiction and in fact, was the crime of kidnapping under English law. The idea was underpinned by the proposition—"No man is *above* the law and no man is *below* it: nor do we ask any man's permission when we require him to obey it." It is ahistorical to claim black people were not British colonists. Revisionist historians have covered up the legal consequence of the Twelve Judges' unanimous verdict in the *Somersett* case in 1772. Claiming that it was the ruling of a man named Mansfield has been an effective tool in an arsenal of weaponry used to shelter slavery's unlawfulness, brutality, and its unrequited assault upon the rule of law and people of Afro-Britons during the 1780s.

"To be Negro in this country and to be relatively conscious is to be in a rage almost all the time". James Baldwin (circa 1968)

Chapter 5
America's Slave Imagined

The British, as a colonial power stood alongside France, Spain, Portugal, and the Dutch Republic. United by England's monarch and governed by Parliament—the Kingdom of Great Britain fell under British military and economic control. During the period of salutary neglect... colonial legislators paid the governor's salary; this was known as control of the purse and it supremely influenced the governor's decisions. This practice became the principal reason for colonial corruption and hereditary slavery. Colonial assemblies operated as if it was a one chamber legislature. However, colonial legislative structures had bicameral legislative bodies throughout North America and by colonial charters were obligated to secure the King's assent upon colonial laws—but, due to their unique relationship with colonial governors—who were all deemed the head of the colonial judiciary—the colonial assemblies forewent this requirement.

Salutary neglect had led to systemic institutional corruption and graft within the American colonies. However, once England changed its internal policies towards the American colonies around 1763——so did its ranking amongst colonial powers.

The British had not been enforcing established laws within the American colonies. This failure in governance had created a species of colonial tyranny called hereditary slavery and white supremacy. The British euphemistically referred to its failures as a period of salutary neglect that focused on import, export duties to control trade and the promotion of mercantilism. Then by way of the Declaratory Act in 1766——British imperialism abandoned this unwritten policy by focusing upon revenue raising, internal taxation, the enforcement of English laws and elimination of colonial control of the purse. The British made clear in the Declaratory Act in 1766 that Parliament should "legislate over the colonies in all cases whatsoever" but hereditary slavery continued to operate extrajudicially. The British recognized that its absented enforcement of English law had allowed slavery and discriminatory practices against ethnic people and women colonists to harden. This created varied species of colonial tyranny and a culture of hooliganism directed at everyone within colonial America——except white Englishmen.

Britain's enactment of the Declaratory Act in 1766 and then exercising direct management and enforcement of the rule of English law by issuing the *Somersett* decision encapsulated the rift between colonial leadership. Legal scholar Stephen Wise posits that the *Somersett* decision "was the beginning of the end of slavery" and this was true. [66] In fact, the *Somersett* decision was an emancipatory judicial judgment for all black slaves throughout the Kingdom. However, too many historians have puzzled and then mistakenly concluded that colonial America's slaveholders' calmness in the wake of the ruling—not publicly expressing fear and outrage was inculpatory that the ruling did not attach to the American colonies. This was a major misapprehension of fact and human nature. First, the Twelve Judges had declared Virginia's slave laws were unlawful and had conferred legal status unto a Virginia born slave. Second, slaveholding Americans had never been under any illusions as to the question of the legality of its slave practice. Moreover, colonial slaveholders within the American colonies recognized that the institution of slavery was underpinned by criminal graft and colonial corruption and after the Twelve Judges ruling had rejected its legality—they merely acted as any seasoned criminal would under similar facts and circumstances; they kept their mouths shut.

Post-verdict, all they could impact was the sentence and behaving fretful or expressing outrage could have raised unwanted attention or scrutiny of them. Such antics would not have changed anything. Parliament's Declaratory Act and the Twelve Judges' rulings in the *Somersett* case were pure manifestation of imperial governance—nothing more elegant than that.

The first court reported case of slavery in the American colonies was the African named John Punch in the year 1640, whose punishment for a crime of escaping his indentured servant's contract was a life sentence as a slave for the remainder of his life. He and two white men—a Scotsman named James Gregory and a Dutchman named Victor, stood trial in 1640 for the crime of running away. All three men were contracted to a Virginian named Hugh Gwyn, and each performed similar tasks. They felt so exploited, they were willing to take risks to pursue freedom and run away.

Though fleeing away from their master as a group—the punishment of the runaways differed, as the white men's terms were only extended by four years, but "... the third being a Negro named John Punch" was sentenced to "... serve his said master or his assigns for the time of his natural life." Edgar A. Toppin, in *A Biographical History of Blacks Since 1528*, writes: "Thus, the black man, John Punch became a slave unlike two white indentured servants who merely had to serve a longer term." England had abolished slavery by a general charter of emancipation in 1381, and by Virginia's colonial charter binding it to common law prohibiting slavery on English soil. [67] Punch's sentence was unlawful, and this July 9, 1640 verdict gave rise to targeted repression of people of African ancestry within America's courts and is deemed the first judicial sanctioning of lifelong slavery in the American colonies. The *Punch* decision was not reversed, nor was it overruled by Virginia's colonial governor—as it should have been, since life-long slavery was not permitted on British soil, and the sentence was arbitrary. Thus, John Punch was *"Negro Zero"* when it comes to documented slavery and disparate treatment of blacks in American courts.

Virginia's 1662 chattel slavery law provided:
> *WHEREAS* some doubts have arisen whether children got by any Englishman upon a negro woman should be slave or free, be it therefore enacted and declared by this present grand assembly, that all children borne in this country shall be bond or free according to the condition of the mother.

This colonial law decreed that a child of a "negro woman" would have the legal status of the mother;

not the father. However, Virginia's colonial charter bound the legislative assembly to England's traditions of *partus sequitur patrem* and *jus soli* and because this law was "repugnant" to the common law; it was unconstitutional. The common law tradition of *partus sequitur patrem* was a structured patrilineal descent system under which a child always claimed lineage through the father—even those born without the legitimacy of marriage.

Importantly, under English law, fathers were legally responsible for supporting their children. *Partus sequitur ventrem* purported to change common law and institutionalize the power relationship between white men and black women. White men with mixed-race children were released from the legal responsibility of financial support. The practice of allowing white men to sell their children or put them to work as slaves was extrajudicial, misanthrope, and morally wrong.

Further, *jus soli* was an inalienable grant of British citizenship unto all children born on English soil, which the colony of Virginia was deemed. And a recent case involving a bi-racial woman named Elizabeth Key had addressed any previous doubts as to what English law authorized. England's king was the king because of a patrilineal descent system and Virginia's colonial charter that provided:

"Declare by theise presents that all and everie the persons being our subjects which shall dwell and inhabit within everie or anie of the saide several Colonies and plantacions and everie of their children which shall happen to be borne within the limits and precincts of the said several Colonies and plantacions shall have and enjoy all liberties, franchises and immunities within anie of our dominions to all intents and purposes as if they had been abiding and borne within this our realms of Englande or anie other of our dominions".

Virginia's legislative assembly never lawfully created a bond class in the colony of Virginia. The failure of the assembly to decriminalize the assaulting and kidnapping of "negroes" foreclosed the creation a class known as "bond". [68] This needed to be done as a condition precedent. [69] Doubly, even if Virginia's legislative assembly had done so, this hereditary slave law passed in 1662 required the King's assent. The legislative assembly failed to secure the King's assent to this 1662 law. Virginia's legislative assembly had no legal authority, real or imagined, to pass a law authorizing slavery, or to change the patrilineal descent system to a matrilineal based upon race. Such laws were nugatory.

The bicameral legislative system made the King an indispensable party to enacting hereditary slavery or to change English law of *partus sequitur patrem* or *jus soli*. Berkeley, in his capacity as Virginia's governor and head of the colonial judiciary only gave protection from prosecution to slave owners. He did so for payment. He and other British officials used their public offices to effectuate, sustain and expand the unlawful practice of hereditary slavery. However, under English law, a government official's actions only have the force of law when the person acts within the rule of law. Thus, none of Berkeley's actions in furtherance of this scheme made hereditary slavery a lawful practice. Graft and corruption of government were the nature and substance of the criminal conspiracy—first between Virginia's governor Berkeley, and Virginia's planter class led by Richard Lee, who held the title Secretary of State—a position next in authority to the colonial governor and then subsequent governors throughout the American colonies.

This scheme fostered, and promoted excessive levels of lawlessness, physical, and sexual abuse toward black women. Under English law, during colonial times, when a government official, such as Berkeley acts without the imprimatur of law, he or she does so by the sheer force of personal will and power.

The first Africans in Virginia—after serving their indentured terms fell into a well-established socio-economic system which carried with it no implications of racial inferiority, or repression. That came later. But in the interim, a period of two generations or so, the original Africans accumulated land, voted, testified in court, and interacted with whites on a basis of equality in the new colony in the Chesapeake Bay region, where indentured servants were more common. An example is Anthony Johnson who came to Virginia in 1621, or thereabout and served as an indentured servant until 1635, or thereabout. Then he became an Englishman under the rule of law, and a major property owner, owning two-hundred and fifty acres of fertile land and holding five indentured contracts by 1651.

Furthermore, Johnson married an African named Isabella—she gave birth to the first recorded black American in 1623 or 1624, who was a freeborn Englishman, by law. No different from today... born in colonial America made you an Englishman—pursuant to English law, with liberty protections under English law. His name was William Johnson, the first of a long line that would swell to millions christened in the Church of England.

Virginia's 1645 Taxation Act provided: "All negro men and women and all other men from the age of sixteen to sixty shall be tithable." However, in 1652 "an unfortunate fire" caused "great losses" for Johnson, and he applied to the colonial court for tax relief. And without regard to his African origin, the colonial court granted relief on February 28, 1652. They then exempted Johnson's wife, Isabella and his two children from paying taxes "during their natural lives," the same as white women, who were not taxed in Virginia... evidencing that black people—and even those who were born in Africa had rights under English law in early colonial America.

Then in 1654, Johnson even prevailed in Virginia's colonial court against a white colonist named Robert Parker. The replevin case involved John Casor, a black indentured servant whose contract was owned by Johnson—but released under duress. Parker had intervened on behalf of Casor, claiming Casor's indentured contract had expired seven years earlier and that he was being illegally held.

Johnson who was illiterate freed Casor since keeping indentured servants past their term of servitude was considered a serious matter... a person could be severely punished for such an offense. But afterwards, Johnson changed his mind, brought a lawsuit when he found out that Casor and Parker had tricked him, and that Casor had signed a seven-year term of indenture to Parker. He then sought the return of Casor.

The court initially ruled in favor of Parker, but Johnson appealed, and in 1655, the colonial court reversed its ruling. The court found that Johnson did not release Casor from his indentured servitude contract and reinstated the contract and extended Casor's term to natural life. Parker was required to pay court fees.

In sustaining Johnson's legal claim brought against Parker, the colonial court established that black Englishmen and/or people of African ancestry could bring suits in colonial courts and prevail under English law.

Kidnapped Africans being subjected to a term of indentured service, and then becoming a British citizen, and a possible landholder, along with the way they were treated in colonial courts, such as Johnson's application for tax relief, and his lawsuit against Parker to recover his indentured servant Casor during the 17th century were significant because they establishes the normal social status accorded to people of African ancestry who became British citizens during colonial times... a status that was practically, and theoretically incompatible with a system of racial repression. Nonetheless, upon

Johnson's death in 1670, a colonial judge ruled he was "not a citizen of the colony," because he was black, and he gave Johnson's plantation to a white man, rather than his lawful children. Johnson's children should have inherited their father's estate since they were citizens of the colony of Virginia—freeborn Englishmen by birth. Although there was no legal basis to make such a ruling—the court so ruled.

The Twelve Judges' decision in the *Somersett* case liberated all black people suffering as slaves in the American colonies since it was a self-executing ruling. The tribunal evaluated the legal sufficiency of Virginia's slave laws as the slaveholder Stewart claimed ownership of this black man based upon colonial slave laws. The decision, under English law was self-executing—meaning a ruling that immediately comes into effect without other action being needed for enforcement. Thus 15,000 people suffering as slaves in England and Wales were immediately freed, as those realms honored English law. The tribunal rejected the legal sufficiency of Virginia's slave laws and as it was a self-executing ruling—British citizens in colonial America who continued to enslave black people or Africans in the American colonies, even with colonial government complicity, they became criminals under English law.

Though the slave masters from the American colonies appeared resolute in their continued support of England—they were not. Secretly, they'd joined forces with rebels in the northern colonies to cover themselves. England discovered that they were aiding revolutionists and supporting radicalized ideologues like John and Samuel Adams of Massachusetts. England recognized the actions of slave masters to be one of betrayal and afterwards, withdrew any pretense of supporting colonial slavery. Slave masters continued to assault English law, even after Dunmore liberated black people in the North American colonies in November of 1775. Having lost the support of the British government, slave masters had no other viable option—but to push for a declaration of independence. It was even more urgent after King George III stated that "blows must decide" whether the Americans "submit or triumph".

The founding generation debated the reasonableness of declaring themselves an independent nation and during the debate Thomas Paine and James Otis denounced the tyranny of both English and slave owners. Paine said slavery was no less immoral than "murder, robbery, lewdness and barbarity" and urged the founding generation to "discontinue and renounce it, with grief and abhorrence." He rejected the idea of "divine right," where God chose kings and queens to hold power over their subjects and he rejected slavery on the same grounds.

In general, Paine thought that kings and queens should never rule. They claimed power over other people, saying their subjects were less important than they were. But when humans first appeared on Earth, Paine argued, they were all equal. Splitting people into different groups—king, slave master, slave was a "distinction for which not truly natural or religious reason can be assigned". The slave masters during colonial times were scofflaws—contemptuous of the rule of law. They knew English law prohibited slavery on English soil and that no one on English soil was *above* or *below* English law. These planters knew that the colonial assemblies were all contractually bound to secure the King's assent during colonial times to make any colonial law lawful and that none of the slave laws had the King's approval. Moreover, under English law that was adopted by the First Congress, ignorance of the law was no excuse for breaking the law.

The founding generation gathered in the summer of 1787 to draft a new federal constitution, and while

Enlightenment ideals influenced the drafting, another key influence on the Framers was the subjugation of black people and repression. America's heroes of its revolution who elegantly wrote of and fought for liberty—yet exploited legally free black citizens—whom they knew to be legally-free under the rule of law are not worthy of being revered as great men. The definition of greatness is when one rises above their circumstances. Yet to a man—all of America's slave mastering patriots were born into an entrenched, lawless system which they benefitted from greatly, and they worked through words and deeds to sustain a misanthrope system that the rule of law had criminalized. And though long dead, that system still churns—as historical revisionists jealously protects America's heroes from imputations, insinuations and possible castigation.

This has caused the miseducation of America and as our historians prefer legends to men, their bibliographies are crafted, with a character arc—that's been finely air-brushed by historiographers no less committed, vigilant than a Knight Templar searching and lest discovering them to be flawed men—transforming America's heroes of the *Glorious Revolution* into something much, much less. Thus, it came to pass... people who did not respect the rule of law and obscurants rose to unduly sculpt

America's post-Revolutionary War policies in the United States. And through the persuasiveness of fables and their policies—even the Catholic Church was seduced by the siren call of slavery, as the Vatican allowed the Jesuits at Georgetown University to operate their own slave plantations beginning in the late 1700s.

America's doctrine—the rule of law applied not only to kings, but also to legislative bodies, judges and future presidents of the United States, who professed to own other human beings. The origin of the doctrine is the Magna Carta and has always stood for the proposition—no man is *above* the law and no man is *below* it, nor do we ask any man's permission when we require him to obey it.

In *Federalist 54* James Madison, the United States' fourth president justified the Three-Fifths Compromise to his "Southern brethren," listing aspects of slaves supporting the conclusion that they were property. Their labor was compelled for a master, they were sellable from one master to another and their liberty restrained, much like animals, which under the law were considered property. At the same time Madison highlighted that under Anglo-American law, slaves' lives were protected against bodily harm, they could be punished for doing harm to others, they were not an irrational creature... such as domesticated animals and they were seen by the law, as a member of society: hence, slaves were also persons. Madison concluded that because of these "mixed" characteristics, the Constitution should treat slaves as both persons and property. And since the proposed constitution did so, the people should support the Compromise, or so he reasoned.

Decidedly, the founding generation knew slavery violated English laws during colonial times... knew chattel slavery was a crime under English law... practiced only by criminals since everyone born in colonies had an inalienable right to liberty and that black people were legally entitled to liberty under the Treaty of Paris of 1783. And though knowing what was legal, and morally right the founding generation agreed and allowed for the enslavement of black citizens. They prevented black citizens from participating in an "American Dream"; denied them due process under law, and subjected them and their children to tyranny, institutionalized repression and disfranchisement. The effect and consequence of U. S. slavery has never really been extinguished in this multiethnic body politic.

America's slave holding colonists were well-compensated henchmen of England's King George III. And leading the charge was the author of the Declaration of Independence—Thomas Jefferson who brought his companion bill to supplant English law with Roman law in 1776. In his *Notes on the State of Virginia*, Jefferson made the argument that political equality for blacks was impossible because "the real distinction that nature has made" between the races went beyond color and other physical attributes. Race, more than their status as slaves, doomed blacks to permanent inequality. In *Notes*, Jefferson asserted that a harsh bondage did not prevent Roman slaves from achieving distinction in science, art, or literature because "they were of the race of whites"; American slaves could never achieve such distinction because they were not white. Jefferson claimed Native Americans had "a germ in their minds which only wants cultivation" and yet, he thought that they were capable of "the most sublime oratory." However, he had never found a black who "had uttered a thought above the level of plain narrative; never seen an elementary trait of painting or sculpture." He found "no poetry" among blacks. And Jefferson had argued that blacks' ability to "reason" was "much inferior" to whites, while "In imagination they are dull, tasteless, and anomalous," and "inferior to the whites in the endowments of body and mind." Jefferson conceded blacks were brave, but this he claimed was due to "a want of fore-thought, which prevents their seeing a danger till it be present."

Jefferson understood that the English constitutional structure did not accommodate slavery in the colonies, rather, slavery was underpinned by graft and corruption of government. English law threatened slavery. And while patriot John Adams of Massachusetts wryly quipped that "facts are stubborn things; and whatever may be our wishes, our inclinations, or the dictates of our passions, they cannot alter the state of facts and evidence", the claim can be made that he and other Founding Fathers that compromised on the rule of law do share equal culpability for the horrors of black slavery here in the U. S. They were guilty of misprision: the deliberate concealment of a felony since each legislator failed to faithfully discharge their duties as U. S. rule of law officials and just went along with the narrative. Thus, Adams and others do not get free passes because they refused to own a slave, or to use slave labor. They were collaborators and complicit in the misanthrope practice, and there are "stubborn facts", such as Adams opposing black people enlisting in the Continental Army because slave holding patriots opposed it. Adams spoke against a bill to free black people in Massachusetts in 1777, saying that the issue was then, too divisive, and so the legislation should "sleep for a time". He slavishly kept the issue of slavery out of national politics, because of the then predictable response, during tumultuous times, as Adams was of the belief unity was needed to sustain political relationships. This was textbook collaborative behavior and criminal complicity.

Misconduct in public office was an offence at common law, dating back to the 13th century. The tort of misconduct of public office can be traced to a case in 1703, Ashby v. White, [70] a case decided by Chief Justice Sir John Holt that ruled in favor of a landowner who wanted to sue a police constable who deprived him of his right to vote. The elements of the offense are when: (1) a public officer acting as such; (2) willfully neglects to perform one's duty and/or willfully misconducts oneself; (3) to such a degree as to amount to an abuse of the public's trust in the office holder. The U. S. rule of law officials were required to use the same protocols used by Virginia's officials in 1619 when they dealt with the arrival of the first nineteen Africans. Rather, each gave in to bias, personal aggrandizement, or mob rule and enslaved legally free people, who had the right to liberty under the rule of law. This was misconduct in public office.

The personal behavior known as slavery was not legal and was incompatible with established constitutional rights when the thirteen American colonies declared themselves independent in 1776. The bicameral structure of the colonial legislative system; the Twelve Judges' ruling in the *Somersett* case in June 1772 that slavery was not "allowed and approved by the laws of this Kingdom" and Dunmore's proclamation of liberation of people suffering as slaves in November 1775 were legal problems, hurdles for slavery since none of the colonial assemblies promulgated a "positive law" that authorized slavery. Thus, no American colony ever created a legal condition known as "slave". The absence of authority and/or the failure to promulgate a law authorizing slavery in their respective colonies, in the first instance meant none of the subsequently enacted hereditary slave laws were ever lawful. It is wholly counter intuitive and without legal support that a legal condition of "slave" existed by virtue of promulgated positive municipal law in colonial America.

Based upon a careful review of Virginia's legislative history and that of the other twelve colonial assemblies——the Twelve Judges' ruling in the *Somersett* case clearly struck down all colonial slave laws. The ruling announced that any colonial slave law in the Kingdom had to be authorized by "positive law." Bound to English law, by virtue of colonial charter——the slaveholders in the American colonies could no longer use colonial customs, tropes, or its nomenclature to legitimize the misanthrope practice known as "slavery". They as colonial citizens and public officials had an affirmative legal obligation——duty to liberate black people, as they were free Englishmen under English law since slavery was not based upon positive law.

The Declaration justified independence by listing twenty-seven colonial grievances against King George III. The first three grievances related to the King withholding his assent to colonial laws. The Declaration and acts of the First Congress established legal rights and obligations. The adoption of English law in 1776 meant black people held rebuttable U. S. citizenship since slavery had never been lawfully constituted in the American colonies.

History supports that ninety-five per cent of all slaves living in the American colonies in 1776 were native-born black people and forty percent of blacks lived in Virginia. They were all victims of British tyranny and the passage of time did not and could not make slavery lawful——*Quod ab initio non valet in tractu temporis non convalescet"*. It means, whatever is done in contravention of a law is void from the start cannot be made legal or enforceable, although the nullity be not formally directed. The ultimate legacy of the *Somersett* case, whether solely determined by Mansfield or the Twelve Judges... circumscribed and limited or not is the fact that it pushed the Framers of our Articles of Confederation and the

Constitution to try to legitimize slavery at the national level.

Looking back at early colonial times, one must be struck by what can only be called equality of oppression. Not the least among the things that framed this period was that England's colonial power structure made little or no distinction between black and white servants, who were assigned the same tasks, and were held in equal contempt. Working together in the same fields, sharing the same huts, the same situation, and they had the same grievances. The first people to live in America, aristocrats excepted—developed strong bonds of sympathy and mutuality. There was, to be sure, prejudice, but it was largely English class prejudice, which was distributed, without regard to race, creed, or color. There were also, prejudiced individuals in the colony, but—and this is the fundamental difference between prejudice and racism—their personal predilections, quirks, and obsessions were not focused, and directed by the organized will of the community.

Social anthropologists and other scientists agree that the concept of a "white race" and its progeny, white supremacy developed in colonial Virginia in the late 1700s. Prior to that time, white colonists did not seem to know that they were white. [71] The laboring class of European Americans in the American colonies showed little interest in "white identity" before the institution of the system of race-based privileges at the end of the seventeenth century, as observed by Theodore W. Allen, in his seminal two-volume study *The Invention of the White Race*. Allen explained that his research of Virginia's colonial records did not reveal that there was an official use of the word "white," as a token of social status prior to 1691. He also found that the "white race" as we know it was not, and could not, have been functioning in early Virginia. He then described how, in the wake of Bacon's Rebellion in 1676, the British "white race" policy was invented as a ruling class social control formation. This policy defined and established the "white race" and it also implemented racial proscriptions against free people of African descent—who were prospering in colonial America.

European traditions and caste system mores made the policy successful. Within European traditions, darker-skinned people were universally stigmatized, as being laborers and servants, as it was a characteristic of most who worked outside in the sun and elements. With the rise of the "natural-born" black population in colonial America, those biases, and those traditions were seamlessly adopted to support an informal race-based hierarchy that became entrenched throughout colonial America's social structures and institutions.

England's "white privilege" narrative assaulted English law and it transformed basic rights——the presumption of liberty, the right to get married, the right to carry a gun, the right to read and write, the right to testify in legal proceedings, the right of self-directed physical mobility, and the enjoyment of male prerogatives over women. It criminally deprived colonial blacks of these common law rights... and protections that were self-evident during Anthony Johnson's lifetime, in early colonial America.

England's race-based policy altered the distinct social classifications by conferring upon poor whites, "white privilege". This policy soon divided colonials based upon race and over time, racialized attitudes and racism became institutionalized. England's "white race" narrative was a major policy initiative and its center-point was the claim that in having African blood made a person inferior. The white race narrative helped England on two fronts; 1) society order and 2) institutionalized tyranny. It became an accepted, and durable part of North America's culture. The British did so, in violation of the rule of law to further its colonization initiative.

The ideology of white supremacy was integral to the expansion of hereditary slavery. Prior to such time——no European regarded themselves as "white," but rather defined their race, ancestry or ethnicity in terms of their nationality. Allen posits that the laboring class of white colonists within the American colonies showed little interest in "white identity" and therefore could not see themselves as being superior before England instituted the system of race-based privileges towards the end of the seventeenth century that *post*-date chattel slave laws. The creation of a new species of tyranny... hereditary slavery that existed extrajudicially, coupled with British policies of disparate treatment in colonial courts, white-skinned privilege, and the narrative that those unearned privileges of being "white" entitled them to discriminate against any and all people of African ancestry grew to influence social, political, legal and labor systems throughout Atlantic World Societies. This is core to the dogma of white supremacy and discourse here in America.

England's Parliament passed the English Bill of Rights on December 16, 1689 guaranteeing certain rights and liberties to all British subjects. The bill limited the power of the King and Queen and was lawful *ex post facto* legislation that retroactively changed the legal consequences of actions that were committed, or relationships that existed before the enactment of the law.

The Bill of Rights incorporated into law the growing conviction that although some Englishmen may inherit privileges, all Englishmen enjoy basic rights—in particular, "liberty" that even England's King could not take away, abrogate or interfere with.

This bill reinforced the Petition of Rights of 1628 and the Habeas Corpus Act of 1679, by codifying certain rights and liberties. The rights expressed in these Acts had already become associated with the idea of the rights of Englishmen and were described as Fundamental Laws of England. These liberty rights attached to everyone born in colonial America.

Virginia's slavery laws were prodigious and by 1691 was supplemented with a law that condemned mixed-race children of free white women to serve as indentured servants for a period of thirty years and subjecting the white mother to a fifteen-pound sterling fine. The mother would be indentured for five years... if the ascribed fine was not paid within a month of the birth. These extrajudicial laws were targeted at black and mixed-race children, as well as white women, these Virginia laws constituted the foundation of racial and gender discrimination in America. But as these colonial laws were the product of corruption, enforced in derogation of English law and violated its colonial charter... none were lawful. The tyranny of Great Britain allowed this law and other colonial laws to function, as if they were the law of the land throughout colonial America and as such, race, and sex discrimination, as well as white supremacy dogma all share a common criminal origin: Virginia's 1662 law of *partus sequitur ventrem*. While many have heretofore used the benign term white privilege to describe our political, economic and cultural system in which white overwhelmingly control power and material resources—but, such usage is moored to conscious ideas of slavery's lawfulness and innate white superiority. This euphemism changes with the acknowledgment of its true origins and it topples it. Thus, as white racial power here in the U. S. owes its allegiance to colonial hooliganism and a criminal species of tyranny known as hereditary slavery—it can no longer have any indicia of legitimacy.

"The truth is like a lion; you don't have to defend it. Let it loose; it will defend itself".   Augustine of Hippo (*circa* 423 A.D.)

Chapter 6
America's Original Sin

The English Civil Wars began in 1642... fighting that took place in the British Isles between supporters of the monarchy of King Charles I and his successor Charles II and opposing groups in each of the realms. The first war was settled with Oliver Cromwell's victory for Parliamentary forces at the 1645 Battle of Naseby. The second phase ended in December 1648 when King Charles I was arrested, charged with treason and then was beheaded in 1649, and in 1651 the English monarchy was suspended. During the decade of turmoil, and civil chaos, ordinary Englishmen took advantage of the dislocation of civil society. For example, communities in England seized timber, and other resources on the sequestrated estates of royalists, and Catholics, and on the estates of the royal family and the church hierarchy. While three thousand miles away in the American colonies—ordinary colonists took advantage of black people by creating a species of tyranny— hereditary slavery.

History supports—the *American Revolution* during the 1770s was the fourth English civil war. Englishman versus Englishman. The earlier wars were fought the years 1642 to 1645, 1642 to 1649, and 1649 to 1651 in England. The prevailing narrative had been that the English civil wars of the 17th century were the result from centuries-long struggles between Parliament, especially the House of Commons, and the Monarchy, with Parliament defending the traditional rights of Englishmen, while the Stuart monarchy continually attempted to expand its right to arbitrarily dictate law. However, an accurate *locus classicus* explaining the actual cause of these wars were not forthcoming until 1973—three hundred and thirty-one years later. England, and throughout the American colonies it became received wisdom that these civil wars were just a single war called the *Puritan Revolution*—challenging the repressive Stuart Church, and preparing the way for religious toleration in the Restoration. Thus, Puritanism was posited as the natural ally of the English people, preserving their traditional rights against arbitrary monarchical power. In the wake of the rebellion within the American colonies, this narrative was adopted by the founding generation.

Then in 1973, in the seminal treatise titled *The Origins of the English Civil War*, historian Conrad Russell redirected focus upon the minutiae of the years immediately preceding the civil war, there returning to the contingency-based historiography. Russell's works challenged received wisdoms, claiming, and proving that factional war-allegiance patterns did not fit. Parliament was not inherently progressive with the events of 1640—a precursor for the *Glorious Revolution*, nor did Puritans necessarily ally themselves with Parliamentarians.

Many members of the bourgeoisie fought for the King, while many landed aristocrats supported Parliament. Thus, starting in the 1990s—three hundred and fifty years after England's first civil war began scholars have supplanted the historical title *"English Civil War"* with the titles *"The Wars of the Three Kingdoms"* and *"The British Civil Wars"*. And some of these scholars now even posits that the cause of the wars were the doctrines of politics, and conflicts that arose from science that disputed those political doctrines. This was a major academic shift.

The rethinking of origins of earlier British civil wars informs and directs the U. S. to focus on the minutiae of the years immediately preceding the rebellion within the American colonies—the fourth civil war, and to return to a contingency-based historiography in discerning America's origins. This approach both explains and can contextualize the passage of two-hundred and forty-three years, and offers perspective and context for the durability of America's revolutionary narrative especially after America's Civil War. The descendants of the founding generation of slaveholders took control of the narrative and committed themselves to historical disinformation and propaganda. "The readiness with which Southern [slavers and accessories] prefer the most false and audacious claims... exhibits a state of society in which truth and honor are but little respected," [72] and "After the war, former Confederates [had] wondered how to hold on to their... pride after [the] devastating defeat... So they reverse-engineered a cause worthy of [their] heroics. They also sensed... that the end of slavery would confer a gloss of nobility, and bragging rights, on the North." [73] Thus, they resolved on denial and disinformation, including pretending that slavery had been constitutional.

History supports, in 1639 Virginia's House of Burgesses excluded black people from being required to possess arms. Then in 1642—the legislative assembly enacted a law that started taxing black women—creating a distinction between colonial black and white women. Subsequently, Virginia's Assembly Committee, its colonial court was faced with Elizabeth Key's claim in 1654 that she was a free-born citizen, as her father was a free white Englishman. She was granted her freedom. [74] The *Key* decision created discourse, so in in 1662, Virginia's legislative assembly enacted a hereditary slave law called *partus sequitur ventrem*. However, Virginia's legislative assembly was only one chamber of a bicameral legislative system and did not bother to secure the King's assent. This law purported to change the patrilineal descent system of *partus sequitur patrem* to a matrilineal system. The King was the king because his father was king; yet, Virginia's legislative assembly purported to change English law—in violation of the colonial charter. This colonial law was "repugnant" to England's common law and Virginia's legislative assembly had no jurisdiction to diverge from the common law. Thus, there was never any legitimacy to this hereditary slave law. This slave law operated extrajudicially.

Berkeley, Virginia's governor as chief justice of the colonial court could have immediately vetoed Virginia's hereditary slave bill of *partus sequitur ventrem*, as it was repugnant to England's common law tradition of *partus sequitur patrem*. But he did not. However, his failure to do so was immaterial as to its lawfulness, as the legal consequence of the legislative assembly purporting to enact a law which was "repugnant" to the common law and also, in doing so failing to secure the King's assent; made Virginia's 1662 hereditary slave law an absolute nullity. Black people born within the colony of Virginia who were relegated to the status of a slave at birth were crime victims.

Virginia's hereditary slave law model became endemic throughout the American colonies. But destructive to hereditary slavery's lawfulness was the fact they all were repugnant to England's common law and none of the colonial assemblies bothered to secure the King's assent. As one of Somersett's lawyers put it, colonial slavery was a "new species of tyranny...created entirely by Colony government." Hereditary slavery was created in the colony of Virginia due to graft, government corruption and a culture of hooliganism, however, the rule of law was implacable and remained a durable guardrail against such an assault.

The legislative assemblies within colonial America never sought, nor acquired assent from King James II, nor any subsequent monarch or Parliament to legalize slavery within the colony. This, in and of itself militated against colonial slavery ever becoming a legal institution. Then every colonial legislative assembly failed to adhere to the bicameral legislative structure. The legislative assemblies did not and could not change the patrilineal descent system of *partum sequitur patrem* to *partum sequitur ventrem* under the colonial charter. The withholding of jurisdiction to change England's common law and the colonial legislative assemblies' failure to secure the King's assent delegitimize the practice of hereditary slavery. Virginia's hereditary slavery law, which at best was nothing more than a bill was an extrajudicial scheme and it changed the ethos of colonial America to one of hooliganism, tyranny, and white privilege.

Lord North, England's Prime Minister approved the false narrative that the *Somersett* decision had no legal consequence upon Englishmen in the British colonies and that it was ramrodded by a rogue "negro-loving" judge named Lord Mansfield, who had a bi-racial niece living in his home at the time. However, Lord Mansfield had referred the contentious *Somersett* case to the Twelve Judges procedure *before* entering judgment and in so doing, this was the "Mansfieldian Moment". David Waldstreicher in his important work titled *Slavery's Constitution: From Revolution to Ratification* [75] posited differently, suggesting that the *Somersett* decision was Mansfield's alone and that it inaugurated "the modern constitutional politics of slavery" by alerting slaveholders throughout the empire that "never again could British slaveholders reassure themselves that everybody (who mattered) believed in slavery as a traditional form of property." It was much more than that, as the Twelve Judges specially looked at colonial slave laws and then ruled [colonial] slavery was not "allowed and approved by the laws of this Kingdom" and can only be lawfully instituted by virtue of "positive law". Lord Mansfield's use of the Twelve Judges procedure in the *Somersett* case was the "Mansfieldian Moment" as it preempted the false and enduring narrative that the *Somersett* decision was Mansfield's alone.

Further, the *Somersett* decision created financial and political uncertainty for slave masters throughout the Kingdom, and while it fueled revolutionary rhetoric within the American colonies and the formation of the Continental Congress in its aftermath, it was not the same in the West Indian colonies. Matthew Mason in his work titled *North American Calm, West Indian Storm: The Constitutional Politics and Legacy of the Somerset Decision* recognized the schism and has offered an important observation. [76] He stated that "[O]ne indicator that West Indians charged well ahead of North Americans is the outright silence that reigns in some places one would expect to find alarmed North Americans joining West Indians in defense of their property rights and racial privilege. Leading white Virginians were particularly mum."

Generally, the American colonists who owned slaves were horrified by the *Somersett* decision but settled for England's narrative that this was a Mansfield's decision and they collectively averted everyone away from first principles; that colonial slavery had existed extrajudicially and that the *Somersett* decision had indeed abolished slavery since colonial slavery was not based upon "positive law". None of the colonial legislative assemblies within the American colonies had ever secured the King's assent and they knew that such a jurisdictional defect was not curable. They saw the *Somersett* decision as being an "olive branch" to slave owners and were appreciative of its obliqueness. These white Virginians, in knowing slavery had never been lawfully constituted, and in being clear-headed about slavery, set about the business of the continuation of this practice.

Lord North wanted slave owners to stay the course—but these learned, enlightened Englishmen were unpersuaded. They knew slavery had been exposed as being criminal, and in knowing the seriousness of the crime of hereditary slavery and having no viable legal options—each one felt the weight and pang of the inadequacy of North's narrative and they initiated and established a back-channel of communication with leadership in the other colonies, to discuss forming a Continental

Congress. They were cognizant of the overarching colonial complaints of British tyranny and a movement for independence in Massachusetts and committed resources—but once Lord North became aware of their activities with northern rebels he was infuriated, and directed Lord Dunmore to declare martial law and to free Virginia's slaves exercising *executive* authority that had the legal consequence of being a proclamation of liberation of all slaves throughout the American Colonies.

Under English law, Lord Dunmore's proclamation of liberation on November 7, 1775 had the legal effect of being a colonial-American wide writ of habeas corpus—that delivered legal liberty to everyone suffering as slaves in the American colonies. Dunmore's executive proclamation liberated everyone suffering as slaves under English rule of law. Under English law, no different than the liberation of the 15,000 slaves in England and Wales in the immediate aftermath of the *Somersett* decision, the proclamation liberated all slaves in the American colonies similarly situated. Dunmore's proclamation forced colonial America's slave master class who had only tepidly thrown-in with the Massachusetts rebels to fully embrace the independence movement.

The *Somersett* decision was the flashpoint of the American Revolutionary War... a civil war that pitted Englishman versus Englishman. The northern and southern colonies joined forces, and what cemented the Faustian deal were promises of financial support to northern patriots. Slave master patriots like Washington, Jefferson, Marshall, and others pledged to invest their ill-gotten wealth in northern colonial rebellion, in exchange for their support and assistance with continuing slavery. The Founding Fathers were not selfless heroes of democratic ideals. England's Twelve Judges' ruling in the *Somersett* case that slavery was not "allowed and approved by the laws of this Kingdom" transformed the extrajudicial practice of slavery into a criminal enterprise in June 1772, as a matter of law. Although it became a crime, the slave masters did not free the black people suffering as slaves. Then Lord Dunmore issued a proclamation on November 7, 1775, a writ of habeas corpus that legally purged, terminated and extinguished all vestiges of ownership of black people living in colonial America, as a matter of law, even if one subscribes to the narrative that somehow... the *Somersett* decision did not outlaw slavery in the American colonies in 1772.

The colonial legislative system was bicameral, yet, colonial legislative assemblies did not secure the King's assent on slave laws, and consequently, slavery was not a legally authorized condition during colonial times. Dunmore's *executive* actions were dispositive, as the slave masters pursued no legal redress to challenge the proclamation. They were obligated to do so and did not and it framed the question——on what legal basis, if any did Virginians George Washington, Thomas Jefferson, John Marshall, James Madison, Richard Henry Lee and Patrick Henry and other alleged heroes of the American Revolution continue to claim legal ownership of black people, at any relevant time before the Declaration of Independence. And while Dunmore's proclamation of liberation can be attacked as being conditional, targeted and punitive——nonetheless, it was still lawful.

Doubtlessly, law-abiding colonists could not just ignore Dunmore's legal proclamation. The on-going rebellion did not suspend the rule of law. Slave owners could not use the fog of war, the Declaration of Independence, eight months later or the treaty to deflect or insulate. English rule of law required slave owners to meet a standard established by Lord Mansfield in the *Stapylton* case, as a condition precedent. Slave owners could not prove ownership of black people since slavery was prohibited on English soil and colonial legislatures all failed to secure the King's assent to relevant slave laws, and the Twelve Judges of the King's Bench ruled slavery was not "allowed and approved by the laws of this

Kingdom" in the *Somersett* case in 1772; four years before the Declaration of Independence.

The Englishmen in colonial America refused to abide by the law and belatedly Lord Dunmore provided relief to black citizens. No seasonably, timely legal objections were made during colonial times. Dunmore's actions were conclusive when one considers the fact that the defendant in the *Somersett* case opposed Somersett's freedom in 1772 based upon the alleged legality of Virginia's slave laws which the Twelve Judges specially ruled was not lawful in the Kingdom. Then they went further by declaring that slavery can only be lawful within the Kingdom based upon "positive law" and hereditary slavery did not meet the standard. After three years, Dunmore, as a lieutenant of His Majesty King George III and Royal Governor of Virginia on November 7, 1775 liberated black colonists suffering as slaves.

The First Congress formally adopted English law *after* declaring itself the legislature of the United States in 1776. English precedent, *Stapylton* and *Somersett* became controlling and became conclusive since the founding generation did nothing to legally appeal the *Somersett* decision, or to legally challenge Dunmore's liberation of black people during colonial rule, and certainly thereafter slavery was a crime by July 4, 1776.

The Declaration espoused the core principles of liberty, equality, and popular consent... a set of principles by which democratic nations came to be judged by and was a compact with all Englishmen in colonial America. The Declaration fell into obscurity until it was rediscovered eighty-seven years later... during America's Civil War. President Abraham Lincoln's *Gettysburg Address* recasted the Declaration's phrase... "all men are created equal" as, this country's creed and questioned whether a nation "conceived in liberty," and "dedicated to the proposition" of equality could "long endure." And by framing the Declaration's use of the word "men" to mean "humanity" Lincoln used the Declaration to galvanize the Union—but the Confederate leadership fiercely challenged his interpretation.

The Confederates advanced its view that the phrase in the Declaration meant "white men," and went on to claim that poor whites, women, Native Americans, and enslaved blacks were never contemplated to have citizenship in the United States. But in truth, Lincoln and the Confederate leadership's interpretations were both wrong; the founding generation used the word "men" to connote "Englishmen"—not humanity or white men of wealth and property. Nothing else makes sense, and as well the question of the meaning of the phrase "all men are created equal" was easily resolvable since the thirteen original colonies were British, and all signatories to the Declaration conceded their status as Englishmen and each state then adopted English law in 1776. The Founding Fathers were not globalists, and nowhere within the four corners of the Declaration are any ethnic or poor Englishmen carved out or excluded. This simply was not the case.

The Declaration spoke to lawlessness, tyranny, and unconstitutional treatment of colonial Englishmen. Nothing evidenced more aptly the lawlessness of colonial times than hereditary slavery. This was the overarching basis for the Declaration that is supported by the contemporaneous writings of John Adams—the second President of the United States in the *Novanglus Essays*.

First, Adams published in February 1775, in which he discussed the constitutional, and legal relationship between Britain, and her American colonies. He claimed colonists were being treated like second-class Englishmen, and later in his seventh *Novanglus Essays* he stated "...the British constitution is much more like a republic than an Empire. Adams stated that "being a government of laws, and not of men. If this definition be just, the British constitution is nothing more, nor less than a republic, in which the king is first magistrate... We are a part of the British dominions, that is, of the King of Great Britain, and it is our interest and duty to continue so."

Anxiously, America's slave master class had pushed the Continental Congress to craft and proffered a declaration of independence in July 1776. All erstwhile Englishmen, now Americans being created equal under the law became America's first principles.

> "When, in the course of human events, it becomes necessary for one people to dissolve the political bands which have connected them with another, and to assume among the powers of the earth, the separate and equal station which the laws of nature and of nature's God entitle them, a decent respect to the opinions of mankind requires that they should declare the causes which impels them to the separation... We hold these truths to be self-evident, that all men are created equal, that they are endowed by their Creator with certain inalienable rights that among these are life, liberty, and the pursuit of happiness."

It is illustrative that the first three grievances in the Declaration are directed towards the King's refusal to give his assent to laws enacted by colonial legislatures. These three grievances and the following twenty-four explained the Founding

Fathers' reasoning and offers the best insight, as to why they cited every possible source to establish and legitimize their right to claim independence and to do so on behalf of all other colonial Englishmen. They came from "powers of the earth," from "laws of nature and of nature's God", they were "self-evident," and "endowed by [a] Creator." By investing the rights with divine origins, the Declaration of Independence sought to change, redefine, and recast them as being not mere legal or political rights. That these rights were higher, transcendent rights that were "inalienable," and if the rights were God-given, they could neither be denied, nor withdrawn by the target of the Declaration—England's King George III. This supports the supports the notion that black people were not excluded from the Declaration.

In early 1776, Thomas Paine had argued in the closing pages of the first edition of *Common Sense* that the "custom of nations" demanded a formal declaration of American independence if any European power were to mediate a peace between the Americans and England. Foreign courts needed to have American grievances laid before them persuasively in a "manifesto" which could reassure them that the Americans would be reliable trading partners. Without such a declaration, Paine concluded, "[t]he custom of all courts is against us, and will be so, until, by an independence, we rank with other nations."

Declaring independence, he believed, could also bring an end to the rebellion. At the time, the rest of the world still saw the American colonists as British subjects rebelling against their King. By declaring independence, the rest of the world would see America as a separate country. Foreign nations would then be more likely to help the colonists and treat them as equals. And over time, Paine wrote, "nothing but independence... can keep the peace of the continent." According to historian David Armitage, the Declaration of Independence is a document of international law, influenced by Emerich de Vattel's *The Laws of Nation, Or, Principles of the Law of Nature, Applied to the Conduct and Affairs of Nations*, a work of political philosophy and international relations. And declaring the United States independent was a necessary first step—if the emerging nation was to have any hope of attaining the recognition it sought from the European powers.

In January 2015, a poignant story about 3,000 black former slaves who left the United States aboard English ships, right before the ratification of the Treaty of Paris of 1783 by the Congress... was dramatized in a mini-series called *The Book of*

Negroes. Their names were listed in Generals Guy Carleton and George Washington's *Book of Negroes*. It was broadcasted by the Canadian Broadcasting Corporation (CBC) and then re-broadcasted in the United States by Black Entertainment Television (BET) during Black History month in February 2015.

The mini-series chronicled an African slave toward the end of the American Revolution, who acted as a scribe... recording personal information about 3,000 black people that managed to leave the U. S. and then migrate to Canada. The story challenges myths surrounding the days leading up to the exodus of the 3,000 souls in 1783. It pointedly challenges America's historiography that slavery was inherited from England and that the colonial Englishmen, who became Americans did lawfully enslaved 500,000 black people upon the end of the Revolutionary War. The U. S. prevented black people from leaving this hostile and then profane country.

The mini-series is based upon true events, and the existence of England's *Book of Negroes* held in its National Archives in London, and America's version preserved in the National Archives and Records Administration in Washington D.C. legitimizes the international controversy and frames the dispositive question: did England steal 3,000 black slaves from America in 1783 and if not, The *Book of Negroes'* real story has always been America's retention and exploitation of 500,000 British subjects. The two versions of this registry legitimate this international dispute. This unflattering——but true story provides historical context regarding America's violation of the Treaty of Paris, the misanthrope enslavement of black people and their disfranchisement here in the U. S., who then became the bedrock of its slavery pool.

Article 4, § 4 of the Constitution is a guarantee "to every State... a republican form of government." It is a guarantee of fundamental rights of all people to self-determination and participation in the governmental process. In James Madison's Papers he referenced writer Johnathan Swift who espoused its necessity "For in reason, all government without the consent of the governed is the very definition of slavery."
In Article I, section 9 of the Constitution recognize and adopt habeas corpus——the right the Framers knew had been and was being used by putative slaves including non-citizens to obtain freedom. *Somersett* was controlling judicial precedent of English law. The Framers knew about habeas corpus, knew that England's highest court struck down slavery on that basis and that legal scholars of the day believed it was the writ of habeas which made slavery implausible under English law. The Twelve Judges' ruling in *Somersett* was the supreme law of the land——making all forms of slave laws enacted by the Congress or state legislatures, in the absence of rejecting

Somersett meant slavery in the U. S. was extrajudicial. George Van Cleve posits that while the *Somersett* decision "directly challenged the legitimacy of slavery as an imperial institution"…"slavery emerged from the Revolution stronger than it had been within the framework of the empire, especially after *Somerset*." [77]

Then there is the Second Amendment to the constitution that was enacted to provide lethal protection to further slavery. The relevant language provides… "A well-regulated Militia, being necessary to the security of a free State." A militia was nomenclature for a slave patrol and the need for a militia was a direct result of the Framers' compromise that enslaved 500,000 legally free British citizens. James Madison, the "Father of the Constitution" and other Virginia politicians were at the ratifying convention in Virginia in 1788.

Their main concern was that Article 1, Section 8 which gave the federal government the power to raise and supervise a militia, could also allow that federal militia to subsume their state militias and change them from slavery-enforcing institutions into something that could even, one day, free the slaves. Their concerns were real.

Dunmore's militarization of black people—coupled with the booming rhetoric of abolitionists made southern colonial leadership and the populace fearful of slave insurrections. Without a doubt, the tried and true tool used to control slave rebellions during colonial times were militias. The militia was important since black slave populations often exceeded the white population in regions like eastern Virginia. Lord Dunmore, twelve years earlier, in November 1775 had liberated and armed blacks against patriot slave owners. History supports that even during the dark parts of the revolution—southern colonies had refused to commit its militias to fight against the British out of fear that, if the militias were deployed, slaves would revolt. Militias were creatures of erstwhile colonial governments and the then new constitution changed that.

It was during a debate that George Mason and Patrick Henry claimed that the new constitution gave Congress the power to subvert the slave system by disarming the militias. Henry then claimed, "[I]n this state, there are two hundred and thirty-six thousand blacks, and there are many in several other states. But there are few or none in the Northern States... May Congress not say that every black man must fight? Did we not see a little of this last war?"

He knew the majority attitude in the North opposed slavery, and he worried they'd use the constitution to free the South's slaves. They then argued that because the Constitution gave the federal government the power to arm the militias, only the federal government could do so. "If they neglect or refuse to discipline or arm our militia, they will be useless... the states can do neither... this power being exclusively given to Congress" said Henry. "The power is concurrent, and not exclusive," said Madison——but he was wrong. The constitution expressly doled out different powers over the militia to Congress or the states. The misapprehension was brought to Madison's attention and he was chagrinned. The constitution was ratified by a close vote.

In the fall of that year, Madison was challenged for his congressional seat. His opponent excoriated him for not including a bill of rights in the constitution. He previously opposed a bill of rights, but since a bill of rights was widely popular, he switched his position. Madison made a campaign promise that if elected, he would write one. He won and made sure it was unambiguous that the southern states could maintain their slave patrols.

The Second Amendment has powerful supporters and the constant, recurring defense is that a prior reasoning for this amendment cannot taint an American fundamental right to protect themselves and freedom.

This argument is vulnerable under English law, applicable in 1780s that required an observance of "good faith" in the exercise of governmental powers, and it is expressed in the maxim "what cannot be done directly cannot be done indirectly". If a legislature is prohibited from violating any constitutional provision, it cannot do so even "under the guise, or the pretence, or in the form of an exercise of its own powers". In other words, "the legislature must not under the guise of dealing with one matter in fact encroach upon the forbidden field". All this is implied in the application of the maxim "what cannot be done directly cannot be done indirectly." This maxim, as such, has played a significant part in determining whether a piece of legislature in question is within the competence of the legislature enacting it. The compromise with slaveholding states, on behalf of slave holding Americans disfranchised thousands of people, who held British subjecthood and was supposed to "set at liberty" pursuant to a treaty. Or alternatively, held U. S. citizenship and were entitled to due process before being subjected to slavery, as no Englishman could be made another man's slave. Their disfranchisement was done for a corrupt motive and in violation of the rule of law, and arguably, but for this wrongful conduct, purpose and/or complicity of others this amendment would have fell.

The U. S. never proved that their citizens owned black people. Carleton's position on behalf of England that black citizens were Englishmen and entitled to be unmolested per British "Proclamation and promises" under the Treaty of Paris of 1783 were thus conceded. The countless black citizens should not have been assaulted, kidnapped and imprisoned. And in all circumstances, each was entitled to have a due process hearing to legitimate their British citizen status.

The British government had no deal-making authority since liberty of all on English soil was legally protected, and thus even——if the U. S. had sought, and secured England's permission to assault, kidnap and imprison black citizens, any such agreement would have been legally unenforceable since both sovereigns were controlled by English law that recognized liberty as a personal right. The U. S. government knew their citizens' actions were violating the treaty——but was of the belief that many of His Majesty's ministers and its aristocracy were extremely supportive of black slavery. The government of the U. S. gambled England would not go back to war——in response to Americans assaulting and recapturing former slaves. The U. S. needed to recreate their economy as quickly as possible, but failed to contest, and to prove black people were not entitled to be unmolested during the armistice period. These seasonably raised claims of the treaty construction were corroborated by English law that prohibited slavery on British soil; the Twelve Judges' ruling in the *Somersett* case that slavery was not "allowed and approved by the laws in this Kingdom" and Lord Dunmore's liberation of all slaves before the Declaration of Independence. The rebuttable presumption of liberty for British subjecthood citizens meant that they were entitled to certificates of freedom under the Treaty of Paris. Thus, while both nations quietly withdrew from publicizing Carleton's attestations of renewed "hostilities" and the black citizens' entitlement to liberty under the treaty *before* ratification in January 1784——the U. S. failure to contest and sustain its burden of proof had legal consequences under international law.

England's ministers were mindful that Carleton's treaty violation dispute could unravel the ratification of the treaty and worst still, possibly ensnarl British colonial interests in the West Indies: a major sugar exporter that was dependent upon slave labor. It is a fair statement—West Indian planters and their representatives were panic-stricken and had been that way since the *Somersett* decision. [78] Many West Indian planters was of the belief that the Twelve Judges' ruling in this seminal case had removed any legal basis for slavery throughout the Kingdom and as scholar David Brion Davis observed that it made it "no longer possible to take for granted the universal legality of slave property". [79] The British government also knew that the government of the U. S. was controlled by pro-slavery men who'd aggressively oppose liberating black people since slave labor was indispensable in reestablishing America's *post*-Revolutionary War economy and sustaining their personal wealth.

However, once the treaty was ratified in January 1784, one of their main concerns went away. Although varied congressmen came to domestically challenge England's evacuation of 3,000 black citizens by way of Carleton's evacuation in November 1783. They only advanced a naked argument that "slaves" were illegally "smuggled" out of the U. S. and called for compensation from the British government, promised by Carleton and substantiated by Washington's *Book of Negroes*. It was just a naked assertion that the British's proclamation of liberation, and promise of liberty were somehow unenforceable, but they did claim financial injury due to the unlawfully deprivation of "property"... per the rule of law and in consequence, they wanted to be compensated.

The nationality of the 3,000 "slaves" that Carleton removed from the U. S. was English and as it relates to the question of their liberty status, if uncertain—the founding generation should have applied the same protocol used when the first Africans arrived in 1619. That's what the U. S. rule of law officials of the federal constitution were required to do—per law. The adoption of English law by the First Congress in 1776 bound the U. S. to England's common law as announced in the Magna Carta of 1215 that placed the duty to adhere to promulgated laws upon lawmakers, magistrates and the judiciary... not strangers in the land, or uneducated victims: habeas corpus.

The question of who held British subjecthood during colonial times was clearly defined by English law. The 500,000 black citizens who'd slave masters continued to treat as slaves after the revolutionary war met the legal definition of being British "subjects" and were entitled to liberty. Doubtlessly, there were no lawyers aboard the slave ship *White Lion* giving legal advice to the Africans in 1619.

None of the kidnapped Africans arriving on Virginia's shores had a clue, perspective, or an understanding of the legal condition known as indentured servitude, or English law that prohibited slavery. But the Africans were not required to know their legal rights in the American colonies to be shielded by them, as rights and protections were enumerated by promulgated law. Such is the purpose and function of the rule of law officials. Being treated as the promulgated law authorizes is the legal consequence of a true republic—governed by the rule of law.

Further, it was the duty of the Framers of the federal constitution to recognize, define and to scrupulously defend all implicated legal rights, protections of liberties that inured to black citizens, without regard to mob rule, or racial bias. But the Framers forsook their duty, in furtherance of preserving this new nation—inaugurating a tyrannical reign directed at black people—who came to be the bedrock of its slave-based institution. However, the cornerstone ideal of a free society is its limits on government authority—the rule of law. This assault compromised the nation. This was why a nationalistic narrative developed, and with the help and cooperation of our historians—America has mis-educated everyone.

The erstwhile Englishmen who became America's founding generation were quite practiced at the politics of personal aggrandizement and of course, collectively were capable of grave personal misconduct. They had affairs——they bribed British officials——they dissembled, and brokered deals. And all their very human failings, weaknesses, and insecurities were exposed when news of the treaty arrived in colonial America in the winter of 1782. Despite the treaty, there were wholesale attacks upon black citizens, and few respected the rule of law. And as Congress had formally adopted English law in 1776, the founding generation had forever lost all putative authority, power or right over any and all black people within the U. S. and Congress could not even enact laws that could abrogate, limit or interfere with a black colonist's liberty or legal rights, without due process. America's Congress could not *ex post facto* enact a federal law that in effect, turned black people into "slaves".

Yet these American lawmakers, politicians with all the baggage that the word "politician" implies, and although giving great lip service to the "rule of law"——they were ruled by all of the same forces that afflict modern politicians——greed——self-interest and regional and commercial interests. And at the constitutional convention in 1787——the Framers even turned individual dreams of black colonial soldiers into nightmares, by reneging on congressional conference of U. S. citizenship to America's native sons who fought in the Continental Army—all in violation of the Anglo-American rule of law.

Just two generations ago, President John F. Kennedy observed that "the great enemy of truth is very often not the lie; deliberate, contrived and dishonest, but the myth; persistent, persuasive, and unrealistic; too often we hold to the clichés of our forebears... we enjoy the comfort of opinion without the discomfort of thought." Susan Sontag felt truth was overrated—"An idea which is a distortion may have a greater intellectual thrust than the truth; it may better serve the needs of the spirit, which vary. The truth is balance, but the opposite of truth, which is unbalance, may not be a lie."

Necessarily, then the question of restorative justice for slavery was encapsulated in a metaphor by President Lyndon Johnson during the 1960s: it was that of a hundred-yard dash, and one of the two runners has his legs shackled together. He has progressed ten yards while the unshackled runner has gone fifty yards. At that point—the judge decides the race is unfair. He halts the race. How should the judge rectify the situation? Should he merely remove the shackles and allow the race to proceed? Then he could say that "equal opportunity" now prevails. But one of the runners would still be forty yards ahead of the other; and he would most certainly win if the judge allowed the race to proceed without a remedial plan. Would it not be the better part of justice to allow the previously shackled runner to make up the forty-yard gap or should the judge start the race all over again? And what would be the remedy if the runner at the fifty-yard line is the one who shackled the other runner? Should the judge disqualify him or make them switch places? And what if it came to light that the judge himself shackled the runner?

This point to the importance of having accurate facts and circumstances, as a condition precedent in furtherance of a restorative justice initiative. Facts must be relied upon to decide remedies and clearly it is necessary with respect to fashioning a remedy for the horrors of black slavery and the threshold question: were colonial slave laws rendered void ab initio by virtue of the *Somersett* decision?

"[W]ho will tell the negro that he is free? Who will take him before [a] court to test the question of his freedom? In ignorance of his *legal* emancipation he is kept..." Abraham Lincoln (*circa* 1854)

Chapter 7
America's True Legacy

It was Britain's first Prime Minister, Sir Robert Walpole's belief in 1721 that "[I]f no restrictions were placed on the [American] colonies—they would flourish." [80] Although Walpole held this belief—America's colonists were still expected to hold fealty to English law and all colonial legislatures were legally constrained by colonial charter to English law and a bicameral legislative system. But America's colonial legislators woefully ignored English law and purported to enact colonial slave laws without acquiring the King's assent, as required by colonial charters during this period of salutary neglect; that was later coined after the *Somersett* decision on March 22, 1775 from Edmund Burke's "Speech on Conciliation with America" that was given in the House of Commons.

Historians John E. Findling and Frank W. Thackeray in the book *Events That Changed America in the Eighteenth Century* takes the position that this "neglect" wasn't entirely deliberate and may have been really caused by the fact that the British were overwhelmed and incompetent in regulating the American colonies. Certainly, the vast distance between England and the North American colonies supports their view and having been left to their own devices, the colonial government created a species of tyranny called hereditary slavery targeted at black Englishmen. However, it has never been a question of intent and as to whether salutary neglect was a policy of *laissez-faire* towards the American colonies, the British being overwhelmed—or just a belated alibi for its aristocracy's financial entanglement in this misanthrope and unsavory practice, [81] the dispositive fact remains that no colony in North America had *carte blanche* authority to run amok and to make slave laws.

The American colonies were bound by colonial charters to English law that repudiated slavery, as well as to the resulting Twelve-Judges' decision in the *Somersett* case that declared slave laws had not been lawfully enacted and that slavery was not "allowed and approved by the laws of this Kingdom" in June 1772. England stuttered in its enforcement of the *Somersett* decision but exercised executive authority by way of Dunmore's proclamation of emancipation of black slavery in November 1775. The slaveholding patriots assumed that the "rights of Englishmen" pertained to all black slaves and acted accordingly as Thomas Jefferson's final iteration of the Declaration of Independence reflected this reality as he blamed King George III, stating slavery was a "cruel war against human nature itself, violating its most sacred rights of life and liberty in the persons of a distant people who never offended him, captivating and carrying them into slavery in another hemisphere..." and then he excoriated King George III for being their emancipator. He then conflated Britain's role in the African slave trade with hereditary slavery stated: "...exciting those very people to rise in arms among us, and to purchase that liberty of which he has deprived them, by murdering the people on whom he has obtruded them; thus paying of former crimes committed against the Liberties of one people, with crimes which he urges them to commit against the lives of another." Jefferson did not acknowledge the difference in legal status and condition of native Africans and that of black Englishmen and did not ascribe upon himself or his fellow slaveholders even a whit of culpability for Virginia's creation and propagation of the species of tyranny—hereditary slavery. However, these and other wording were edited out of the approved Declaration by his proslavery colleagues and Jefferson would write in

1823 that his colleagues' actions with respects to edits "mangled" the Declaration. Yet, when the Founding generation violated the Treaty of Paris, by renewing "hostilities" against black Englishmen, beginning in late 1782 that included assaults, battery, rape and kidnappings; Jefferson was mum.

These coordinated acts by the Americans, targeted at English citizens were brought to the attention of the U. S. and resulted in negotiations by and between British General Guy Carleton and George Washington in May 1783. Washington made the bare claim that black Englishmen during colonial times were not British subjects and they only held a status of slave. Washington was ignoring the law, as being a "slave" during colonial times was an extrajudicial status that violated English common law; had never been legally authorized by a colonial bicameral legislative process and had been rendered unconstitutional by the Twelve Judges' decision in the 1772 *Somersett* case. The rule of English law, as well as Jefferson's attestation in his submitted Declaration that King George III had indeed emancipated all former slaves during colonial times by way of Dunmore's emancipation of black slaves were pushed aside——as proslavery Americans such as Washington convinced others to disfranchise and relegate 500,000 black English citizens to toil as slaves in the U. S. They were legally required to release *all* Englishmen pursuant to the Treaty of Paris of 1783. The U. S. was obligated to "set at liberty" all Englishmen and thus black loyalists should have been freed due to their British subjecthood. Decidedly, black Englishmen had legal rights and under any circumstance they were entitled to a due process hearing; this did not happen. Their English subjecthood controlled—not racial identity and while a final treaty came to have language prohibiting the "carrying away of Negroes" or words to that effect, the threshold legal hurdle was the renewed hostilities by U. S. citizens targeted at black loyalists *after* the preliminary and *before* a final treaty was entered early in 1783. And as liberty was a personal right under English law to all people including black Englishmen and Africans; they should have had a due process hearing before disfranchisement and enslavement.

Moreover, as the First Congress had adopted English law, *after* declaring itself the legislature of this new sovereign nation in 1776—all questions of emancipation, status and legal rights—possibly inuring to black Englishmen under English law, as well as the actions of King George III during colonial times, although edited out by Jefferson's proslavery colleagues were facts and circumstances to be analyzed through the prism of English common law. The language in Jefferson's proffered Declaration, notwithstanding the removal of such language is probative and in fact is inculpatory.

> "We hold these truths to be self-evident, that all men are created equal, that they are endowed by their Creator with certain unalienable Rights that among these are Life, Liberty and the pursuit of Happiness."

Somersett was the controlling judicial construction of English law. American colonists were bound by English law that made slavery in the American colonies a criminal act in June 1772. Congress debated, and then adopted English rule of law in 1776. The resulting congressional act bound the U. S. to English law, yet erstwhile American colonists still purported to own slaves. And U. S. rule of law officials went along with them. They brought forth no evidence to support ownership claims, and throughout the American Revolutionary War... the founding generation from northern colonies supported slaveholding patriots. Benjamin Franklin's essay published in the London Chronicle... began by first praising metropolitan Englishmen as being "generous humane persons" who had aided Somersett's bid to obtain "liberty by law," he expressed his wish "that the same Humanity may extend itself among Numbers, if not to the procuring Liberty for those that remain in our Colonies, at least to obtain a Law for abolishing the

African Commerce in Slaves, and declaring the Children of present Slaves free after they become of Age." Franklin then reminded the metropolitan readership that the nation held 850,000 slaves and trafficked over 100,000 Africans yearly. He then wrote:

> "Pharisaical Britain! To pride thyself in setting free a single slave that happens to land on thy coasts, while thy merchants in all thy ports are encouraged by thy laws to continue a commerce whereby so many hundreds of thousands are dragged into a slavery that can scarce be said to end with their lives since it is entailed on their posterity!"

David Waldstreicher has settled on calling Franklin's relationship towards slavery as being complex during the Revolutionary era—but it was not complex. [82] Franklin was a collaborator, a dissembler and his hyperbolic tone was only proffered to obfuscate and to shift focus away from the dispositive fact that the American patriots were engaged in the trafficking of black Englishmen—their countrymen. The *Somersett* decision in 1772 rendered hereditary slave laws within the American colonies void—as none of the colonial assemblies within the American colonies had enacted "positive law," as none had the King's written assent to any purported change of English law. Thus "setting free a single slave" happening on England's shore by the highest court in the Kingdom made slavery a crime in the American colonies and Franklin knew it.

The American Revolutionary War was an English civil war that the Treaty of Paris of 1783 ended. The war was about slavery and freedom. It is true that the British government's initial war aims were to preserve the American colonies. It is also true that the Founding Fathers claimed to fight for some abstract term like "no taxation, without representation." But these were subterfuges. On both sides the leaders understood what was at stake. The revolutionary war was the first time in recorded human history when slaveowners revolted to keep their slaves——as opposed to slaves rebelling to gain freedom.

The founding generation agreed to cease all hostilities against British citizens, and to "set at liberty" all captive Englishmen. However, by the spring of 1783, Americans had resumed hostilities, and in May of 1783, British General Guy Carleton filed a protest. He informed General George Washington of mass assaults, kidnappings, and the detention of black British citizens. He claimed such actions were violative of the peace treaty. Washington disagreed. Washington's position was that his countrymen were merely recapturing legal "chattel slaves" pursuant to the treaty. He stated that organized repossessions of pre-war human property were lawful, authorized, and therefore, Americans were not violating the treaty. He provided no proof.

Carleton went on to explain to Washington that liberty was a personal right under English law, that the word "slave" had only a colloquial connotation. He stated that all such people were British citizens—protected by the treaty and entitled to their liberty. [83] Dissatisfied, Carleton declared his intention to provide safe passage, and transport for all former "slaves" who wanted to leave the U. S., but Washington bristled at the suggestion, and in an effort to deescalate the situation, Carleton suggested that each side keep a registry of black people removed from the U. S.—a *Book of Negroes*. He obligated England to pay the U. S., if he was proven wrong. Washington agreed to inform the U. S. Congress of this international dispute, and he did. [84] However, the U. S. used militias, slave patrols and dragnets, to stop the mass exodus of black people, who were committed towards leaving North America. Carleton left America with only 3,000 black souls in November 1783. [85] The preservation of Carleton's *Book of Negroes* at the National Archives in London, England, and Washington's version at the

National Archives and Records Administration in Washington, D. C. are inculpatory. [86] Carleton's attestation of treaty violations in May of 1783 and Washington's claim of Americans owning black people under English rule frames the restorative justice debate. This was never just a theoretical issue.

In his book titled *The Character and Influence of the Roman Civil Law*, legal scholar Peter Stein observed: "Immediately after the Revolution, there was a widespread feeling that efforts should be made to develop a particular American jurisprudence, which would not be just a slavish imitator of the English common law, but would be eclectic—selecting the best principles and methods from whatever system they might be found in." And pulling the strings within Congress to develop a uniquely American jurisprudence was Judge George Wythe, a Founding Father who signed the Declaration of Independence, attended the Constitutional Convention, and Thomas Jefferson's mentor—who served as his point man. The initiative within Congress to sever ties with English law was multi-faceted and the thorny issue of colonial slavery and its coveted integration in the new nation played an integral role—but was rejected by the First Congress in 1776. There were overarching reasons, embodying continuity of contracts, legal processes, economics and in part, the notion of being in some sort of continuity with an Anglo-Saxon past gave erstwhile Englishmen— now Americans the impression that they were elements of a linearly expanding people pursuing liberty. However, the adoption of English law resolved all lingering questions in favor of black people. English law was an anathema to slavery, as it made black people equal to white people and legally barred them from claiming differently.

Whyte and Jefferson's well-organized push to adopt Roman rule in 1776, and its rejection evidenced an informed polity that English law was the objective will of the founding generation. It was common knowledge that black people were never legal slaves here in colonial America. The Declaration's twenty-seven grievances proves that its signatories knew that no law enacted by a colonial assembly, in the absence of the King's assent was positive law. Slavery is an obvious flashpoint since ninety-five percent of all colonial blacks were native-born—Englishmen by law and their status and condition as slave, was based upon colonial laws. Whyte and Jefferson sought to supplant English law, as only then would slavery—their wealth, power and culture have a chance of surviving were their thoughtful views.

Anglo-Saxonism for Wythe, and Jefferson was nothing more than a dead patrimony to be bequeathed intact from fathers to sons. They were concerned about wealth, power and according to Jefferson, abandoning English law was more important to the living, than growing familiar with Greek or Roman cultures. "No man ever left behind him a character more venerated than George Wythe," were some of the words Jefferson used to describe his teacher. "His virtue was of the purest tint; his integrity inflexible, and his justice exact; of warm patriotism, and, devoted as he was to liberty, and the natural and equal rights of man, he might truly be called the Cato of his country." Wythe also taught John Marshall, and Henry Clay.

The Declaration set-forth twenty-seven grievances against King George III and asserted certain legal rights as justification. Per Declaration, as the threshold declarant was liberty for all under English law, a personal right and as each colony had been bound by colonial charter to English law that criminalized assaults and kidnappings—slavery had no chance of being a legal institution, if English law was formally adopted by Congress. Abraham Lincoln made it the basis of his policies, and argued its preamble announced principles by which the constitution was to be interpreted. However, legal historian John Phillip Reid in his book *The Irrelevance of the Declaration* posits that the Declaration was not a political philosophical manifesto about natural rights, rather, that it was a legal document; an indictment against King George III.

The founding generation knew colonial governors, the head of the colony's judiciary should have vetoed slave laws. They also knew that they were violating black Englishmen liberty rights. The southern colonial assemblies steadfastly refused to respect the jurisdictional shortcomings of colonial slave laws, even though the King never gave his assent to slavery and the Twelve Judges in the *Somersett* case stated slavery was not "approved and allowed by the laws in this Kingdom" and can only be lawful by virtue of "positive law". The king not giving his assent to the decriminalization of kidnappings and to colonial slavery, or to matrilineal laws that accommodated hereditary slavery made the practice totally criminal. The founding generation knew that the bicameral structure of the colonial legislature made colonial slavery extrajudicial and totally beholding to governmental corruption, graft, and British tyranny. Ownership claims of black people became criminal by virtue of the Twelve Judges' ruling in the *Somersett* case, as none of the colonial slave laws had been lawfully promulgated. They were all void *ab initio*. Lord Dunmore liberated black citizens suffering as slaves using executive authority in November 1775, and then by Congress' adoption of English law in 1776. Wythe and Jefferson were self-assured that every black suffering as a slave would be transformed into an American, once and if English law was formally adopted by the U. S. legislature. Such was a major reason that they pushed for supplanting English law, but once the First Congress formally adopted English law in 1776… their concerns turned to dread. Black people became Englishmen and citizens of the U. S. and could not legally belong to white Americans. They recognized that such citizens would have a litany of pending legal claims against them. This was the lawful consequence—once Congress adopted English law, or so they believed

Contributing to Whyte and Jefferson's consternation was Article XIII of the Articles of Confederation. America's first constitution provided that "Every State shall abide by the determination of the United States in Congress Assembled, on all questions which by this confederation are submitted to them." The choice of English law was formally decided by Congress and it defined, limited, and constricted Congress' legislative powers, authority to change any congressional act involving black people in the U. S. and in furtherance thereto, Article

VI, clause 2 of the U. S. Constitution also called the Supremacy Clause provides:

> The Constitution, and the Laws of the United States which shall be made in Pursuance thereof; and all Treaties made, or which shall be made, under the Authority of the United States, shall be the supreme Law of the Land; and the Judges in every State shall be bound thereby, any Thing in the Constitution or Laws of any State to the Contrary notwithstanding.

Under U. S. law, these three are the supreme law of the land. Thus, the federal constitution by its own text created a trinity... the Constitution... *laws of the United States*... and *Treaties made*.

History supports—no one being *above* the law or *below* the law were core to English law. And the debates to supplant English law with Roman law in 1776 and 1787, where Thomas Jefferson—the author of the Declaration of Independence, George Washington—the father of the United States, James Madison—the father of the Constitution, John Marshall—America's first Chief Justice of the Supreme Court and George Wythe—America's First Law Professor, and other slave owning Founding Fathers unsuccessfully pushed the First Congress to abandon English law in 1776— advocating for a clean break from English jurisprudence is first principles in addressing slavery's true origins.

The Three-Fifths Compromise of 1787 calculated population by adding "the whole Number of free persons, including those bound to Service for a Term of Years, and excluding Indians not taxed," and "three fifths of all other Persons." Those "other Persons" of course were black "slaves"——who were British citizens and in real terms entitled to be counted as full U. S. citizens, pursuant to Congress' legislation in 1776. This Compromise was *per se* unlawful because it diminished the humanity of Englishmen with black blood and it surrendered disproportionate representation in the House of Representatives to the southern slave states, relative to the voters in Free states until the Civil War. Take for instance, southern slave states had 47 of the 125 congressional members in 1793——but would have had only 33——if seats had been assigned based upon free population. And in consequence, slave states had disproportionate influence on the presidency of the United States, the speakership of the House, and the Supreme Court all the way up until the Civil War.

Thomas Jefferson won the election of 1800 over John Adams——but if there had been no Compromise, Adams would have won the election.

This was because of the Electoral College that gave a state the same number of votes, as it does representatives in the House. During the federal constitutional convention in Philadelphia, James Madison said that with a popular vote, the Southern states, "could have no influence in the election on the score of Negroes." The Electoral College process was a product of the Compromise.

Additionally, but for the Three-Fifths Compromise——slavery would have been excluded from Missouri... Andrew Jackson's Indian removal policy (The Trail of Tears) would have failed... the Wilmot Proviso would have banned slavery in territories won from Mexico... the Kansas-Nebraska bill would not have been enacted and the Confederate South would not have attacked Fort Sumter in South Carolina in April 1861——shortly after Lincoln was elected President. The Civil War led to citizenship and voting rights for black people.

The federal constitution did not authorize slavery, and there was no need to abolish slavery by way of the Thirteenth Amendment. The failure of the federal judiciary to enforce anti-slavery provisions of the constitution gave states the green light to introduce slave laws. Since its enactment, the Electoral College system have cost five candidates the presidency, after they received the popular vote.

Most recently, Hillary Clinton lost to Donald J. Trump in 2016.

The U. S. violated the law of nation when it stopped black people from leaving this new nation at the end of the Revolutionary War in accordance with the Treaty of Paris. Objectively, the Framers of the constitution failed to honor the rule of law during the 1780s. Such decisions ripples, impacting the enactment of the Fugitive Slave Act through the Thirteenth Amendment to the extent the same class of people's congressional representation was reduced by two-fifths in the United States and it also inveigled the Second Amendment.

The fractionalization of rights, role and status of black people embodied in the Three-Fifths Compromise also violated the Treaty of Paris, and earlier laws and congressional guarantees that "law will be king" in the United States. Lord Coke's seminal opinion in *Calvin's Case* offers a definitive statement of how one became a subject of the King of England. The case held that a person's birthright subjecthood was immutable, perpetual, and could not be abandoned or interfered with. Congress' adoption of English law in 1776 meant questions of British subjecthood and ownership of human beings during colonial times was well-settled and as the rights, role and status of all British subjects not leaving the U. S. were subject to laws promulgated by Congress, black people were U. S. citizens, by tacit consent.

All British subjects remaining here were legally conferred citizenship in the United States and as a matter of law; Congress could not and did not pass a law that in effect changed the rights, role and status of black people. The Three-Fifths Compromise was nugatory—as a matter of America's rule of law. It is an undeniable fact—erstwhile Englishmen like George Washington and Thomas Jefferson were self-proclaimed, unrepentant slave masters who exercised the power of life and death over natural-born black colonists during colonial times—but slavery remained a serious violation of English law.

Chief Justice John Marshall's observation in *Wheaton v. Peters,* [87] was that "... the framers of the constitution having been acquainted with the principles of the common law and acted in reference to them. Most of them were able lawyers; and certainly able lawyers drew up, and revised the instrument... This case, and all the law on this subject, discussed and decided by it, must have been known to the lawyers of the [constitutional] convention." With respect to legal rights under the treaty, the rule of law officials were obligated to apply the law as to all questions. This did not happen, as the founding generation disfranchised black citizens in derogation of Anglo-Saxon jurisprudence and the Treaty of Paris in the 1780s. This decimated America's creed of being a government of laws, and not of men. Enslavement without due process ran afoul of Law of Nations doctrine, founded on the treaties, and Customary (common) Law of the modern nations of Europe, and it remains first principles.

Congress' adoption of English law in 1776 meant black people could not be fractionalized either for population, taxation or any other purpose—as a matter of federal law. And as a threshold consideration, the Supremacy Clause of the United States Constitution rendered the controversy that led to the Three-Fifths Compromise moot—as it established that the Constitution, federal laws made pursuant to it, and treaties made under its authority, constitute the supreme law of the land. . . Even state constitutions are subordinate to federal law.

Doubtlessly, the placement of black people who were citizens of the U. S. *below* the rule of law explains much, but it also taints and pollutes the constitutional process since the First Congress bound this new nation to the rule of law and equal representation for all—by way of the Declaration of Independence. However, Article 1, section 2, clause 3 of the United States Constitution, also called the

Three-Fifths Compromise runs afoul of the "Treaties made" proviso of the federal constitution by purporting to enact a positive law allowing slavery on United States soil and devaluation of black people's humanity in obvious violation of America's rule of law, and the Supremacy Clause of the United States Constitution.

Alexander Hamilton who supported abolishment of slavery stated:

> "Much has been said of the impropriety of representing men who have no will of their own... They are men though degraded to the condition of slavery. They are persons known to the municipal laws of the states which they inhabit, as well as to the laws of nature. But representation and taxation go together. . . Would it be just to impose a singular burden, without conferring some adequate advantage."

In June of 1772, the Twelve Judges ruled in the *Somersett* case that slavery was not "allowed and approved by the laws of this Kingdom" and colonial slavery became criminal since it was not the product of positive law. The question of colonial laws lawfulness was the dispositive legal issue before the King's Bench. Although bound by colonial charter to abide by English law, Washington and others slave masters did not release people who they knew to be legally free Englishmen. Lawlessness continued even after the governor of Virginia; Lord Dunmore issued a writ of habeas that liberated slaves in the colony of Virginia. However, Dunmore's proclamation of November 1775 had the legal consequence of liberating all slaves in colonial America under the rule of law—but colonial Englishmen throughout the American colonies refused to free black Englishmen suffering as slaves—showing disdain, and utter contempt for the rule of law. They claimed that they legally owned black people, yet the rule of law had plainly stated that colonial slavery was unconstitutional throughout the British empire.

In July of 1776, the American colonies declared themselves the United States of America, and although the slave holding founding fathers are remembered as noted disciples in making Anglo-Saxon law a civil religion in the United States—a guarantor of American liberties, in late summer of 1776 Thomas Jefferson and other slave masters advocated for this new nation to sever its historical, legal ties to English law. They urged the first Congress to supplant English law with Roman law, which recognized the tradition of *partus sequitur ventrem*: chattel slavery. The enlightened Jefferson, and his supporters understood that a democracy by its very nature could never exist with a slave-based economy and thought Roman Law——if adopted by Congress would offer the new nation a way to reconcile the two. However, Jefferson's initiative was squarely rejected in 1776, and then English law was adopted by the First Congress.

Although this was a dispositive legal defeat for slave masters, it did not resolve the slavery question, as delegates in favor of supplanting English law in favor of Roman law continued to lobby, and were able to cajole enough delegates to agree to a compromise during the federal constitutional process in the late 1780s. Through inaction, the Framers legitimated the Americans' ownership claims of black people and by doing so, abandoned the rule of law——assaulted this democracy and fouled the new federal constitution.

With respect to U. S. history... constitutionalism in both its descriptive and prescriptive sense, has slavishly focused on the period surrounding the enactment of the federal constitution. Indeed, a routine——but a mistaken assumption of scholars has been that American constitutionalism entails only the thought that went into the drafting of the federal constitution, and the American experience with that constitution since its ratification in 1789. But pre-Declaration of Independence constitutionalism offers a broader and more precise insight into constitutionalism in the United States.

The Declaration of Independence was a new thing—never seen in the world, and it served as a social contract tendered to all colonial American colonists. It was evidence of how the new government would work and bound the founding generation. To grasp its true significance, we must draw back for a moment and view it against the background of the American Revolution, which produced a new nation.

The founding generation conferring U. S. citizenship unto all legally free Englishmen and foreign inhabitants in 1776 was a substantial compact. In other words, the Declaration was a compact with all free Englishmen in colonial America in July 1776, and since England's high court ruled slavery was not "allowed and approved by the laws of this Kingdom" and Congress adopted English law—it was the sole prism to analyze the question of nationality of black people, and entitlement to U. S. citizenship, as a matter of law *after* the Revolutionary War ended.

History supports, America's original thirteen colonies were divided into three geographic areas consisting of the New England, Middle, and

Southern colonies. The Southern colonies, which consisted of Virginia in 1606, Maryland in 1632, South Carolina and North Carolina in 1729, and Georgia in 1732, were all crown colonies. The colonial governor, appointed by the king was the ultimate authority in each colony, and each colony was constituted as being "a government of laws and not of men." The colonies were bound by English law and had no legislative authority to enact a law that which was "repugnant" to England's common law. Each colony in America had a bicameral legislative structure; the King and the colonial assembly. They were all financially reliant upon slavery and had no real quarrels with British rule.

Notably, this British ideal of being "a government of laws and not of men" was adopted by the First Continental Congress in 1774, and was enshrined by John Adams——the second President of the United States in the *Novanglus Essays* published in February 1775, in which he looked at the constitutional relationship between Britain and her American colonies. Novanglus was a pen name Adams used in replies to essays published by Daniel Leonard, a loyalist lawyer who wrote under the pseudonym Massachusettensis, and it was in the seventh *Novanglus Essays* that stated:

"...the British constitution is much more like a republic than an empire. They define a republic to be a government of laws, and not of men. If this definition be just, the British constitution is nothing more, nor less than a republic, in which the king is first magistrate...We are a part of the British dominions, that is, of the King of Great Britain, and it is our interest and duty to continue so."

Adams' core contention in his *Novanglus Essays* was the claim that Massachusetts' colonial assembly should be the Supreme power of the colony and that the colony of Massachusetts, just like the other twelve colonies were only connected to Great Britain through the King. The "no slavery allowed" pillar of English law embodies a Roman law principle that "captivity and servitude are both contrary to the law of nature; for by that law all men are born free." "The air in England is too pure for a slave to breathe; if their lungs receive our air, that moment they are free; they touch our country and their shackles fall" is a poetic expression of English common law during colonial times. The trope "law is king" was English common law, and in the classic treatise *Commentaries of the Laws of England* penned in 1765——Sir William Blackstone opined "If an uninhabited or infidel territory was colonized by Britain, then English law automatically applied in this territory from the moment of colonization." The Magna Carta of 1215 and English common law was the law of the land in colonial America and was even adopted as the basis of America's legal system——after the thirteen colonies declared themselves an independent nation in 1776.

The colonial charter defined, bound and limited the power of the colonial assembly to enact laws. Laws passed by all legislative assemblies within the American colonies required the King's assent. No British monarch contemplated surrendering sovereignty over colonial affairs to legislative assemblies. Each properly promulgated colonial law required the King's assent, and by being only one chamber of a bicameral legislative system, the American colonies could not change the patrilineal descent system to *partus sequitur ventrem*. Colonial assemblies did not divest black people of their British subjecthood, nor did they legalize slavery within the American colonies during colonial times. Pursuant to the Treaty of Paris of 1783——each black person had a liberty right, or at the minimum, was entitled to have a due process hearing under the rule of law.

With respect to the U. S. enslaving 500,000 people that England claimed were British citizens and entitled to liberty per the Treaty of Paris of 1783, freedom was a liberty right during the 1780s: a right which did not entail obligations on other parties, but rather only freedom or permission for the right-holder. Yet there were claim rights too that entailed responsibilities, duties, or obligations on other parties regarding the right-holder. They were symbiotic: a world with only liberty rights, without any claim rights, would be a world wherein everything was permitted, and no act or omission was prohibited; a world wherein none could rightly claim that they had been wronged or neglected.

Alternatively, a world with only claim rights and no liberty rights would be a world wherein nothing was merely permitted, but all acts were either obligatory or prohibited. The ideal that people have a claim right to liberty—that people are obliged only to refrain from preventing each other from doing things which are permissible, their liberty rights limited only by the obligation to respect others' liberty. This was a central thesis of liberal theories of democracy and justice.

For example, to assert a liberty right to pursue happiness is to assert that you have permission to be happy; that is, that you are not doing anything wrong by being happy. But that liberty right does not in itself entail that others are obligated to help you be happy, or even that they would be wrong in stopping you from being happy. And under the rule of law it is the party infringing upon a liberty right who has the burden of proving powers and immunities. In *R v. Stapylton*, (K.B. 1771, unreported) Lord Mansfield ruled in this criminal case of assault against a black person—the black victim was conferred the presumption of liberty and was afforded all legal protections of English law. The defendant's bare claim of legal ownership of another human person was deemed legally insufficient; it required proof. Likewise, Lord Mansfield's 1771 ruling in this foregoing case was controlling precedent for Carleton's 1783 treaty violations dispute and is dispositive of the U. S. disfranchisement and enslavement of 500,000 black people during the 1780s.

In U. S. constitutional history, the legal theory that a state has the right to nullify or invalidate any federal law which that state has deemed unconstitutional with respect to the United States Constitution is called nullification. Federal courts in rejecting the doctrine of nullification have held, the federal constitution was established directly by people of the United States and points to the preamble... "We the people of the United States." This is also true of the Declaration of Independence's preamble... "When in the course of human events it becomes necessary for one people to dissolve the political bands which have connected them with another..." Such raises a compelling inquiry into the federal constitution, if 500,000 black citizens were willfully denied representation during the constitutional process.

> "Those who have no record of what their forbears have accomplished lose the inspiration which comes from the teaching of biography and history". Carter G. Woodson

Chapter 8
Below The Rule of Law

The tropes or short metaphors, "rule of law" and "law is king" are expressions of the same ideal that everyone was bounded, limited, and protected equally by English law. An early example of its application came in 1619, when the first Africans disembarked from a slave ship as indentured servants—not slaves. The rule of law officials abided by English law and certainly, the legal classification of indentured servant for captured Africans, and their ensuing treatment within the colony once becoming free were rousing testaments to the ideal of equal protection under English law. The Africans thrived, owned land, and prospered within the colony of Virginia *after* their terms as indentured servants terminated. Their children were freeborn Afro-Britons under English law and Virginia's colonial charter. There were no then popular passions against Africans, mulattoes, or systemic corruption of colony government. That came later.

Lerone Bennett, Jr. observed in his seminal book *Before the Mayflower*—that the Declaration of Independence "scattered four revolutionary seeds to the four corners of the earth". He observed:

1. "That all men are created equal and are endowed by their Creator with natural and inalienable rights no man or government can bestow or take away.
2. That to secure these rights men creates civil communities and civil authorities, who derive just power from the consent of the governed.
3. That members of the community are colleagues and not subjects and that legitimate government consists in the dominion, in short, of people over themselves and not in the dominion of communities over communities or groups over groups.
4. That when governments are destructive of these ends as evidenced by bad faith ("a long train of abuses and usurpations pursuing invariably the same object.") it is the duty of citizens to alter or abolish these governments."

These ideals, coupled with the First Congress' adoption of English law, and then each of the thirteen states following suit in 1776—had the legal consequence of delegitimizing all trappings, vestiges and claims of ownership of black people under Anglo-American jurisprudence. This thesis had received powerful reaffirmation once England's Twelve Judges ruled in the *Somersett* case—that slavery had not been lawfully enacted within the American colonies by their colonial legislatures; as well, the tribunal's ruling that slavery was not "allowed and approved by the laws of this Kingdom" and explained that it can only be lawful by way of "positive law". The High court's ruling established slavery was only an extrajudicial institution within the Kingdom and rendered all colonial slave laws void *ab initio,* as a matter of law since no King had ever allowed and approved a colonial slave law within the American colonies. But despite the *Somersett* ruling, the slaveholding colonists within the North American colonies refused to voluntarily release the wrongfully enslaved black colonists—thus His Majesty's lieutenant Lord Dunmore came to liberate all black people within the American colonies who were suffering as slaves. He did so by exercising executive authority of habeas corpus in November 1775—eight months *before* the Declaration of Independence in July 1776. The rejection of Jefferson's bill to supplant English law with Roman law and English law's formal adoption by the First Congress in 1776 were defining legislative acts of the U. S. Congress.

Slavery in the U. S. was an act of sublimation, transitioning an illicit, misanthrope practice into an otherwise respectable enterprise, without reconciliation with the rule of law. However, the rule of law stood resolutely. Black people and all other Englishmen were not compelled to leave the U. S. and could not be disfranchised of any legal rights. Citizenship through tacit consent was conferred unto all English citizens who continued to reside in the United States. The conference of U. S. citizenship unto all colonial Englishmen was underpinned by the "no slavery allowed" aspect of the British constitution and English law that espoused the principle that citizenship "ought to be uniform, and without invidious gradations and it ought to confer equal rights." It followed that in the absence of sustaining the legal burden of proving black people were not Englishmen or were being carved out as being exempted Englishmen in the Declaration, they held full U. S. citizenship under the rubric of tacit consent. They were the countrymen of George Washington, Thomas Jefferson, James Madison, John Marshall, and Patrick Henry, under English American rule of law.

Modern American political discourse beginning with Richard Nixon's successful presidential run in 1968 infused conservative legal dogmas of constitutionalism, originalism, and textualism into the lexicon—emphasizing judicial restraint, and fidelity to the original intent of the federal constitution. It became a Republican crucible, although once Nixon appointed four justices that seemed to be true to this philosophy—one of them shifted leftward and another became a moderate. Gerald Ford's presidential campaign distanced itself from this issue, but Ronald Reagan's candidacy rebounded by promising "strict constructionists" and all three of his Supreme Court nominees fell into this category. And every Republican presidential hopeful since Reagan have promised to appoint strict constructionists to the Supreme Court—but it's a specious, metaphysical term and a vacuous pledge.

The threshold notion that U. S. presidents should only appoint Supreme Court nominees who hold fealty to the Framers' intent when they failed to begin with first principles illuminates the speciousness of the label... strict constructionist and the practice. A member of the Supreme Court ought to express fealty to the rule of law, not mere Framers of the law. This is apparent since any descriptive focus obligates a careful historian to begin with English antecedents... going back to the English Magna Carta of 1215, and then from that point, explore the presence and development of ideals of liberty rights, individual freedoms, privileges, and protections through colonial charters, and English law. The use of any other data point, rather than first principles and then identifying revolutionary declarations, and constitutions, documents, and judicial decisions during the Confederation period, and the formation of the federal constitution is a flawed process.

Likewise, there can be no meaningful claim of prescriptive focus——since within the four corners of the federal constitution there is a Supremacy Clause, Article, VI, clause 2. It provides "all treaties made, or which shall be made, under the authority of the United States shall be the Supreme law of the Land." This Supremacy Clause specifies certain national acts, regardless of whether a conflicting law, or interest comes from Congress, courts, administrative agencies, or constitutions takes priority over all interests that conflicts, and all acts and interests lay prostrate before the art. VI, cl. 2 of the Constitution. Yet black people's liberty rights, individual freedoms, privileges, and protections have been blithely ignored, lest of all factored, valued or have been given weight.

Doubly, British colonization policies during the 17th and 18th centuries, its bicameral legislative structure that required the King's assent to all colonial laws passed by a colonial assembly to be deemed legal, and the protracted period of colonial government corruption, tyranny and hooliganism associated with slavery is the "smoking gun". The historical struggles of all Englishmen to be recognized by its monarchy beginning with the Magna Carta during the 13th century, its civil wars during the 17th century and the enshrinement of a Bill of Rights for all Englishmen in the year 1679 provides insights, not only as towards liberty rights, but are probative of constitutional order, and construction. It is a fair statement to make that England's historical struggles for constitutional acknowledgement of its citizens' liberty rights, freedoms, as well as protections against government overreach have been ignored.

In *Federalist* No. 44, James Madison defended the Supremacy Clause, as being vital to the functioning of the nation. He noted that state legislatures were invested with all powers, not specially defined in the Constitution, but also, he declared that having the federal government subservient to various state constitutions would be an inversion of the principles of government, concluding that if supremacy were not established:

> "it would have seen the authority of the whole society everywhere subordinate to the

authority of the parts: it would have seen a monster, in which the head was under the direction of the members."

Yet, a constructive focus upon constitutionalism in the U. S. have always demanded a fair, unvarnished interpretation of all facts and reconciliation of Carleton's attestation of treaty violations in 1783 through the prism of English law. Only by first bridging the U. S. Constitution through the Treaty of Paris of 1783——Articles of Confederation——the Declaration and colonial charters that granted the founding generation the legal right or basis to declare themselves independent nation in 1776 can this be achieved.

First principles regarding slavery's origins is a challenge to U. S. constitutionalism, which is synonymous with the legitimacy of this government and the country's enslavement of 500,000 black English citizens during the 1780s. This necessarily triggers a reexamination of this outstanding treaty dispute and slave-based provisions and compromises since Carleton made a formal attestation of treaty violations in May 1783 *before* ratification. English law obligated anyone claiming ownership of a black person during the 1780s to prove it pursuant to Lord Mansfield's holding in the *Stapylton* case. The U. S. could not rely upon colonial practices to legitimate their claim of ownership of black people to resolve this treaty dispute.

In *Ware v. Hylton*, [88] relying upon the Supremacy Clause, the United States Supreme Court struck down a Revolutionary War-era law enacted in 1776 in the state of Virginia. The law extinguished debts owed to British citizens. The Supreme Court declared that such a law was null and void since Virginia's law conflicted with the Treaty of Paris of 1783. America's highest court held "An individual citizen of one state cannot set up the violation of a public treaty, by the other contracting party, to avoid an obligation arising under such treaty; the power to declare a treaty void, for such cause, rests solely with the government, which may, or may not, exercise its option in the premises." The *Hylton* case is controlling U. S. precedent, to address legal standards, consequences, and legitimacy of all founding generational claims of ownership of black citizens, as the Treaty of Paris of 1783 controls.

The slave owners controlled colonial assemblies throughout the southern colonies and were in criminal league with corrupt British officials. Their relationship spanned generations. Collectively, colonial legislators knew the extent of their lawful authority to enact colonial laws. They all knew slavery was not a lawful practice—as colonial laws did not have the King's assent. However, through institutionalized graft a legal fiction called "slave" was created and to what extent the British policy of salutary neglect constituted actual neglect, as the term suggests, or be it a social experiment of self-rule that courted the colonists' better angels and/or an initiative to further slavery; certainly the policy initiative failed from a British imperial perspective. Nonetheless, the American colonies and its people were legally bound by the *Somersett* decision that declared slavery was not "allowed and approved by the laws of this Kingdom" and could only be lawful by way of "positive law."

America's Revolution that gave rise to this *"The Shining City on the Hill"* called the United States was more than revolutionary rhetoric—it was a movement of mankind, an eviction notice to all men of ill-intent who would pervert humanity and natural law. But after the Twelve Judges' ruling in the *Somersett* case in 1772—the slave owning Englishmen hi-jacked America's Revolution, and though it was understood that these men were criminals under the rule of law, an anathema to Thomas Paine's penned "cause of all mankind" because they were enslaving legally free Englishmen—not Africans; yet they allowed these people to become leaders of this new nation.

In the book *Slave Nation: How Slavery United the Colonies and Sparked the American Revolutions*, the writers Alfred and Ruth Blumrosen observed that many patriots were anti-slavery and professed to hold enmity towards slavery on moral grounds—but capitulated to proslavery interests for the sake of unity. However, the Framers, as rule of law officials had a legal obligation to apply the law and could not capitulate to pro-slavery interests and enter a compromise to further unity and to avoid disharmony. Nonetheless, that's exactly what they did.

The compromise allowed black people to be disfranchised; people who had liberty rights under the treaty. The Framers assaulted the rule of law by putting black people *below* it and elevating slave masters *above* the rule of law. All signatories to the Declaration knew slavery was not a lawful condition, as colonial slave laws did not have the King's assent and the Twelve Judges had ruled in the *Somersett* case that slavery could only be lawful by way of "positive law". These revelations mandate a recalculation of America's creed, and more importantly, its historiography.

In late spring of 1787, the erstwhile Englishmen to the federal constitutional convention gathered for the announced purpose of reforming the Articles of

Confederation. And in debates between May 25 and September 17, the delegates invoked Roman history, legal principles, and institutions as they debated the future constitutional order of America. Some of the founding fathers raised concern about looking to the Roman Republic because it had collapsed and became an empire. But historian Reinhold Meyer notes in *Classica Americana: The Greek and Roman Heritage in the United States* that the classics were important to the founding generation because they were looking for "a lamp of experience in ancient history" and political thought to validate the political conclusion that they had from contemporary thought and reason. However, it was a renewed, orchestrated effort by Jefferson and others to supplant English law that criminalized hereditary slavery, and to protect portended rights, and potential losses of status and wealth.

Jefferson, who was learned in the classics had occasion to note that in Rome:

> "I am immersed in antiquities from morning to night. For me the city of Rome is actually existing in all the splendor of its empire. I am filled with alarms for the event of the irruptions daily making on us by the Goths, the Visigoths, Ostrogoths, and Vandals, lest they should reconquer us to our original barbarism."

He notes in this quotation that Rome fell after foreign invasions—reminding delegates that internal divisions among the Roman people significantly contributed to the fall of the Roman Republic, and Empire. Jefferson was speaking to the division existing between the delegates, and the certainty of collapse, lest they pull together on the question of what to do with black people.

The delegates who invoked Roman history at the federal constitutional convention supported enslaving black people, despite knowing of Carleton's claim of British subjecthood and the Treaty of Paris violations. The First Congress had bound the U. S. to English law and the *Somersett* decision and common law—that a person's birthright citizenship was immutable, perpetual, and he/she were children of the nation. They knew all black people were British subjects by English law—entitled to liberty under the Treaty of Paris of 1783, and that the enslavement of the 500,000 black Englishmen would never be anything other than extrajudicial.

Initially, it was not about protecting personal liberty or autonomy. The essential idea, long before a modern understanding of individual liberty had developed was about government tyranny. The need to restrain the sovereign's awesome power has been a perennial struggle for societies as long as they have existed. There are three distinct components in a democracy. The first theme is the government's fealty, or lack thereof to promulgated laws. The second theme is the notion of formal legality. The third theme is the classic expression: "No man is above, nor below the law." And certainly, the theme that a democracy is limited by its promulgated laws is a thread that has run for over 2,000 have years, as ancient Greek and Roman civilizations political ideas have survived through texts of history and philosophy. These texts explore ideals of democracy, republicanism, and citizenship that not only endured, but also significantly influenced the formation of the Constitution.

The effort to impose legal limits on the sovereign raises an ancient dilemma: How can the creator of law be bound by the law? Nonetheless, there developed two distinct strains of the notion that the sovereign, and government officials must operate within a limiting framework of law. The first strain is that officials must abide by the positive laws currently in force. The law may be changed by authorized rule of law officials following appropriate procedures—but it must be complied with until it is changed.

The second strain is that even when government officials wish to change the law, they are not entirely free to change it in any way they desire. There are restraints on their law-making power. The fundamental import of this second strain is that the sovereign's power over enacting positive law is itself subject to higher legal restrictions. This underscores why the defeat of Jefferson's bill to supplant English law in 1776 was so significant.

The U. S. was legally constrained by English law and could not cast away protections put in place by the Magna Carta of 1215 and common law. The rule of law required U. S. lawmakers to apply the exact same protocol used by the colony of Virginia's rule of law officials when it dealt with the first Africans arriving on their shores in 1619. They were indentured servants—not slaves under English law. However, one hundred and fifty-six years later, in connection with enacting a new federal constitution—lawmakers did just the opposite in acceding to the demands of southern slave holding states, and the citizens.

The second theme, formal legality goes to the nature of rules—what rules are and how they operate. Friedrich A. Hayek posits in his book *The Road to Serfdom* that the rule of law makes "it possible to foresee with fair certainty how the authority will use its coercive powers in given circumstances and to plan one's individual affairs on the basis of this knowledge." This allows people to know in advance which actions will expose them to risk of sanction by the government apparatus. A growing body of evidence indicates a positive correlation between economic development and formal legality, which is attributed to the enhancement of predictability, certainty and security.

A legal system that lacks these qualities cannot constitute a system of rules that bind officials, and citizens. Formal legality provides predictability through law. And with respect to this theme, the violation of the Treaty of Paris of 1783; Congress's failure to address General Carleton's attestation of treaty violations that implicated the liberty of 500,000 U. S. or British citizens, in derogation of the rule of law, coupled with the rule of law officials unwillingness to enforce the anti-slavery provisions of the Constitution was a regime of laws with inequitable—evil intent. It was misanthrope, and consistent with authoritarian, or non-democratic regimes with respect to people of African ancestry here in the U. S. An unjust set of laws is not made just by adherence to formal requirements.

On the contrary, the U. S. had black codes and later Jim Crow laws. These laws encouraged racial repression and lawlessness. Their formal legality brought about a greater evil because the government was dedicated to carrying out these unjust laws, and vigilantism helped in that regard.

The rule of law can be used to strengthen the grip of an authoritarian regime upon a group by enhancing its efficiency, and by providing it with the appearance of legitimacy. These arguments can be easily made here in the U. S. when one considers the prison population, recidivism rate, and disparity in wealth based upon the population. An effective system of the rule of law is wholly responsible.

The third theme—"No man is *above*, nor *below* the law" is core to a democracy. This commonly phrased idiom is put different ways: "the rule of law, not of man"—"a government of laws, not men"—"law is reason, man is passion" and "law is king". The inspiration underlying this ideal is that being under the rule of law is not to be subject to the unpredictable vagaries of other individuals—whether monarchs, judges, government officials, or fellow citizens. It is to be shielded from the familiar human weaknesses of bias, passion, prejudice, error, ignorance or whim. This sense of the rule of law is grounded upon fear, and distrust of others.

The inevitability of human participation in the application and interpretation of rules provides the opening for the reintroduction of the very weaknesses sought to be avoided by resorting to law in the first place. The indeterminacy of law and language suggest that this opening can never be shuttered completely. The standard solution to this concern is an independent judiciary that serves as a foundation for the rule of law and democracy. The rule of law means that all authority and power must come from an ultimate source of law.

With respect to this theme— "No man is above, nor below the law," an independent judiciary has been proven illusory, as it was a member of Virginia's judiciary, Virginia's Governor Berkeley who first succumbed to graft in the 1660s and unleashed slavery in the American colonies. And although Congress adopted English law in 1776, and conferred citizenship upon all Englishmen living in the United States—the judiciary did not overturn repressive laws that were foreclosed by that congressional act. The legacy of enslaving people protected by the Treaty of Paris of 1783, ratified by America's Congress in 1784 has been a blackening cloud—gathering and floating ominously in the distance future that has stained the men as hooligans, and the U. S., as being a maladroit nation.

Although airbrushed out of history books—racial repression are enduring reminders, and in a 2016 study of a United Nation affiliated group based in Geneva observed America's colonial history is the continuing link between the dark chapters of America's history, and "contemporary police killings and the trauma that they create are reminiscent of the past racial terror of lynching." The study by the United Nations' Working Group of Experts on People of African Descent—an independent body that reports to the international organization's High Commissioner on Human Rights found "In particular, the legacy of colonial history, enslavement, racial subordination, and segregation, racial terrorism, and racial inequality in the United States remains a serious challenge, as there has been no real commitment to reparations, and to truth and reconciliation for people of African descent."

The findings of the United Nation are significant, in pointing out that the linchpin for addressing social ills, such as police killings of blacks is America's colonial history: where many of their ancestors were placed outside the rule of law. Thus, requiring the fealty of blacks to the flag without reconciliation or acknowledgement that the U. S. government put black people *below* the rule of law, institutionalized the wrongful act—while simultaneously pushing ideals of fairness, liberty and equal justice under the rule of law is perverse and profane. No one should expect blacks in

America to have the same patriotic zeal for our flag. And in having formally adopted English law and accorded U. S. citizenship to all free Englishmen in the country in 1776 the Framers could not legally authorize slavery on American soil in 1787 or legally deprive black people, who were British citizens of their liberty, without procedural due process.

The rule of law was designed to protect everyone, and the federal judiciary should have overturned Congress and the varied state legislature's enactment of slave laws. This revelation can and do cause cultural dissonance for people who have long believed in an independent judiciary, as slavery was illegal during colonial times, and unlawfully insinuated in the U. S. during the 1780s, yet no federal court struck them down, or even alluded to this fact.

America's historians have sculpted the biographies of Washington, Jefferson and others slave owning patriots, as being heroes of the American Revolution. But historian Andrew Burstein notes that a "biography is never a faithful record. It is a construction, a clandestine effort to refashion memory, to create a new tradition, or sanction yet another myth about what is past." Myths are quite durable, and while some will claim it to be a reckless assault upon America to question our heroes' biographies—such is not the case, especially in the case of America's slave mastering heroes from the commonwealth of Virginia. They are not immunized due to the passage of time, or high office, as each man had to know slavery was a criminal scheme when the Declaration of Independence was proclaimed in July 1776. Lord Dunmore's proclamation of liberation in November 1775 was a clumsy, a ham-handed attempt to purge England of its culpability, and its role as the mastermind behind this criminal scheme.

The salient facts were unaffected by England's role, and motive to liberate black people during colonial rule or the slave owners' protestations—black people had legal rights, and protections under English law. Black people were legally free since slavery was never lawful in colonial America and England's Twelve Judges so declared in the *Somersett* case in 1772. By the end of the war, the U. S. was legally obligated, required to "set at liberty" all black loyalists free or legally justify why such people were enslaved, in derogation of the Treaty of Paris of 1783. The enslavement of 500,000 British citizens, without conferring due process to them is America's history.

In the book *Fallen Founder: The Life of Aaron Burr*, Nancy Isenberg made the salient observation that "these were our founders: imperfect men in a less than perfect nation, grasping at opportunities. That they did good for their country is understood, and worth our celebration; that they were also jealous, resentful, self-protective, and covetous politicians should be no less a part of their collective biography. What separates history from myth is that history takes in the whole picture, whereas myth averts our eyes from the truth when it turns men into heroes and gods."

Yes, but no one was meant to be above America's rule of law, nor *below* the rule of law, and the misanthropic enslavement of British citizens and their systemic repression is a cautionary tale. But it is their promotions to the status of heroes of America's Revolution that prevents slave owning American patriots from being described as mere "imperfect men" and be given a free pass.

The schism is perfectly housed in two James Baldwin's quotes: "To accept one's past... one's history is not the same thing as drowning in it. An invented past can never be used—it cracks and crumbles under the pressures of life like clay in a season of drought" ... "To be Negro in this country and to be relatively conscious is to be in a rage almost all the time." The essence of justice is truth, and if America is conceived in liberty—it cannot truly claim itself an exceptional nation without admitting, confronting and owning its truths.

The history of slavery is a tale of systemic government corruption during colonial times—but a new species of tyranny and a fissure developed in the aftermath of the rulings in the *Somersett* case. The learned slaveholding colonists within the American colonies were of one mind with respect to the core ruling in the *Somersett* case: it placed them outside the rule of law because it made the unqualified declaration that slavery was not "allowed and approved by the laws of this Kingdom". The American colonies were within the kingdom—therefore slavery was not lawful were their conclusion. The British government minimalized the decision and encouraged them to proceed normally, claiming that Lord Mansfield had left colonial slavery alone—as it was established and protected by positive law. However, that was the rub, it was not protected since the colonial legislative assemblies had all failed to secure the King's assent. Slavery was extrajudicial and they knew it.

Adding to the Afro-Briton calculus was Queen Charlotte—King George III's wife who herself was black, and their son George Augustus, who was the Prince of Wales and heir to the British throne.

Historian Mario De Valdes y Cocom have observed that Queen Charlotte was directly descended from a black branch of the Portuguese royal family: Alfonso III, and his concubine, Ouruana—a black moor. [89] Thus, Queen Charlotte's bi-racial heritage troubled the slaveholding colonists, not only because she was honored by black native sons—who were convinced from her portraits, and likeness on coins that she had African ancestry—rather, England's Council of Regency had passed a law in 1765 that would make Queen Charlotte the *de facto* sovereign of the Kingdom—if her husband, King George III became unable to do his duties, or to function as England's monarch. King George III was not a man in good health and Parliament enacted the *Minority of Heir to the Crown Act of 1765* in recognition that there were three minor children in line to be the ruler of England. By law—Queen Charlotte would have all the power of the throne, until the child heir reached the age of majority. And only apart from some acts of Royal prerogative, such as declarations of war or the signing of peace treaties that required a majority vote of the Council of Regency, Charlotte would wield His Majesty's powers. This concerned slave masters within the American colonies where eighty-per cent of the hereditary slaves lived as the *Somersett* decision had ruled colonial slavery had not been lawfully enacted by colonial assemblies.

The colonial slave masters... who profited from the exploitation of black people recognized the obvious; having a Queen with black blood undermined slavery's core rationale of racial superiority and if Queen Charlotte became regent and head of England's church, she'd have the constitutional power to liberate black people in any colony and to jail slave masters since slavery was not based upon valid slave laws and was ruled not "allowed and approved by the laws of this Kingdom" by the Twelve Judges in 1772. The slave masters would have no viable legal recourse, if the Queen did so because colonial slave laws did not have the King's assent, and enslaving British subjects was a serious criminal violation of English law.

Alternatively, those profiting from slavery believed, even if Queen Charlotte displayed reluctance to forfeit the total benefit of the revenue generated from colonial America's slave-based economy, she could liberate America's native sons—men, women, and children born in colonial America and then seek to fill England's treasury by blackmailing colonial slave masters for their transgressions against Afro-Britons, or taxing African slaves and their colonial exports. Everyone that owned slaves in colonial America felt that any of these scenarios was bad and would totally decimate their personal wealth and colonial control.

A generation ago President John F. Kennedy challenged America...

> "Let us not seek the Republican answer or the Democratic answer, but the right answer. Let us not seek to fix the blame for the past. Let us accept our own responsibility for the future."

President Kennedy tasked each American with the responsibility to seek right answers and baselined our search, by first coming to terms with America's actual history, albeit painful or disillusioning. And though many young Americans were then motivated, the dogma of Joseph Goebbels—a chief propaganda lieutenant of Germany's leader Adolf Hitler that "if you tell a lie big enough, and keep repeating it, people will eventually come to believe it" has eclipsed Kennedy's charted path.

Slavery within the American colonies was repugnant to England's common law as declared by Chief Justice Holt's ruling in 1765—Mansfield's predecessor "that as soon as a negro comes into England, he becomes free: one may be a villein in England—but not a slave". Chief Justice Holt's ruling was consistent with England's Magna Carta of 1215, the *Cartwright's* Case of 1569 and the trope... no one is above, nor below the rule of law—announced in England's Magna Carta. The "law being King" was an ideal embodied in English law represents an ideal of advanced government. However, only by having honest and effective law-abiding public officials could this ideal of "law being King" be realized. That's exactly what happened when the first Africans arrived in Virginia in 1619——honest and effective, law-abiding rule of law officials made the 19 kidnapped Africans indentured servants——not slaves. Things went well for one generation of black people living in the American colonies, but the British policy of salutary neglect, colonial government corruption, and a culture of hooliganism destroyed the rule of law ideal. Exploitation of Afro-Britons whose only transgression was that they were physically identifiable became institutionally repressive and endemic. Nonetheless, historians continue to suggest colonial slave laws were jurisdictional, supported directly by the sovereign's prerogative, to diverge from common law so long as it was not "repugnant" and that to deny the local legitimacy of colonial laws would be to deny the power of the monarch over his dominions. Too many scholars ignore or feign confusion about an immutable truth——colonial slave laws were "repugnant" to English law and in failing to have the monarch's assent they violated the bicameral colonial legislative structure and *Somersett* ruled that they were not allowed or approved within the Kingdom.

"In the end, we will remember not the words of our enemies, but the silence of our friends". Dr. Martin Luther King Jr.

Chapter 9
Commander to Commander

In accordance with their grant of power, and authority, the American Peace Commissioners, Benjamin Franklin, John Adams, John Jay and Henry Laurens, a U. S. congressional delegation entered an armistice with England to end the Revolutionary War on November 30, 1782—called the Treaty of Paris of 1783. [90] The armistice bound both sides to cease all "hostilities," but upon hearing the news of a pending peace treaty by late January 1783, Americans began assaulting, kidnapping, and attacking black Englishmen and loyalists.

A black loyalist named Boston King summarized the times thusly:

> "... the horrors and devastation of war happily terminated and peace was restored between America and Great Britain, which diffused universal joy among all parties' except us, who had escaped from slavery and taken refuge in the English army; for a report

prevailed at New York, that all the slaves, in number 2,000 were to be delivered up to their masters altho' some of them had been three or four years among the English. This dreadful rumour filled us all with inexpressible anguish and terror, especially when we saw our old masters coming from Virginia, North Carolina, and other parts, and seizing upon their slaves in the streets of New York, or even dragging them out of their beds. Many of the slaves had very cruel masters, so that the thoughts of returning home with them embittered life to us."

England's military leader Sir Guy Carleton, who had replaced Sir Henry Clinton as Commander-in-Chief of all British forces in North America on March 2, 1782 was flummoxed by these widespread practices, and finally, at a May 6th meeting with General George Washington to arrange for the implementation of those parts of the Treaty of Paris relating to the evacuation of New York City, Carleton... discussed the unsavory practice, and plight of black loyalists.

The armistice had covenanted cessation of all hostilities directed at Englishmen and Carleton complained that these actions was renewed "hostilities"——a violation of the armistice. Washington scoffed at Carleton's assertion that such actions were violating the armistice and claimed that his countrymen were merely gathering up their lawful human property——their slaves. However, Carleton claimed that these black people were Englishmen by virtue of English law and as the *Somersett* decision had declared that slavery was not lawful within the American colonies in June 1772; which rendered all colonial slave laws void, they could not be molested during this period of time for any reason——real or imagined.

History support, that nearly ninety-five percent of the black people in the American colonies, suffering as slaves were Englishmen by birth. England by virtue of Dunmore's proclamation, exercising *executive* authority freed all blacks suffering as slaves living in the American colonies on November 6, 1775 and by law, their British subjecthood had not been affected while suffering as slaves.

The First Congress adopted English law——after declaring their independence. It is significant that subsequent U. S. courts such as *Littleton v. Tuttle*, 2 Dane Abr 413 (1796) would rule that the Declaration of Independence abolished slavery in colonial America. [91] Such is consistent with the state of Massachusetts' constitution, specially declaring in its first article, "All men are born free and equal." People of African ancestry were not carved out as being exempt, and based upon the Massachusetts Constitution, in the lawsuit of *Elizabeth Freeman, et al v. John Ashley* (Great Barrington Mun Ct. Aug 1781) the court declared the same. [92] This precedent, along with the *Quock Walker* cases were pre-federal U. S. constitutional cases, consistent with the Twelve Judges' *Somersett* decision and England's common law.

Carleton claimed protection for black Englishmen under the preliminary treaty—while Washington's rejoinder involved matters outside the confines of Article 7 of that treaty. Article 7 in the preliminary treaty provide: "Prisoners of war on both sides are to be released, and all property left by the British army in the United States will remain unmolested"... This treaty was ratified by Congress on April 15, 1783 and did not have language prohibiting the British from "carrying away any negroes or other property of the American inhabitants". At the relevant time, the question then was not one of whether Americans owned former black slaves. Rather, the issue was that during the agreed cessation of hostilities period, this class of Englishman should not have been facing assault, kidnapping and imprisonment at the hands of the Americans as Article 7 did provide..."all hostilities both by sea and land shall.... immediately cease; all prisoners on both sides shall be set at liberty". Washington did not respond to Carleton's claim that the actions of his countrymen were *per se* violations of Article 7 that warranted the cessation of hostilities against all and releasing His Majesty's subjects.

Washington then learned Carleton had permitted some black loyalists to embark upon one of His Majesty's vessels and sail away ten days earlier. He seized upon this fact to complain that this too was a violation of the treaty. Carleton stated that if this proves to be a violation of the finalized treaty, then compensation would have to be paid to the U. S., however, he explained that it was his belief that "it could not have been the intention of the British Government...to reduce themselves to the Necessity of violating their Faith to the Negroes who came into the British Lines under the Proclamation of his Predecessors." However, as Washington's wealth was inextricably linked to this unsavory practice of black slavery, he doubled downed by requesting the surrender of all black people under Carleton's care, control, and custody. Carleton refused to do so and then demonstratively, explained to Washington that everyone born within the American colonies were Englishmen by law and that the state of being a slave was not a legal condition, and to Washington's chagrin, that he did not see any provision in the articles of peace, as being a relinquishment, or an abandonment of Britain's policies of liberation of the colonial black population.

Carleton then went on to explain to Washington's horror that it would be a breach of honor for him not to respect the rule of law, or England's proclamation of liberation and promises that conferred British subjecthood unto alien Africans in the colonies. Carleton stated that he planned to evacuate all black people from the U. S., if they wanted to leave, but, as an olive branch to Washington stated that if his removal of blacks proved to be a misapprehension of law, or fact on his part, and a violation of the Treaty of Paris, then compensation would have to be paid to the U. S. government by England's government. And in consideration of that possibility, he proposed to register each person—so that "owners might eventually be paid for the slaves who were not entitled to their freedom by British Proclamation and promises." Washington reciprocated and both men generated separate registries, called *"Book of Negroes"* listing their names, ages, and occupations of each black person, along with the names of their former masters. This exchange and the resulting agreements, by and between Carleton and Washington are first principles: were Carleton and Washington's agreements to each maintain a *Book of Negroes* and to compensate the offended nation for any misapprehensions of the preliminary treaty terms binding upon their respective nations?

There had been numerous threshold jurisdictional problems with Washington's claim of ownership of black Englishmen under his construction of the treaty, inasmuch as, liberty was a personal right under English law, and the state of being a slave was a criminal condition. Under English law, such a provision is unenforceable because the purpose of this provision tries to achieve an illegal end. [93] Thus, the section of the treaty, if interpreted as being one that condemned black Englishmen to suffer as slaves to Americans, it was a legally unenforceable provision. The unlawfulness of this condition was the reason that the first nineteen Africans that arrived on to America's shores in 1619 were indentured servants—not slaves. The practice of slavery was criminal and the usage of the term "slave" had evolved extrajudicially within the American colonies, and although colonial assemblies had passed slave laws—such laws were fatally defective, as each colonial charter by construction did not grant colonial legislatures the lawful authority to enact laws "repugnant" to England's common law or to enact laws without the assent of the monarch.

The colonial legislative structure was bicameral: the monarch and the colonial legislative assembly. The legislative assemblies only had jurisdiction to propose a bill for the monarch's assent. The colonial assemblies did not secure the monarch's "Assent" upon their bills authorizing slavery or to change the patrilineal descent system——to make such bills "positive law". Further, even if the monarch had given his assent, in June 1772, the Twelve Judges in the *Somersett* case struck down colonial slave laws. Mansfield delivered the *Somersett* decision for the Twelve Judges, ruling slavery was "odious" and can only be lawful by "positive law" and as it considered the lawfulness of Virginia's slave laws——it overturned colonial slavery when in determined the condition of slavery was not "allowed and approved by the laws of this Kingdom. [94]

Secondly, Lord Dunmore liberated black people in November 1775——*before* the Declaration of Independence. Dunmore was wielding executive power of His Majesty King George III, and as *Somersett* was controlling precedent his proclamation was tantamount to a writ of habeas. During November 1775, the American colonies were under British rule and the Treaty of Paris concedes this material fact.

Thirdly, pursuant to the subsequent ruling of the U. S. Supreme Court in *Littleton v. Tuttle*, 2 Dane Abr 413 (1796), the Declaration of Independence affirmed rights, and liberties of all Englishmen within the American colonies, and abolished slavery. This included all black Englishmen. Jefferson proposed a bill to adopt Roman law as America's jurisprudence, but it was defeated. If Roman law was adopted, the U. S. could have severed itself from English law, and its anti-slavery precedent. Under Roman law, *partus sequitur patrem* could have been nullified. Whether it was the founding fathers putting the needs of the people before personal needs—respecting the nobility of public service, or an unwillingness to reject whole cloth a jurisprudence that they had committed their entire professional lives to—the First Congress rejected Jefferson's bill, and then formally adopted English law. This ratified the rulings of the Twelve Judges in the *Somersett* case and guaranteed procedural due process to all black people within the nation. Such being the case, under the rule of law all "recaptured" former slaves were entitled to due process hearings. They were not given any hearing before being relegated to U. S. slavery. Pursuant to the precedent in *Stapylton* that bound the U. S., the American slave owner had the burden to prove their legal ownership claims.

Lastly, England's civil war raged and in June 1779, British General Henry Clinton reiterated Dunmore's proclamation of liberation for black people; it declared that liberation had not been conditional. The rationale behind Clinton's proclamation was that the Americans were claiming Dunmore's proclamation of freedom was a conditional emancipation of the black slaves and limited to people of fighting age. Further, the British wanted to stimulate mass desertion of black slaves and specially indicated that the former slaves could pursue "any occupation which he shall think proper". Many blacks left captivity. The U. S. sued for peace in November 1781 and within the four corners of the resulting Treaty of Paris of 1783 acquiesced on the issue of British governance during the revolutionary period. Such an acquiescence——with respect to *post*-Declaration of Independence governance implicates and legitimize every one of England's proclamations and promises. Integral is the fact that Carleton announced to Washington that all former slaves were British subjects by law and entitled to certificates of freedom based upon the "Proclamation of his Predecessors".

A careful student of early American history would realize Washington and Carleton both understood the difference between a violation of the preliminary treaty and the final treaty executed in September 1783. The failure of each colonial assembly to secure the monarch's "Assent" upon its law purporting to change the patrilineal descent system to *partus sequitur ventrem* forever robbed hereditary slavery of any badge of being a legally enacted institution. The Twelve Judges' of the King's Bench explicitly determined same in the *Somersett* case in 1772, when it ruled that slavery was not "approved and allowed by the laws in this Kingdom" and can only be made lawful by "positive law". [95]

Washington on behalf of the U. S. understood Carleton's position, as being a treaty dispute... and in a book titled *The Writings of George Washington from the Original Manuscript Sources 1745-1799*, the writer John C. Fitzpatrick highlights a letter he sent to Carleton:

> "Whether this Conduct is consonant to, or how far it may be deemed an infraction... is not for me to decide... I cannot however conceal that my opinion, is that the measure is totally different from the Letter and Spirit of the Treaty... I find it my duty to signify my readiness... to enter into any Agreements, or take any Measures which may be deemed expedient to prevent the future carrying away any Negroes or other property of the American people."

Subsequently, Carleton appointed four officers to serve as British Commissioners to meet "every Wednesday at ten o'clock [to hear] any Person claiming property embarked, or to be embarked...Should any Doubts arise in Examination the circumstances of the case to be minuted down" for a possible settlement in the future. [96] However, the British Commissioners refused to consider any claims made by the American delegation, taking the position: no property was going to be delivered until it was shown to be in danger of being carried away. In a letter to Washington they complained:

> "It appeared to us improbable that Sir Guy Carleton ever intended to afford Redress against his own Orders and Measures...We cannot forbear observing to your Excellency that in our sentiment no valuable purpose will be effected by representing, at this juncture, violations of the Treaty — Cases where we are certain Redress will be denied when we have it not in our power to enforce." [97]

Historian Bob Ruppert in an article titled *How Article 7 Freed 3000 Slaves* highlights the early 1780s in the U. S. that includes the signing of the preliminary articles of peace on November 30, 1782, that resulted in the Treaty of Paris of 1783 through Carleton's departure from New York in November 1783. [98] It does not address the threshold treaty dispute: was America's "round-up" of former black slaves *after* the preliminary treaty was signed and *before* the execution of a final treaty in September 1773 an objective violation of peace terms? Squarely, Carleton rejected Washington's explanation and recognized the "round-up" of then freed loyalists for what it represented.

The assaults, kidnapping and enslavement of black people after the preliminary articles of peace was signed and before the final treaty was executed in September 1783 was in fact a violation of the Treaty of Paris. All black people living in the erstwhile American colonies were Englishmen and certainly, the actions of the Americans qualified as renewed "hostilities". The rounding up of former black slaves violated the treaty and certainly, liberty for black people *per* the Treaty of Paris were legal questions to be addressed through the prism of English law; that Congress had adopted. The U. S. claimed legal ownership of black people—yet colonial slave bills to legalize slavery during the 17th and 18th century were never lawfully enacted. The Twelve Judges in the *Somersett* case in 1772 ruled slavery was not "allowed and approved by the laws in this Kingdom" and then Dunmore, exercising *executive* power liberated all people suffering as slaves in November 1775. Dunmore resolved the slave ownership issue *before* the Declaration of Independence—eight months later. At a minimum, black people living in colonial America had a legal dispute with the Americans.

Ruppert points out that Article 7 "fell under the direction of General Washington" and thus, Carleton's claim that black people were legally entitled to liberty under the Treaty of Paris was raised at the highest level of the U. S. government. His position was supported by controlling English precedent. Certainly, anyone rounded-up as being a former black slave during this period would be defined as a "prisoner" and entitled to due process under Anglo-American jurisprudence. Carleton's evacuation of 3,000 former black slaves in November 1783 framed the reparatory justice debate. He placed the U. S. on actual notice of treaty violations... mass kidnappings of black people during the spring of 1783... resumption of "hostilities" and putative infringement upon liberty rights of black citizens and his duty to respect and honor based upon earlier "Proclamation[s] of his Predecessors," which were Dunmore and Clinton. These issues should have been resolved in accordance with English law. These black people were all entitled to due process. Carleton and Washington on behalf of their countries each kept a registry—*Book of Negroes* and while 3,000 people left the U. S., the international dispute implicates the legal status of the 500,000 people who were disfranchised and made slaves.

And although England was complicit in colonial slavery, and their role forestalled liberation of black people suffering as slaves in the aftermath of the *Somersett* decision—it is an irrelevancy since English law stood resolutely.

The final treaty was signed on September 3, 1783 at the Hotel d'York in Paris by Benjamin Franklin, John Jay and John Adams, along with Sir David Hartley, a member of the British Parliament on behalf of King George III. The final treaty had language "...his Britanic Majesty shall with all convenient speed, and without causing Destruction, or carrying away any Negroes or other Property of the American inhabitants..." However, Carleton on behalf of England ordered everyone under his command to "remain on duty until every man, woman and child who wanted to leave the United States is safely moved to British soil." This was reasonable when one considers that the spirit of that language in the finalized Article 7 was to prohibit the British from carrying away property owned by the Americans, but they owned no slaves by virtue of the *Somersett* decision and Dunmore and Clinton's proclamations of freedom. However, through detention, coercion, and doggedness the U. S. prevented the mass evacuation of black people out of America. And when Carleton left the U. S. on

November 28, 1783——he had only 3,000 black people on his manifest, and he settled them in Nova Scotia, the Caribbean, and England. [99] Similarly situated, 500,000 black people were prevented from leaving the U. S. and then suffered the horrors of institutionalized slavery.

The Treaty of Paris ended the American Revolution, and nearly 500,000 black Englishmen were languishing as "prisoners" when Congress ratified the Treaty of Paris on January 14, 1784 at the Maryland Statehouse in Annapolis, Maryland. Afterward, the U. S. Congress issued a proclamation of ratification, providing in relevant part:

> "By the United States in Congress assembled, a proclamation: Whereas definitive articles of peace and friendship, between the United States of America and His Britannic Majesty, were concluded and signed in Paris, on the 3rd day of September, 1783... we thought proper by these presents, to notify the premises to all the good citizens of these United States... Given under the seal of the United States, witness His Excellency Thomas Mifflin, our president, at Annapolis, this fourteenth day of January, in the year of our Lord one thousand seven hundred and eighty-four."

The First Congress in 1776 foreclosed any potential conflict of laws issues between England and the U. S. when it formally adopted English law and then each state followed suit. It was an axiomatic principle of English law, that since slavery was banned by law and liberty was conferred upon the enslaved by writ of habeas corpus—no payment to the slaver. The U. S. lawmakers were presumed to have knowledge of judicial construction of existing constitutional provisions and the rule of law. [100] Ignorance of the law was never an excuse and as the Twelve Judges' ruling in the *Somersett* case was controlling judicial precedent concerning colonial slavery and the existing constitution in 1776; slavery was a crime. Congress's adoption of English law in 1776 was dispositive of the two questions, as to whether the Americans were entitled to financial compensation for the 3,000 former slaves that Carleton's transported out of the U. S. in 1783 and whether, the U. S. should have set at liberty the 500,000 Afro-Britons who became the bedrock of America's slave pool during the 1780s. The founding generation was bound by these precedents, in having adopted English law in 1776.

Subsequently, a new federal constitution was enacted in 1788. The Framers of this federal constitution were also presumed to have knowledge of judicial construction of existing constitutional provisions and controlling judicial precedent, as they began its Preamble with an all-encompassing statement; "we the people" excluding nobody, and stating the Constitution's purposes, including to promote liberty for all by a "more perfect" government than existed under the Articles of Confederation. Alvan Stewart in his book *Legal Argument for the Deliverance of Persons from Bondage* makes the observation that "[T]he purpose of a constitution is to defend, not subvert rights." Slavery was diametrically opposed to the declared objectives of the federal constitution. Edmund S. Morgan observed; "The men who came together to found the independent United States, dedicated to freedom and equality, either held slaves or were willing to join hands with those who did... None of them felt entirely comfortable about the fact, but neither did they feel responsible for it. Most of them had inherited both their slaves and their attachment to freedom from an earlier generation, and they knew the two were not unconnected." [101] Thus, while U. S. slave masters are the parallax to discern and address the ongoing discourse regarding restorative justice for the misanthrope institution of black slavery—they have remained outside the field of depth and have been jealously protected and inscrutable throughout our historiography.

Historians Thomas Paterson, Garry J. Clifford and Shane J. Maddock in the book *American Foreign Relations: A History to 1920,* describes the Treaty of Paris of 1783 as being "exceedingly generous." Point in fact, the treaty only took on a favorable character when the U. S. unilaterally refused to "set at liberty" 500,000 black Englishmen, as the treaty mandated and then exploited these Afro-Britons and their descendants for generations. It was the U. S. that fashioned the narrative that England had recognized the U. S. as a future major trading partner and thus had made the terms of the treaty favorable. Which then——and not by chance, nor coincidence, their major ally France, through its Foreign Minister Charles Gravier, Count of Vergennes supported this narrative, stating, "The English buy peace rather than make it." This was a coordinated attempt to put forth a narrative——spun by the U. S. and its closest ally France that liberation for black people had been abandoned by the British. However, the treaty was quite draconian, if the U. S. had honored the treaty and released the 500,000 Afro-Britons.

The self-congratulatory assessment of the Treaty of Paris, as being favorable to America did not square with England's position, as Carleton communicated to Washington *before* ratification that by "Proclamation and promise" that the people who'd suffered as slaves during British rule were entitled to liberty. Carleton's position was consistent with English common law that made slavery illegal on sovereign soil, and the *Somersett* decision. The Congress was required to substantively address the claim that recapturing liberated black people were violations of the Treaty of Paris. Such acts constituted renewed "hostility" against Englishmen, and it had horrific consequences for 500,000 legally free people. The failure of the U. S. to respond to Carleton's claim was purposeful, misanthrope and a waiver of its objection to this claim.

England had never lost a colony, and feared revolt in other colonies if they appeared, or acceded to terms favorable to the U. S. and this eviscerates the suggestion that England molly-coddled the U. S. in furtherance of entering this treaty. From the outset, England had put the five-member treaty negotiating commission of John Adams, Benjamin Franklin, John Jay, Thomas Jefferson and Henry Laurens on notice that freedom for all British citizens was extremely important to King George III. The U. S. delegation knew that this issue would be thorny, as the sustainability of slavery engulfed both the U. S. and its leadership. And since nationality and race were compatible under English law—the American delegation was not hopeful, although releasing prisoners of war had gained popularity during the late 17th century. The impetus was favoring the furtherance of this international practice and this suggested that negotiations would be difficult.

The U. S. delegation was unsuccessful in trying to carve out black people, as being outside the classification of being Englishmen under the treaty. British subjecthood was not denied to people of African ancestry and as Queen Charlotte the lawful wife of King George III was of African ancestry, such a concession they found to be totally unobtainable. This type of concession was fundamentally incompatible with rights guaranteed to all subjects throughout the empire. The consequence of this reticent position meant that the U. S. leadership was unhappy with the preliminary treaty, especially after months of negotiations because they knew black slavery figured mightily in its post—war economy and it was agreed upon—all people who met the legal definition of being a British citizen within the American colonies at the time of the Declaration would be "set at liberty." Realizing that this was probably the best deal that could be made and with internal British opposition teeming… the terms and conditions were reduced to writing and placed in the Treaty of Paris that Congress ratified in January 1784.

Pursuant to colonial charters all people were guaranteed rights, and liberties of Englishmen, and equality of all people in terms of fundamental rights. Singularly, African ancestry was not set-forth as a disqualifying factor for being denied liberty under the treaty. British subjecthood was established and defined by English law—and as English law had been adopted by the U. S. Congress in 1776—it was controlling and not subject to any facile disputes.

This reality foreclosed all substantive legal bases, and defenses as slavery was not lawful during colonial times and as slave labor was to be integral to the post-war U. S. economy, a binary choice loomed—either liberate black Englishmen or pretexually enslave them. The resolution of this conundrum caused the U. S. to ignore Carleton's attestation of treaty violations, as well as all due process protections provided for under English law, and to place Afro-Britons *below* the rule of law. This assaulted the rule of law.

Some scholars have parroted the British government's narrative that the southern colonists in North America that the *Somersett* decision had limited consequence and did not apply in the colonies. [102] However, nothing was further from the truth and in fact, the Twelve Judges' determinations in the *Somersett* case should have resulted in the criminal prosecution of colonial slave masters and only greed, self-interest, and graft foreclosed that possibility or any type of justice for the victims. And, if North American slave masters such as Washington, Jefferson, Madison and Marshall had been charged, tried and punished for violations of existing criminal laws, arguably, there wouldn't been an American Revolution, and slavery would have ended.

The unique species of colonial tyranny called hereditary slavery spawned a culture of hooliganism, white supremacy and likewise, in allowing colonists to operate above English law it had a natural and foreseeable consequence of forging an American ethos that English law and rules do not bind colonial America and a resulting revolt against belated English governance was the natural consequence. [103] Thus, after generations of salutary neglect the slave holding colonists were fully committed to a slavocracy by the time that His Majesty's King's Bench rebuked slavery in the *Somersett* decision. Thus, it is counter-intuitive to suggest British officials were surprised by the colonists' actions. However, personal behavior throughout the American colonies, what people do, was not the standard of what was lawful during colonial times. The standard was the promulgated laws—defined within legal and constitutional limits. It evidences circular, wrong reasoning to conclude that practice, history, or a tradition is what the law allows, and yet that has been America's enduring defense of black slavery. This was fallacious, even if it was initially reinforced by the unwritten British policy of salutary neglect since England purged this practice during colonial times during the 1760s; colonial slave laws were not lawfully promulgated and during the year 1772—Somersett's legal right to liberty was specially based upon colonial slave laws. Stewart's opposition to Somersett's application for liberty placed nascent colonial slave laws *before* England's Court of King's Bench. The enslavement of black native-born peoples in colonial America was tyranny based upon corruption, graft and hooliganism. Such being the case, it is counter-intuitive to embrace the notion, least of all the conclusion that colonial slave owners within the American colonies became legal owners of black people—absent the promulgation of colonial laws that legitimized (1) slavery and (2) changing the descent system on British soil during colonial times. These preconditions were even more daunting, as the Twelve Judges specially ruled in the *Somersett* case that as of 1772, slavery was not "allowed and approved by the laws of this Kingdom". Stewart claimed Somersett to be a slave based upon colonial laws. The Court of King's Bench had original jurisdiction over colonial legislatures and its laws, as the justiciable issue before the Twelve Judges involved the enforceability of Virginia's slave law; that was devoid of the King's assent. Such colonial laws implicated the power of the monarchy over his dominions.

The Twelve Judges proclaimed slavery was so "odious" "that it is incapable of now being introduced by Courts of Justice upon mere reasoning or inferences from any principles, natural or political; it must take its rise from positive law," and it had to decide the question of whether Virginia's slave laws were legally constituted in furtherance of establishing conflict of laws standards throughout the Kingdom. Slave laws within the American colonies became void a*b initio*, as the bicameral colonial legislative structure required the King's assent to be deemed "positive law" and the tribunal declared slavery was unconstitutional within the Kingdom. Colonial slave laws were not "positive law, as none of the colonial assemblies bothered to secure the assent of the King. Thus, the *Somersett* decision converted the extrajudicial practice of slavery into a full-blown criminal enterprise, when America's slaveowners refused to release their alleged slaves, despite the British government's directives to the contrary. [104] Slavery existed due to tyranny and it was a serious crime under English law. [105] The Twelve Judges ruled colonial slave laws were defective and in consequence, slavery was unconstitutional. Further, as Mansfield's ruling in *Stapylton* was controlling precedent—America's slave owning Founding Fathers were legally obligated to prove their ownership of black people under the rule of law.

Certainly, the *Somersett* decision took on a life of its own. [106] And what has oxygenated the long-enduring debate has been the belief that colonial slavery was the product of lawfully promulgated municipal laws, supported directly by the sovereign's prerogative to diverge from common law. Most people in the legal community were of one mind on this point and thought that to deny the local legitimacy of colonial laws would be to deny the power of the monarch over his dominions. Hence, the *Somersett* debate has endured based upon a core misapprehension of a material fact: colonial slave laws were not the result of England's monarchy exercising dominion over the American colonies, it existed due to colonial hooliganism. The monarchy never allowed or approved slavery, least of all a 1662 law that changed the patrilineal descent system that gave rise to hereditary slavery. These were not lawfully promulgated municipal laws and slavery could not claim to be based upon positive law; pursuant to the *Somersett* decision.

Colonial slavery was the result of a "new species of tyranny... created entirely by Colony government". And in this era of the early 1770s, where the rights and powers of colonial legislatures were front and center in British imperial politics, the fact that a justiciable issue implicating colonial slavery had found its way *before* the King's Bench, and the clear rulings that slavery was not "allowed and approved by the laws in this Kingdom" and that slavery can only be lawful by "positive law" that which the colonial legislatures had blithely ignored, was a dispositive rebuke of colonial slave practices. This resonated with slaveholding colonists as their decision was based upon their review of Virginia's slave laws and garnered a unanimous decision from the Twelve Judges of the King's Bench.

Matthew Mason observes that Mansfield had played a major political role in a 1766 debate on repealing the Stamp Act and had insisted that Parliament represented "the whole British empire" and possessed "authority to bind every part and every subject without the least distinction" in all legislative matters. [107] Therefore, slaveholding colonists in North America knew slavery was over, as the legislative assemblies could not prove that earlier slave laws had been supported by the monarch. This jurisdictional obstacle was daunting enough, but once the British government abandoned its policy of complicity and Dunmore liberated black people, it was disheartening as Mansfield had already expanded the appellate powers of England's complex legal system, that he sat atop. Dunmore had exercised executive authority in proclaiming on November 7, 1775 that "I do hereby declare all indentured Servants, Negroes, or others (appertaining to Rebels) free". This liberation language, in and of itself freed all people suffering as slaves within the American colonies without qualification; as slavery was prohibited on British soil and the *Somersett* decision had so determined. Slavery was legally over under English law, pursuant to Dunmore's proclamation.

The Twelve Judges' ruling in the *Somersett* case was a judicial construction of colonial slave laws lawfulness in the year June 1772 and once Dunmore exercised the *executive* power of habeas corpus in November 1775, freeing black slaves... Dunmore's proclamation stripped slaveholding Englishmen within the American colonies of the legerdemain to continue to claim legal ownership of other human beings. Thus, when the Continental Congress proclaimed all men in the American colonies were created equal, "with certain inalienable Rights" in the Declaration of Independence in July 1776, eight months later—all black people suffering as "slaves" within the American colonies were legally free Englishmen. This is the case, as the dispositive facts are that colonial slavery operated extrajudicially during colonial times; the colonial legislative system was bicameral and the *Somersett* decision rendered all existing colonial slave laws nugatory since colonial legislatures failed to secure the King's assent to these laws. They held rebuttable U. S. citizenship since the First Congress acted on behalf of all English citizens when they issued the Declaration of Independence on July 4, 1776, and conferred U. S. citizenship unto all free English people and with the adoption of English law, this bound all Americans to English precedent and Mansfield's ruling in the *Stapylton* case: "being black will not prove the property." The rule of law officials in the U. S. (the First Congress) was required to use English law to determine if black people within the American colonies were conferred U. S. citizenship based upon English law. The same protocol used to determine the legal status of the first nineteen Africans in 1619 should have been used. This was not done.

> "It is self-evident that no number of men, by conspiring, and calling themselves a government, can acquire any rights whatever over other men, or other men's property, which they had not before, as individuals". Lysander Spooner

Chapter 10
Restitution Opposed to Reparations

Certainly, as a condition precedent, a contemplated policy debate on the reparations question necessitates a return to first principles on the question of the origins of slavery. Virginia's charter specified that the people in the colony of Virginia:

> "shall have and enjoy all liberties, franchizes and immunities within any of [Great Britain's] other dominions, to all intents and purposes as if they had been abiding and born within the realm of England".

Such was the reason why the first Africans arriving in Virginia in 1619 were indentured servants—not slaves. [108] History supports, slavery developed due to corruption, and although it became endemic… no erstwhile Englishman, who became an American legally owned "Negroes" during colonial times. [109] Bound by colonial charters to English law, slavery on its best day was only an extralegal, extrajudicial practice. However, in truth, slavery was a criminal enterprise with countless, unspeakable crimes against people who should have been protected by the rule of law. And although its masterminds and perpetrators were not held to account, nor can they ever be, the use of the term "reparations" is no less crass and offensive as using the "N word" since reparations is an equitable remedy—applicable when an aggrieved party does not have an adequate remedy at law. The misapplication of the word reparations, as it relates to slavery has been transferred intergenerationally, and it is presently an idiom, no less illogical than saying: "Cold War thinking" or "raining cats and dogs". Just a casual examination of the etymology of the word reparations, reveals its abiding kinship to the enduring narrative that slavery was inherited from the British, and lawfully instituted in the U. S. Neither is true and logic leads us to the conclusion that if slavery was not inherited from the British, or if slavery was somehow unearthed as not being lawfully started in the U. S., a change to the meaning and our understanding of the word reparations must follow. The use of the word reparations misdirects the policy discussion because the origins of slavery were criminal in nature—not just a moral failing of a nation.

Enlightenment philosopher Charles-Louis Secondat, Baron de Montesquieu... one of the greatest intellectual influence on the founding generation maintained that "the misfortune of a republic... happens when the people are gained by bribery and corruption—in this case they grow indifferent to public affairs, and avarice becomes their primary passion." England was a nation of laws during colonial times but abandoned the rule of law during the mid-seventeenth century. The British allowed colonial government officials to be gained by bribery, graft, and corruption and while the founding generation was perfectly willing to rid themselves of the tyranny of King George III's government, patriots in the southern colonies championed slavery for black citizens and northern patriots went along... corrupting its core founding precept that all men were created equal, under the rule of law.

James Madison in *Federalist Paper* No. 51 stated—"If men were angels, no government would be necessary. In framing a government which is administered by men over men, the great difficulty lies in this: you must first enable the government to control the governed; and in the next place oblige it to control itself." Madison's point was that men who administer laws must be honest, fearless, and ethical when it comes to upholding the law and the public must zealously commit themselves to making sure that the rule of law remains king. However from inception of this nation the public has abided the practice of the men who administers the law to elevate themselves, and others above the law and say nothing when others were below the law. This was the normalization of tyranny personified since everyone had the same legal rights and status under English law that the First Congress adopted in 1776. The scrupulous application of English law was the reason why the original nineteen Africans who arrived unto the shores of Virginia in 1619 were treated as indentured servants—not slaves. The rule of law worked in 1619, people of African blood were not placed *below* the rule of law—that came later.

The colonial legislature structure was bicameral. A careful student of colonial American history will see that the King, one chamber of the colonial legislature never gave his "Assent" to slave laws enacted by legislative assemblies in the American colonies that purported to normalize the act of "kidnapping" and to authorize slavery. Destructive to the slavery scheme was the fact that each colonial assembly failed to acquire the King's assent unto colonial hereditary slavery laws—first enacted in

1662 by Virginia's colonial legislative assembly, that purported to change the English patrilineal descent system of *partum sequitur patrem* to *partum sequitur ventrem*; they were all nugatory. The King withholding his "Assent" to colonial laws were the substance of the first three stated grievances the founding generation would later allege many times in 1776—one-hundred and fourteen years later in the Declaration of Independence regarding King George III's governance.

The Twelve Judges' in the *Somersett* case in 1772 declared slavery was not "allowed and approved by the laws of this Kingdom" and that it can only be lawful by "positive law". This was a seminal ruling, as it forever struck down colonial slave laws. The *Somersett* case made plain that slavery was not authorized by the laws of this Kingdom, and that the bicameral legislative structure of colonial governance mandated the King's "Assent" upon a promulgated slave law. This case disabused, and informed colonial assemblies within the American colonies that promulgated colonial slave laws needed the King's assent to be "positive law".

Graft, corrupt colonial government and outright hooliganism aided in the continuation of colonial slavery. However, finally on November 6, 1775—eight months *before* the Declaration of

Independence, Lord Dunmore the lieutenant of His Majesty King George III issued an *executive* proclamation liberating black citizens; suffering under colonial tyranny. Dunmore, who was also the Royal governor of the colony of Virginia—wielded the executive power of His Majesty King George III, and as *Somersett* was controlling judicial precedent, Dunmore's proclamation was tantamount to a writ of habeas corpus. The proclamation freed all black citizens. Dunmore liberated all blacks in the American colonies similarly situated, suffering as "slaves". Although habeas corpus continues today, as originally intended for all "persons," regardless of citizenship black people remained slaves, as slave holding colonists refused to respect the common law.

Afterwards, the American colonies declared themselves independent in July 1776, proclaiming "all men are created equal". [110] Then the First Congress formally adopted English law in 1776, and each state followed suit. The First Congress is presumed to have had knowledge of judicial construction of existing constitutional provisions and English precedent. [111] *Somersett* was controlling legal precedent and was a reigning construction of the existing constitution which meant black people suffering as slaves were legally free under U. S. law and now U. S. citizens.

"The citizens are the authors of the law, and therefore its owners, regardless of who actually drafts the provisions, because the law derives its authority from the consent of the public, expressed through the democratic process" was cited in *BOCA v. Code Technology, Inc.*, 628 F2d 730, 74 (CA 1, 1980). [112] And a legislative act founded on a mistaken opinion of what was law, does not change the accrual state of the law as to pre-existing cases. [113]

The Declaration of Independence was a perfect legerdemain to change the slavery narrative, but Congress did not exempt, nor did it exclude Englishmen of African ancestry. *Somersett* was the controlling judicial construction of the existing constitution and this was obvious to Thomas Jefferson who brought a bill in the summer of 1776 to supplant English law with Roman law—making it American law. Roman law could have legitimated hereditary slavery going forward—but Jefferson's bill failed to secure the requisite support to become law, before the First Congress. Adding to this setback, Congress formally adopted English law and conferred U. S. citizenship unto all free Englishmen living in the erstwhile American colonies. English law became king in the United States of America.

Likewise, Carleton's attestation of treaty violations was made to Washington in May of 1783——seven months *before* Congress ratified the Treaty of Paris of 1783. The actions were not disputed, rather Washington asserted a blanket slave ownership defense that Mansfield had been deemed feckless, saving proving legal ownership of the putative slave in the 1771 *Stapylton* case. Further, slavery within the American colonies was subsequently ruled to be not "allowed and approved by the laws of this Kingdom" the following year by the Twelve Judges in the *Somersett* case and the *Somersett* decision was the law of the land in July 1776. The crimes of assault, kidnapping, rape, and trespass were targeted at black citizens during the beginning of the year 1783. The Americans were violating the treaty since no erstwhile Englishman now American ever *legally* owned another human being during colonial rule and the Americans were bound by colonial charter to English law, and even *after* the Declaration of Independence the First Congress had formally adopted English law.

Finally, pursuant to the colonial charter most revolutionary war-era blacks were Englishmen, having been born in the American colonies and had suffered under a species of tyranny...created entirely by Colony Government. The American colonies had the same charter and the same language and were of course law.

> "we take it to be a clear principle that the common law in force at the emigration of our ancestors is deemed the birth right of the colonies unless so far as it is inapplicable to their situation, or repugnant to their other rights and privileges." [114]

The Treaty of Paris of 1783, in Article 7 required the U. S. to "set at liberty" all former slaves as being "prisoners of [civil] war" as the *Somersett* decision rendered colonial slave laws void *ab initio* in 1772, by finding slavery was not "allowed and approved by the laws in this Kingdom" and can only be lawful by "positive law". All colonial slave laws required the King's assent; but none had the King's assent. Thus, slavery operated extrajudicially during colonial times, and slave masters became criminals under English law, once Mansfield issued the *Somersett* decision in 1772. [115]

Deteriorating relations and civil unrest led Lord Dunmore to issue a proclamation of liberation on November 6, 1775 that freed black citizens. England had mixed motives for doing so, but it was irrelevant since within eight months, the American colonies declared themselves independent, officially triggering a civil war on July 4, 1776 and then its legislature immediately adopted English law. English law seamlessly became U. S. law and *Somersett* controlled. It is of demonstrable importance that the First Congress could have severed ties with English law *after* the Declaration of Independence—but it did not. Jefferson urged supplanting English law with Roman law, and as a congressional proponent of Roman law explained "Roman law offers this new republic an opportunity to develop a particular American jurisprudence, which would not be just a slavish imitator of the English common law that is hostile to many a man's interest here in this hall".

The *Somersett* decision remained the controlling judicial construction of the existing constitution, as the legislative debate regarding Jefferson's Roman Law bill in 1776 was unsuccessful. Although being fully advised in the premise and propriety of this proposed law—Congress was not persuaded. Congress then formally adopted English law—the same rule of law that transformed captive Africans into indentured servants in 1619. This was a dispositive legislative act, as it foreclosed the U. S. from making the claim that as a new nation, it was entitled to make their own laws, rules or to claim that they were not bound by the English constitution. [116]

The *Somersett* decision and Dunmore's proclamation of liberation of colonial black people months *before* the Declaration of Independence were enormous, hard-fought victories for basic human freedom. They ended an extrajudicial system of slavery that relegated generations of black Englishmen into bondage, while also providing an inspirational model of how the rule of English law ought to protect everyone equally. But they did not signal the end of the fight against all forms of slavery. Abolitionist Wendell Phillips on the passage of the 13th Amendment during the 1860s... said it best in remarking that "[W]e have abolished the slave, but the master remains." And to the extent that none of the colonial slave masters were punished and in fact appeared to have been immunized by way of the Declaration of Independence eight months later and then elevated to leaders of the American Revolution—slavery morphed and became more durable here in the United States. Doubtlessly, congressional records of the historic debate to supplant English law during the summer of 1776 was dispositive proof that Washington's rejection of targeted hostility, and violence against black British subjects during the spring of 1783 was a baseless protestation and totally without legal merit. [117]

In 1773, after Thomas Hutchinson, Royal governor of Massachusetts overruled a *Somersett* inspired bill to free colonial slaves——he proposed a tea tax that led to a protest in Boston. After the Boston Tea Party, England shut down Boston Harbor, appointed British general Thomas Gage as governor, and limited the power of local governments. Those actions, which the British called the Coercive Acts led to the First Continental Congress and the Declaration of Independence in 1776. *Somersett* was the law of the land, yet Governor Gage overruled another *Somersett* inspired bill to free colonial slaves.

The Declaration of Independence had complicated their predicament, as there were two core ideals; (1) government by consent, and (2) equality status. They were propositions of law and the core predicates of our constitution which the British had abandoned during colonial times. And there was no question, the founding generation did the same. England's downfall within the American colonies should have served as a cautionary warning. The founding generation willingly compromised the Lockean ideal of human equality to establish this nation, and incorporated compromise in the then new federal constitution which caused Founding father Alexander Hamilton to express his concern and Abigail Adams agreed——telling her husband John Adams of Massachusetts that:

> "it always appeared a most iniquitous scheme to me to fight ourselves for what we are daily robbing and plundering from those who have as good a right to freedom as we have."

But Benjamin Franklin of Pennsylvania had already framed their then precarious predicament by reminding them all that they "must, indeed, all hang together, or, most assuredly, we shall all hang separately." Franklin's observation placed matters into perspective, as the rebellion had become mortally personal for all.

The failure of the U. S. to respond to General Guy Carleton's attestation of Treaty of Paris violations in the spring of 1783 highlights an ugly truth: the enslavement and disfranchisement of black citizens during the 1780s was not legal. The Congress, although on notice as to England's treaty violation claim, it took no steps to seasonally address this international dispute.

The U. S. failed to address the May of 1783 attestation of renewed "hostilities" while varied congressmen claimed Article 7 of the Treaty of Paris of 1783 required England, by way of Carleton—England smuggled 3,000 slaves out of New York and gave them refuge in Canada. One notable escapee was Henry Washington, a black citizen that George Washington claimed he owned. He fled from the Mount Vernon plantation in

1776—fought for the British Army during the Revolutionary War and under Carleton's protection, he left America. But 500,000 black people became slaves here in the U. S. and their children suffered the talisman of inhumanity slavery at birth represents. [118]

Millions of innocent people disappeared behind the firewall of slavery in the U. S. [119] The founding generation knew Carleton's claim that black citizens were protected under the Treaty of Paris of 1783 was correct and supportable. Slavery was never legal within the American colonies; slave laws were ruled unlawful by England's Twelve Judges in June of 1772, and Lord Dunmore liberated all Afro-Britons suffering as slaves in November of 1775—eight months before the Declaration of Independence in July of 1776. First principles—the fact that the first nineteen Africans were indentured servants under English law, not slaves illuminate the perverseness of urging the descendants of the enslaved to move on. America's slave narrative has held a vise-like grip on all, as most find historical accuracy tedious, and obstructive to a good story. In this regard, the consternation, recrimination, and uncivil discourse reflecting race relations lay at the feet of the Framers and founding generation—not those who were enslaved or their descendants.

The nation was victimized during the federal constitutional convention, especially since 500,000 black people were entitled to liberty pursuant to the Treaty of Paris of 1783. Their disenfranchisement, enslavement, and institutionalized repression has hallowed out the phrase "equal protection under the rule of law," and moreover, only incidentally and with the air of current phrases are mechanically repeated by lawmakers and judges that no one is above the law. The Faustian deal traded the soul of a nation by placing black people *below* the rule of law. This eviscerated all inference that this country would hold fealty to the rule of law.

Abraham Lincoln, in an October 16, 1854 speech in Peoria, Illinois said "[W]ho will tell the negro that he is free? Who will take him before [a] court to test the question of his freedom? In ignorance of his *legal* emancipation he is kept..." He observed that the common law "is not much known except among lawyers" and made plain that the state of slavery in the U. S. was unlawful. [120] Lincoln likened pro-slavery argument to "the old argument for the "divine right of kings". By the latter [argument], "the king is [allowed] to do just as he pleases... the white man is to do just as he pleases with his black slaves... The two things are precisely alike..." Yet, when Lincoln issued the Emancipation Proclamation in 1863, he carefully worded it to be a military order—only capturing, confiscating "property," and freeing slaves in enemy territory or battle staging areas. Under Article 2, Section 2 of the Constitution as Commander-in-Chief, Lincoln had the inherent power to abolish slavery in war-time enemy territory. And as the Confederacy was referring to itself as a separate nation, he could capture enemy personnel, and by calling "slaves" property, he could confiscate "slaves" or free them as they were being used to carry on the war effort. [121]

The federal constitution was not proslavery and the word "slavery" was not referenced in the federal constitution. Thus, it is reasonable to conclude that there wasn't a need to abolish slavery by constitutional amendment. [122] Abolitionist Gerri Smith said of the Thirteenth Amendment "I never liked [it]. It implies, or seems to imply, that the original Constitution did not forbid the greatest crimes—whereas by the canon of legal interpretation it did [already] forbid it. I should [would] have preferred an Amendment, that simply disallows a Pro-Slavery interpretation of an already Anti-Slavery Constitution".—*Letter to Senator Charles Sumner* (Feb 5, 1866). Under American rule of law, a "practice" [or state law] "not based upon any rule of law" [or Constitution] was unconstitutional. [123]

The "practice" of slavery should have been overruled by the Supreme Court early in the Republic and it raises the unsettling question of "why" was slavery allowed to exist if it was not authorized by the Constitution and "why" abolish slavery by constitutional amendment? [124] Federal and state officials had conspired to ignore the rule of law—in favor of institutionalizing slavery.

There is a legal maxim: "for every right, there is a legal remedy, where there is no remedy, there is no right". There are two categories of remedies, one—a legal remedy for a legal right and two, an equitable remedy. America's judicial system was contemplated to be a legal system, not a justice system and early America's legal system had two distinct types of courts—courts of law and courts of equity.

The courts of law were considered the primary venue for seeking redress for legal wrongs, including breaches of contract, while courts of equity were viewed as courts of last resort. Such courts delivered remedies based largely upon fairness concerns. Presumptively—courts of equity are proper forums when a party does not have a remedy at law and suffers from an injury or injustice.

Quod nullium tempus occurrit regi literally means "no time runs against the King". This English common law doctrine exempts the King and even governmental bodies from statutes of limitations, laches, and statutes of repose. Carleton, on behalf of King George III set-forth articulable treaty violations in May of 1783. They were not subject to staleness or laches defenses. The U. S., as a nation that adopted English law could not just ignore Carleton's attestation of treaty violations made to Washington in 1783. English law obligated the U. S. to use the due process protocol announced in the Magna Carta to expeditiously resolve liberty disputes. Washington, who too had slave trackers in his employ during this time admitted to the contested activities, but he proffered the defense that black people were legally *owned* by Americans. Relying upon English law, Carleton rejected Washington's claim. Washington agreed to forward Carleton's attestation of treaty violations to the Congress and as he would be transporting black citizens out of the U. S., both agreed to keep a registry listing vital information regarding the people taken out of the country, absent him receiving different instructions from England; he never did.

Objectively, Congress could have addressed the matters raised before Carleton left the country in late November of 1783. English law announced in the *Somersett* case refuted Washington's defense to his attestation of renewed "hostilities" against black citizens, and certainly, the Americans were all obligated to substantiate their ownership claims pursuant to Lord Mansfield's ruling in the *Stapylton* case. The bare claim that the Americans were merely recapturing lawfully owned human property required them to prove slavery was allowed and approved by English law during colonial times and that Lord Dunmore's proclamation of liberation of black citizens in November of 1775 was somehow legally ineffectual. Carleton appeared to have been acting upon a "good faith belief,"——but——the same cannot be said for the U. S., as it appears that Congress was comfortable with doing nothing. The disfranchisement of 500,000 Afro-Britons who were legally free people and entitled to a due process hearing under the Treaty of Paris were made slaves and then their children were exploited for generations.

The U. S. elevated slave owners *above* the law by embracing Washington's narrative that enslaving 500,000 Afro-Britons was lawful during colonial times. White privilege throughout the U. S.

reinforced the misanthrope narrative. Within a few decades, Southerners wanted to expand the institution of slavery into other U. S. territories, but more and more people in the northern states, driven by a sense of morality or an interest in promoting federal immigration initiatives to encourage European white migration into the U. S. came to believe slavery must be limited. White southerners feared that limiting the expansion of slavery would mean financial ruin and over a period, the two sides became increasingly polarized. The politicians were less able to address the dispute through compromise. And when Abraham Lincoln, the candidate of the demonstrably antislavery Republican Party, won in 1860 presidential election, seven states—South Carolina, Mississippi, Florida, Alabama, Georgia, Louisiana and Texas seceded, organizing the Confederate States of America.

The American people were led to believe that slavery had been lawfully inherited from colonial rule and that the Civil War was fought over the morality of slavery, when it was the economics of slavery and political control of that system that was central to the conflict. Thus, Lincoln and the northern politicians became convinced as the war raged, that emancipating the descendants of the Afro-Britons by constitutional amendment was a necessary step—in the wake of massive Civil War casualties that exceeded 600,000. They were certain in their belief that there would be a wailing hue and cry of Americans who would express betrayal and disillusionment if it was revealed that slavery had never been a lawful institution. This caused Congress to enact the Thirteenth Amendment, abolishing slavery. A reparations initiative during the 1860s had promised them "forty acres and a mule" that was never honored. The commercial value of black loyalists and their progeny's uncompensated labor to the U. S. economy has been estimated to be between $29 and $40 trillion dollars.

The U. S. adopted English law during the summer of 1776 and in consequence, all 500,000 black people should have been released pursuant to the Treaty of Paris of 1783, or at a minimum, granted a due process hearing. Under English common law and pursuant to each colonial charter—everyone born in colonial America were subjects of the King. Although alien residents in the colonies were not British subjects by birth—each colonial charter professed alien residents in the colonies would eventually become "Our Loving subjects and live under Our Allegiance." And leading up to the break from England, ambiguity in the colonial charters created a debate about the extent of the authority of colonial assemblies to naturalize alien residents. Every colony but except Hampshire enacted naturalization policies, and laws to fulfill their growing demand for new immigrants.

This went on until proscribed by Parliament's directive to governors in the colonies, not to consent to any naturalization bill passed by a colonial legislative body. Such being the case, England could legally naturalize African residents pursuant to each colonial charter. However, history supports, less than five percent of black people were African born when the U. S. declared itself independent, the balance were all native sons.

Without the benefit of English law, the U. S. claimed England's Proclamation and promises did not have the force of law… embodied by Lord Dunmore's *Proclamation* during colonial times was not a mere "promise," rather it was a letter of patent from the British government liberating all slaves and conferring subjecthood unto all Africans held as slaves, here in the U. S. pursuant to English law.

The *Somersett* decision declared slavery was not "allowed and approved" by the laws in this Kingdom *before* America declared itself an independent nation. It was English law that controlled, as most black people were Englishmen by birth under common law——no different than white colonists.

The following wording in the Declaration of Independence, its introduction: "When in the Course of human events, it becomes necessary for one people to dissolve the political bands which have connected them with another..." and "Such has been the patient sufferance of these Colonies; and such is now the necessity which constrains them to their Systems of Government" establishes that *Somersett* was controlling precedent as the Thirteen colonies admits that the American colonies are part of King George III's "kingdom". English law that controlled, as most black loyalists were Englishmen by birth under common law, no different than white colonists. Afterwards, the First Congress then formally adopted English common law in 1776 that had no English statue laws authorizing the holding of slaves, either in England or in the American colonies.

Such being the case, restitution opposed to reparations is not an either, or proposition since institutionalized slavery and its progeny institutionalized racism gave rise to Jim Crow, segregation laws and system-wide disparities that have impacted the U. S. and continues to impact the country. Restitution can complement reparations.

"America is not another word for Opportunity to all her sons".   W. E. B. Dubois, The Souls of Black Folk

Chapter 11
The Legal Right to Restitution

The Englishmen in the colony of Virginia began as forlorn immigrants, desperately struggling for survival on the Atlantic seaboard. They evolved into being the brain trust for the experiment called America in 1776. Their sagacity, attunement to shifting colonial mores was pitch perfect, by first routinely treating and classifying captured Africans as indentured servants in 1619 and then opposing the British changing its unwritten policy of salutary neglect to equal treatment under English law during the 1770s. However, during the summer of 1776—behind the scene, these same men from the colony of Virginia were engaged in conduct no less audacious than a *coup d'état* of this American experiment in democracy, by offering a legislative bill, sponsored by Thomas Jefferson of Virginia to adopt Roman jurisprudence. These men were committed to establishing a slavocracy in the U. S.

and knew to a legal certainty that English law stood in opposition to this desired goal. And while the Roman law bill was defeated, through tenacity, perspicacity and grit they cajoled rule of law officials to authorize enslaving 500,000 Afro-Britons in the late 1780s, in derogation of the rule of law. Such facts, circumstances or averments do frame the question of a remedy for U. S. slavery.

The Declaration of Independence offered erstwhile Englishmen——now Americans an opportunity to start anew and to put into practice that which they had opposed and reviled from British governance in the American colonies. The Magna Carta of 1215 was the cornerstone of America's constitutionalism and was the legal underpinning of the fundamental relationship between a government, and the people it oversees. In England, the principle that the law was king was a prominent feature of the Magna Carta, signed by King John in 1215. It was the essential initiative of a revolt by the nobility against the king, following his attempts to extract more resources from them to fund war in France. Among its many provisions, the Magna Carta also declared, established that no person should be deprived of their liberty, or property "except by the lawful judgement of his equals or by the law of the land". This is the legal concept of habeas corpus the founding generation recognized and adopted in Article I, § 9 of the Constitution. However, the Framers assaulted the rule of law when they placed Afro-Britons *below* the rule of law during the constitutional convention in 1787... and elevated slave holding Americans *above* the rule of law. And while many will say "so what", given the distance America has traveled as a nation since 1787, this was a legal wrong and this nation and many people have suffered greatly.

The "so what" has always been the fact that the founding generation's actions were misanthrope, unlawful and void *ab initio*. They had a sweeping legal, societal and cultural consequence here in America yet to be resolved. This has been a haunting upon our constitutional order, as the law contemplates returning everyone to *status quo ante*; a reversion to the previously existing state of affairs, since the U. S. rule of law officials had no lawful authority over the 500,000 black people, who they turned into slaves after England petitioned for their liberty in 1783. The disenfranchisement and enslavement of free black people in the late 1780s, placed all blacks, both freemen and enslaved below the rule of law and did elevate slave masters, politicians, and wealthy individuals who profited from the new federal constitution *"above"* the rule of law. The compromise sullied this democracy, by undermining public confidence in the U. S.

lawmakers. There can be no compromise on the rule of law for any purpose; yet that is the origins of the federal constitution. Truly, no episode in America's history has left a greater indelible stain on this democracy than U. S. slavery, and one need only consider America's criminal justice system to see the schism created, as a rich person's justice is far superior to others in whole of the nation, and then you have a black man's justice, that's far below the norm. This reality stands in stark contrast to the idiom "no man is above, or below the law".

Doubtlessly, the schism does reflect the logical consequence of the Framers' compromise upon the rule of law. Nonetheless, it remains a sharp contraction that pits history against ideals. This nation could never reconcile the glorious dream of an idyllic egalitarian society—*The Shining City on the Hill,* with the dark nightmare of human slavery and institutionalized inequality. This haunting is the causation of dissonance, polarization, and chaos here in America.

Historians are of the position that Mr. Jefferson's Declaration, and commitment to the institution of human slavery are contradictory… but, they were not. Dealing with real world pressures, Jefferson, as a slaveholding member of the Second Continental Congress was placed into a binary box by

1776—but he had a plan. Jefferson, a lawyer, legislator, and enlightened man for the times recognized the unlawfulness of hereditary slavery at the age of 29. This epiphany started when Britain switched its unwritten policy of salutary neglect to that of enforcing laws strictly, along with more direct management and was capped off by the seminal *Somersett* decision in 1772—declaring slavery can only be valid by "positive law" and that Virginia's slave laws were not "allowed and approved by the laws of this Kingdom". Being so informed, by 1774—Jefferson, while addressing Virginia's legislative assembly stated: "[T]he abolition of domestic slavery is the greatest object of desire in these colonies, where it was unhappily introduced in their infant state." Jefferson fretted that Virginia's legislative assembly never secured the King's assent upon its hereditary slave law in 1662 and that slavery operated extrajudicially. He began to contemplate finding a long-term solution since slavery was not a legally recognized condition in the Kingdom and the *Somersett* decision said so. Jefferson had reason to fret and was the first lawmaker in a colony that was dependent upon slave labor to discuss the hereditary slavery issue in this manner.

While in contemplation—Virginia's Governor, Lord Dunmore liberated Jefferson's slaves—by virtue of his November 7, 1775 proclamation. Dunmore's exercise of executive authority had the legal consequence of being a writ of habeas corpus. Colonists who continued to hold people in a state of slavery were now criminals under English law. It is significant that that in the aftermath, Jefferson did not liberate any blacks, suffering as slaves during colonial times. However, then on June 11, 1776—the Second Continental Congress appointed him, and four others to draft a declaration announcing independence.

Jefferson, the principal author of the declaration understood its importance and when he finished the draft on the first of July—he'd concurrently drafted a bill to supplant English law with Roman law, as America's jurisprudence. If adopted, abandoning English jurisprudence would have allowed Jefferson, and other slaveholding Americans to reconcile the egalitarian principles of equality found in the Declaration, with hereditary slavery.

Singularly, the bifurcation of the Declaration and his Roman law bill have made Jefferson appear conflicted with respect to slavery. Point in fact, he'd arrogantly assumed adoption of his Roman law bill. But the bill to adopt Roman law was soundly defeated before the First Congress, when it formally adopted English law.

The British subjecthood of black people, and the unlawfulness of their condition within the American colonies during colonial times established Jefferson's *mens rea*—guilty mind towards slavery, and it explained his near manic attempt to have English law supplanted with Roman law. The formal adoption of English law by Congress established two important facts; one, the British subjecthood of black people during colonial times, and if ever disputed, or contested, that the dispute would be addressed using English law. And without doubt, the legislative defeat of the Roman law bill before the First Congress—coupled with its formal adoption of English law, and ratification of the Treaty of Paris of 1783 in January of 1784 were dispositive legislative actions concerning slavery, opposed by Jefferson.

America's historians do not hide the fact that America's economy was in dire straits in the 1780s and the founding generation who voted for and approved the federal constitution saw the need to accommodate the institution of slavery, as being critical to preserve the nation. However, all black citizens were Englishmen entitled to liberty under the Treaty of Paris of 1783. The rule of law militated against enslavement and disfranchisement, without due process. Many delegates to the federal constitutional convention had a huge conflict of interest.

James Madison——the Father of the Constitution and the fourth president of the United States claimed ownership of over one-hundred black people. Nonetheless, he drafted the Bill of Rights and officiated over the federal constitutional process. And if those Afro-Britons were not Madison's property how would our view of the constitutional process be affected——if history confirmed that slavery in England's colonies had been declared illegal well before the American Revolution? What if, before the founding of our Nation, everyone held in bondage had been confirmed by England's highest court to possess the full rights of English citizenship? The 'enslavement of black people, who held British subjecthood was a criminal wrong, and ideologically in conflict with the type of nation the founding generation hyped in the Declaration of Independence.

In anticipation of the 1787 Constitutional Convention, Mr. Madison drafted a document known as the Virginia Plan, which provided the framework for the Constitution of the United States.

His plan proposed a central government with three branches that would check and balance each other, keeping any one branch from wielding too much power. No such government had ever been created before, and Madison negotiated with other delegates to ensure that the Convention would produce a Constitution that all states could accept.

There is academic support for the proposition that "the Constitution is best understood... as a means of implementing the rights outlined in the Declaration." [125] But, the nefarious, self-serving intentions of the Framers of the federal constitution is plain when you consider, as an observant student of constitutional history observed that "[t]he Founders deliberately omitted the Declaration's doctrine of equal rights from the Bill of Rights, not because the doctrine was considered more rhetoric, but because its inclusion in the Constitution would have been dangerous to the continued existence of slavery." [126] Negotiations also led to overarching ideals being interwoven in the Declaration and ideals being taken out of the new federal constitution.

And as early as 1788, George Mason of Virginia, drafted a proposed Bill of Rights that took out the most troublesome equal rights language, and conditioned protection of specified rights to "freemen" only. But Mr. Madison of Virginia strongly opposed using the term "slave" or "freeman" in constitutional text and proffered a proposal that became the prefix to the Constitution. Madison's compromise to preserve the union is the baseline for understanding the legal injury inflicted upon black people during the late 1780s, who were Englishmen by law and entitled to full U. S. citizenship, or at least the right to leave America.

The Declaration of Independence in 1776 was America's first promulgated law... that governments derive their just powers from the "consent of the governed" and "all men are created equal." These are at the foundation of the American republic. And there is little question that erstwhile Englishmen now Americans saw themselves as involved in this same process when they ratified the Articles of Confederation in 1781, and the new federal constitution in 1787. America's written constitutions were viewed, as the memorialization of the contract between the government, and the governed and the powers held by government were viewed, as grants from the people.

Rule of law officials, as contemplated in the Declaration purported to provide legal protection for all, even if the person did not know that a law was in existence, or even the concept of rule of law. All persons, institutions, and entities are accountable to laws that are publicly promulgated, and they should be equally enforced. This statement of governance during colonial times was supported by the treatment of the first Africans arriving to America's shores by Virginia's rule of law officials.

The Africans' legal status was that of indentured servants——not slaves. This was not a mistake——but it was English law and after a period, these people were integrated into colonial America's society. The elevation of the captive Africans to that of indentured servant here in the American colonies is a testamentary to the criticality of the role of our rule of law officials and the power of the Magna Carta and English rule of law.

The colonial charter legally tied black people to the American experiment announced in the Declaration. At all times relevant——the children of African women born in the American colonies were free-born Englishmen under English law, although suffering as slaves. Thus, each black person had inalienable legal rights, liberties and subjecthood, conferred by the British monarchy——protected by English law. Hereditary slavery within the American colonies was an extrajudicial practice and was never legally authorized. Such being the case, native-born blacks during colonial times were original Americans——a unique race of people.

The Second Continental Congress memorialized in the Declaration on or about the fourth of July in 1776 that all Englishmen in the American colonies were to be treated equally in the new nation and conferred equal U. S. citizenship. It is without doubt, British subjecthood was defined by English law that made blacks born in the American colonies Englishmen by birth and Africans could be granted English citizenship. Three legislative acts of the U. S. Congress defined their legal status and created a legal right—as well as a legal remedy: the Declaration of Independence, adoption of English law in 1776 and the ratification of the Treaty of Paris, in January 1784. Black people living in early America had legal rights that could not be unilaterally withdrawn, lessened or interfered with by the Framers of the new federal constitution. Nonetheless, the Framers did so, they negotiated a compromise in the late 1780s and did not seek, nor receive the assent of the black people who they enslaved, as all people of African ancestry living in the United States—formerly known as the American colonies were Englishmen under English law and were entitled to liberty under the Treaty of Paris of 1783; or a due process hearing.

Their British subjecthood existed because of their birth in the American colonies, or by a naturalization procedure for Africans authorized by English law *before* the Revolutionary war ended on January 14, 1784. The Framers of the new federal constitution found themselves in a binary box since the question of U. S. citizenship and liberty pursuant to the Treaty of Paris both turned upon the issue of British subjecthood, defined by English law and was substantively decided by the British government. The founding generation calculated that the nation had only one way out... not abide by Law of Nations norms and standards and to place black Englishmen *below* the rule of law in the United States. They did so by shamelessly averring that Afro-Britons——their countrymen and equals under English law were legally owned by white Americans.

The Americans had just been through a period when the making of *ex post facto* laws had been greatly abused in many of the states——like the so-called "pine-barren law" of South Carolina, or the paper money acts of Rhode Island. The sentiment of anger caused the founding generation to be in opposition to *ex post facto* laws because such authority allowed a government to retroactively subject a person to a law. An example of an *ex post facto* law is a law passed, after the Declaration in 1776 that applies to circumstances or acts that occurred during colonial rule. The Framers thought this to be unjust and prohibited Congress from passing *ex post facto* laws by clause 3 of Article I, Section 9 of the constitution. The states were prohibited from passing *ex post facto* laws by clause 1 of Article I of the constitution, Section 10. And even if that was not the case, the international question of subjecthood of black people living in the American colonies involved a dispute between two sovereign powers and by virtue of the First Congress adoption of English law was totally controlled by English precedent. And the process during the late 1780s that applied and should have been used with respect to determining the citizenship of Afro-Britons was the one used when the first Africans arrived in 1619——bearing in mind, the legal status of captured Africans became indentured servants——not slaves under English law. But countless years of exploitative, criminal conduct towards blacks in the American colonies changed the calculus, and instead of applying the rule of law that was in place in 1619——they were placed *below* the rule of law.

Additionally, the prohibition of *ex post facto* laws meant the Framers did not have the power to compromise on the rule of law——that in effect, retroactively declared Afro-Britons to be slaves and interfered with their liberty rights, protected under Article I, Section 9 of the United States Constitution. The Framers proceeded in a manner forbidden by the then new federal constitution. Although in 1798, the Supreme Court determined that this prohibition applies only to criminal laws and is not a general restriction on retroactive legislation, implicit in the prohibition is the notion that individuals can be denied liberty only in accordance with standards of conduct that they might have ascertained before acting and of course, this matter ripened before the enactment of Article III and it must be viewed through the prism of the Treaty of Paris of 1783. [127]

The legal status of black people was defined and established under English law and it was that of erstwhile Englishman with U. S. citizenship, whose legal rights could not be negotiated away or compromised by the Framers. The Americans were obligated to prove their claim of ownership of black people under Mansfield's ruling in the *Stapylton* case. Bound by English law and in the absence of informed consent, the founding generation was obligated to apply the rule of law without prejudice, bias or arbitrarily. Decidedly, the Framers understood the long-term implications of placing black people *below* the rule of law and it caused John Adams of Massachusetts, who never owned a slave to remark:

> "Facts are stubborn things and whatever may be our wishes, our inclinations, or the dictates

of our passion, they cannot alter the state of facts and evidence."

The facts—stubbornly establishes the Framers' *mens rea*, their affirmative, legal duty to respect rule of law and that they were knowledgeable of the dual British and U. S. citizenship of Afro-Britons who lived through the American Revolution—yet they were disfranchised and relegated to endure life-long slavery. Framers compromised the rule of law and congressional records, proposed legislative bills, and the facts proves it. John Adams' warning to delegates at the constitutional convention that "facts are stubborn" were profoundly prophetic and enduring.

The Framers knew black people were then unsophisticated, unaware and ignorant of their legal rights—but under the rule of law that should not have mattered. It was the Framers' duty to hold fealty to the rule of law, and to protect, rather than exploit black people during the 1780s.

> "It is in vain to alledge, that our ancestors brought them hither, and not we... We inherit our ample patrimony with all its incumbrances; and are bound to pay the debts of our ancestors."

These were the sermonized words delivered by Timothy Dwight, the president of Yale University in 1810, early in the Republic. However, over the years——obscurants have successfully undermined Dwight's message as being one of equity, rather than being one for justice and reconciliation.

The Framers of the federal constitution sacrificed the rule of law to save the nation and themselves during the 1780s. They approved unauthorized ownership claims of human beings and elevated these men and others above the rule of law, while putting erstwhile black Englishmen below the rule of law and institutionalized racial repression. Black people were entitled to legal protections under the rule of law and did not consent to being made slaves to save this nation. They had a right to proper notice of charges. [128] They had a right to procedural due process, no different than the first nineteen Africans who arrived in Virginia who became indentured servants——not slaves under English rule. [129] This topples opposition to reparatory justice and allows the idea of restitution for the descendants of black slaves in the U. S. to move forward is clear.

Instructive is the early American federal case of *Ware v. Hylton* where after dismissing a matter——the Supreme Court declared that the question of a violation of the Treaty of Paris of 1783 was a political question. Then the political question doctrine was addressed in the subsequent Supreme Court case of *Marbury v. Madison* that stands for the principle that some questions—in their nature, are fundamentally political and the court must refuse to hear. A federal court have declared that because the matter of reparations been committed to the legislative branch—judicial power was restricted. [130] Unique to this instant matter, the question here too involves the Treaty of Paris of 1783—did the United States break the treaty when it disfranchised and enslaved black colonists in the late 1780s.

The Supreme Court in *Baker v. Carr*, 369 U. S. 186 (1962) established a standard formulation and factors for federal courts to use to dismiss a case for want of jurisdiction under the political question doctrine.

[1] A textually demonstrable constitutional commitment of the issue to a coordinate political department; or [2] a lack of judicially discoverable and manageable standards for resolving it; or [3] the impossibility of deciding without an initial policy determination of a kind clearly for non-judicial discretion; or [4] the impossibility of a court's undertaking independent resolution without expressing lack of respect due coordinate branches of government; or [5] an unusual need for unquestioning adherence to a political decision

already made; or [6] the potentiality of embarrassment from multifarious pronouncements by various departments on one question.

According to Justice Brennan, who delivered the opinion of the Court, "it is the relationship between the judiciary and the coordinate branches of the Federal Government, and not the federal judiciary's relationship to the States, which gives rise to the political question." Thus, the "nonjusticiability of a political question is primarily a function of the separation of powers." "Deciding whether a matter has in any measure been committed by the Constitution to another branch of government, or whether the action of that branch exceeds whatever authority has been committed, is itself a delicate exercise in constitutional interpretation, and is a responsibility of this Court as ultimate interpreter of the Constitution."

Following a discussion of several areas in which the political question doctrine had been used, Justice Brennan continued: "It is apparent that several formulations which may very slightly according to the settings in which the questions arise may describe a political question, although each has one or more elements which identify it as essentially a function of the separation of powers." Regarding the restitution for slavery claim it is predicated upon a dispute or quarrel regarding a treaty entered by

Congress: the Treaty of Paris of 1783. The U. S. bound itself to "set at liberty" and not molest Englishmen in America; but failed in both regards.

History supports that in the spring of 1783, England's General Guy Carleton put the U. S. through George Washington on actual notice of a violation of the Treaty of Paris—the resumption of hostility, by the assaults, kidnappings and false imprisonment directed at black Englishmen.

The Articles of Confederation gave Congress exclusive authority to enter treaties and the power to authorize captures and reprisals against foreign nations, their subjects, and their property. There are those who argue that courts should recognize customary international law as a form of federal common law (the "modern" position), the law of nations applies even if not adopted by the political branches or the states.

For those who contend that state law governs the status of customary international law in the absence of a federal statute or treaty (the "revisionist" position), the law of nations applies only when state or federal law incorporates it. This debate has paid too little attention to other portions of the Constitution—particularly, to specific provisions of Article I and II that require all courts in America, federal and state to apply certain traditional principles of the law of nations.

The Constitution's allocation of powers to the political branches also has implications for the revisionist approach that posits that courts may not apply traditional principles of law of nations absent adoption by the political branches or the states. This approach struggles to explain cases in which federal courts have applied traditional principles of the law of nations that neither the political branches nor the states have adopted. However, the modern view appears to be that any question of applying international law in our courts involves the foreign relations of the United States and can thus be brought with a federal power. The substance of the dispute involves a violation that predates the Constitution that was adopted in 1789 and, arguably neither the revisionist position nor the modern position fully accounts for the application of the traditional law of nations since First Congress had then adopted English law to resolve disputes. And as suggested here, resolution of the question can only be contemplated by relying upon the law of nations in existence at the time of their adoption.

Accordingly, it will be necessary to consider whether there is an alternative explanation of the historical practice that is consistent with the constitutional lessons of *Erie Railroad v. Thompkins* (1938) while also accounting for the Framers abandonment of the rule of law.

Significantly, chattel slavery was a criminal action and many historians draw a comparison to Nazi Germany. There are no appreciable differences between the U. S. and Nazi Germany. It was the chattel principle that underpinned all the brutality of slave labor regimes; that destroyed so many enslaved families; that allowed for the unlimited sexual access of masters to enslaved men and women; that precluded all but the barest recognition of basic human rights for the enslaved. [131] The U. S. slave practices were against another ethnic group——black Englishmen and done in derogation of law of nations standards and its own rule of law.

The German state paid reparations to the Jews in territories controlled by Hitler's Germany, to indemnify them for persecution. In the initial phase, payments included two-billion dollars to make amends to victims of Nazi persecution; nine-hundred and fifty-two million dollars in personal indemnities, thirty-five dollars and seventy cents per month per inmate of concentration camps, pensions for the survivors of victims and eight-hundred and twenty-million dollars to Israel to resettle 50,000 Jewish emigrants from lands formerly controlled by Hitler.

In September 2016——the U. S. State Department announced that it was currently administering a multi-million-dollar World War II reparations program, involving the state-owned French railway, SNCF and the French government, who transported 76,000 Jews, and other prisoners, usually with no food, and only a bucket for a toilet, to Nazi camps. All but about 2,000 were killed——more than seven-hundred claims have been filed, and ninety claims has been paid or approved, including to heirs considered to be "standing in the shoes" of people who died in concentration camps before compensation was approved——reparations for descendants of victims during the 20th century. Descendants of Holocaust victims were awarded reparations. It is irrelevant that slavery was abolished in 1865 or that the Framers of the Constitution only did so to save the union during the 1780s. The rule of law should have stood resolute and prevailed.

Finally, anti-reparations advocates make the claim reparations for slavery would be perceived by nearly everyone as injustice——embittering many and inevitably setting back race relations. This is fearmongering and is based upon the false narrative that the enslavement of black people was lawful, when in fact it was a criminal enterprise and it functioned extrajudicially during colonial times and the U. S. enslaved 500,000 legally free black people in derogation of the Treaty of Paris and did not grant them due process——although authorized under the rule of law. Thus, restitution for slavery is a form of restorative justice for a criminal wrong. The descendants of the enslaved are struggling from the foreseeable consequence of the misanthrope, and unlawful acts institutionalized by the U. S. government. In truth, restitution for slavery can and should be perceived as an attempt to take responsibility for the government's actions and to give it an opportunity to redeem itself. The founding generation lost faith in the rule of law and succumbed to the tyranny of mob rule in the 1780s.

A full open public debate would be good for America, and one that would allow the healing to begin and to chart a constructive course for this nation. In furtherance, to build and improve upon that more perfect union, not toppling it.

The 500,000 black people living in the U. S. during the 1780s were not slaves under the rule of law and all had been conferred dual U. S. citizenship by Congress. This class of Americans were criminally robbed of the benefits of their labors and political voice and power. The baseline for a constructive discussion concerning racial dissonance, restitution for slavery, the disparity of treatment in courts and wealth here in the United States is inextricably tied to addressing the founding generation's suppression of U. S. citizenship to black people in the 1780s. It is undeniable—slave owning American colonists were institutionally placed above the rule of law and black people *below* the rule of law once Congress ratified the Three-Fifth Compromise and the Fugitive Slave Act in the constitution.

The British recognized its unwritten policy of salutary neglect was a failure and tightened its control upon the American colonies during the 1760s. However, in the wake of England's Twelve Judges declaring slavery was not "allowed and approved by the law of this Kingdom" and can only be lawful by "positive law" in 1772... four years later the U. S. declared itself free and independent of England. And certainly, the adoption of English rule of law *after* America declared itself an independent nation in 1776 is the defining legislative act that bound this new nation to English law. It lays bare the legal and moral challenges the founding generation faced—having succumbed to graft, tyranny and corruption with the introduction of slavery several generations earlier.

The struggle with the reparatory justice debate has always been that the U. S. claimed slavery was legal during colonial times—but it was not. Placing black people *below* the rule of law has always been the "smoking gun" and it was inextricably linked to the federal constitutional convention in the late

1780s that purported to give institutional reality to the theoretical ideal that governmental authority should rest on a constitution: one that proceeded directly from the people and that no one would be above the rule of law. But as black people were Englishmen under the rule of law and the delegates coming to the constitutional convention in 1787 understood a constitution—not as a written document, but as the embodiment of long-established laws, traditions and first principles consistent with natural law, their willingness to disenfranchise and enslave black citizens was nothing short of blasphemy.

During colonial times, citizenship or subjecthood and nationality were not, one and the same. Citizenship and subjecthood were defined concepts: they were specific legal relationships between a state and a person. The state gave that person certain rights and responsibilities. Such was the reason why kidnapped Africans arriving in the American colonies became British subjects. And while foreign-born people became citizens or subjects and never possessed nationality, in having nationality by birth guaranteed citizenship or subjecthood—*jus soli* under English law. A person could not be born in a state and not have a legal relationship with that state under English law. The sons and daughters of the enslaved America's native sons are the real party-in-

interest in the restitution discussion, as the founding generation criminally enslaved their ancestors in derogation of the rule of law.

In furtherance, the organization Sons and Daughters of the Enslaved acronym S.A.D.E. is committed to promoting, shaping and advancing public discourse and legal restitution regarding slavery in the United States. The organization's mission statement is to proffer a factual elucidation of slavery's origin in the U. S. and to debunk the enduring narrative that slavery was a legal institution during colonial times. To serve as America's first principles or *locus classicus* that explains how black slavery violated the rule of law and seek to heighten the lineage data point in the erstwhile reparations discussions and promote collegiality, integration and views of the descendants of the enslaved in the national discussion. S.A.D.E. is of Nigerian origin for "honor bestows a crown."

In 1833, the British government passed the *Slavery Abolition Act*—positive law outlawing slavery in most parts of the Kingdom of Great Britain. The country took out one of the biggest loans in history, to finance the slave compensation package, required by the Act. Abolitionists maintained that slavery was a violation of God's law... since every human being possessed a soul. They argued that no human being could be turned into another man's possession, without perverting the divine plan. But some abolitionists, in the Anti-Slavery Society railed against the idea. "It would reconcile us to the crime," wrote one contributor to the *Anti-Slavery Monthly Report* in 1829. "It would be a sap on public virtue," wrote another the following year. Some abolitionists even demanded that compensation be paid to the enslaved. "To the slaveholder, nothing is due... to the slave, everything," said an anti-slavery pamphlet in 1826.

Reparations went to owners of slaves, who were being compensated for the loss of what had, until then, been considered their property. Many notable abolitionists were conflicted about this plan because compensation went to the slave owners. There was not a single dime of reparations, or a single word of contrition, or apology by the British state to the people it enslaved, or their descendants. Some justified it as being reasonable... although being imperfect to achieve a worthy goal. Other slave-owning states, including France, Denmark, the Netherlands, and Brazil would follow the British example of compensated emancipation in the coming decades. But the compensation that Britain paid to slave owners was by far the most generous.

Britain stood out among European states in its willingness to compensate slave-owners, and to burden future generations of its citizens with the responsibility of paying for it. The loan represented forty per-cent of the government's yearly income in those days, equivalent to nine-hundred million dollars today, and was so large——that it wasn't paid off until 2015. Forty per cent of the U. S. income would be a staggering amount, while estimates of slavery's economic value to the U. S. is estimated between 29 to 42 trillion, the figure is much larger when one factors in opportunity losses.

"An educator in a system of oppression is either a revolutionary or an oppressor".   Lerone Bennett Jr.

Conclusion

Slavery was forbidden on British soil. [132] Slavery's unlawfulness was the reason why Virginia's rule of law officials made the first Africans here in colonial America indentured servants—not slaves in 1619. Freedom devolved in colonial America due to England's unwritten policy of salutary neglect:

- 1619   Rule of law officials made Africans indentured servants, who became Englishmen after term of indenture was served and their children were free-born Englishmen, per Virginia's colonial charter.

- 1662   Virginia's House of Burgesses pass hereditary slave law. The colonial assembly did not secure the King's accent to decriminalize kidnapping or to change patrilineal descent system to matrilineal. The slave laws operated extrajudicially due to corruption.

1772   Court of His Majesty's King's Bench ruled slavery within the Kingdom was unconstitutional, and can only be lawful by positive law. Black citizens suffering as slaves are rendered free under law.

1775   Virginia's Governor Lord Dunmore abolish colonial slavery. Colonial slave masters and patriots do not liberate black citizens.

1776   American Colonies declared itself the United States of America—a new nation, and adopted English law. Congress legislated that all free Englishmen will be full U. S. citizens.

1782   England and U. S. entered a treaty that guaranteed liberty for all British citizens. Americans violated treaty, by assaulting and kidnapping black people off U. S. streets and enslaving them.

1783   In May of this year, British General Guy Carleton made attestations of treaty violations to U. S. General George Washington. They agreed to disagree, and each create a *Book of Negroes*.

1783   In November of this year, England left the U. S. with 3,000 black people, who were resettled in Canada. The U. S. refused to release 500,000 black citizens or to give them due process and do not honor the Treaty of Paris of 1783.

Slavery evolved extralegally within the American colonies, and operated extrajudicially, as the colonial legislative assemblies failed to secure the King's assent on varied slave laws. Slavery was never legal. The rule of law officials within each colony succumbed to corruption, as slavery operated illegally for one-hundred and ten years. However, even if legislative assemblies had secured the King's assent, England's Twelve Judges ruled slavery was not "allowed and approved by the laws of this Kingdom" in the *Somersett* case in 1772. The ruling rendered all colonial slave laws void *ab initio* and made slavery criminal. Under English law, adopted by the First Congress in 1776——passage of time did not legitimize a void process——*quod ab initio non valet in tractu temproris non convalescet*. It was through tyranny, graft, and corrupt government practices that slavery continued to exist within the American colonies after the *Somersett* decision——but once Virginia's Governor Lord Dunmore liberated Afro-Britons suffering as slaves in November 1775, by operation of English law *before* the Declaration of

Independence: England repudiated and ceased championing the practice.

The Treaty of Paris of 1783 ended the American Revolution. The parties agreed that hostilities would cease, but the U. S. violated the treaty by assaulting, kidnapping and enslaving countless black people, who were under the protection of this international armistice. The U. S. government did nothing to stop violations of the treaty, even after General Guy Carleton, commander-in-chief of the British forces lodged a formal complaint with a U. S. delegation led by then General George Washington in May 1783. The two military leaders disagreed, as Washington made the bare claim that Afro-Britons were legally owned by Americans.

Carleton had first attempted to debate the issue, but found it to be pointless, and stated to Washington that it remained his duty to transport black citizens out of the U. S., as free Englishmen. He and Washington agreed to keep registries called *Book of Negroes,* but only 3,000 were rescued when Carleton left the U. S. in November 1783. The Washington-Carleton dispute over Afro-Britons, memorialized in each nation's registry of black people ("slaves") framed and established U. S. slavery's criminal origins, and that restitution is the proper remedy—not reparations.

The American Revolution was a civil war, and the legislative record of America's First Congress adopting English law in 1776 supports the legal conclusion that the founding generation did not and could not own Afro-Britons. History supports that the British high court ruled four years *before* the Declaration of Independence that slavery was not "allowed and approved by the laws of this Kingdom". Decidedly, the American colonies were parts of King George III's Kingdom and held fealty to English law even after it declared its independence, as its legislature adopted English law. The laws passed by the First Congress are condemnatory of America's narrative that black citizens were owned by Americans, and exempted from the Treaty of Paris of 1783, and it is probative, conclusive evidence that the founding generation had no legal authority to institutionalize the enslavement of Afro-Britons, and or to deny them due process. Washington knew it——but gambled that Carleton would capitulate and he did.

The disfranchisement, enslavement of legally-free people who were Englishmen under English law, and violations of due process to these British nationals was an assault upon international law. The founding generation used a simple type of legerdemain, the fog of war, and mob rule to rob

500,000 Afro-Britons of life, liberty, and happiness in 1787. [133]

It is a mystery worthy of Erle Stanley Gardner. It had heroic protagonists—hapless victims set upon by government forces, puzzling clues, and the story line of a Perry Mason detective novella. General Carleton's declaration that black people were under British protection *per* the Treaty of Paris of 1783 was the Perry Mason moment—the type of "stubborn," probative fact that Founding Father John Adams warned of during the American Revolution.

Colonial slavery became criminal in June 1772 due to the *Somersett* decision for two reasons; first, slavery was "repugnant" to England's common law, and colonial legislatures were not granted jurisdiction to enact repugnant laws. Second, and even if such laws were not repugnant to the common law, the legislative assemblies needed—but did not have the assent of the monarchy. Due to the bicameral colonial legislative structure—not having the assent of the monarchy meant that the colonial legislature could not enact positive municipal law. Such being the case, all colonial slave laws that suffered one of these defects could not be deemed positive law. The Twelve Judges in *Somersett* had ruled that positive law was required to enact a slave law in the kingdom and specially declared Virginia's colonial slave laws were not allowed and approved by the laws of this Kingdom.

Thomas Jefferson's Declaration of Independence was the *"smoking gun"*. While drafting the declaration during the summer of 1776, Jefferson and all signatories to the Declaration were well aware of colonial slave laws' defectiveness, by publicly claiming that King George III had "refused his Assent to Laws the most wholesome and necessary for the public good"... "he has forbidden his Governors to pass Laws of immediate and pressing importance, unless suspended in their operation till his Assent should be obtained..." and "he has refused to pass other Laws for the accommodation of large districts of people, unless those people relinquish the right of Representation in the Legislature, a right inestimable to them and formidable to tyrants only".

Demonstrably, the American colonies were legally bound to English law by colonial charter. The colonial legislative structure was bicameral, that required the assent of the monarchy. The *Somersett* decision ruled slavery was not "allowed and approved by the laws of this Kingdom," even if a colonial assembly did have the King's assent. *Somersett* "became part of American common law".

[134] And since English law was formally adopted by the First Congress in 1776, the founding generation could not advance a credible claim that they were not bound by the *Somersett* decision. Certainly, then the question of legal status and rights inuring unto Afro-Britons was subject to construction through the prism of English law. Black people should have been "set at liberty," or at least, granted a due process hearing. Slavery violating the Treaty of Paris of 1783 has provocative, sweeping implications to America's historiography.

History supports, black citizens were placed *below* the rule of law, as a compromise to preserve the nation. The founding generation's compromises regarding slavery were not merely ideological. They also compromised the rule of law, in favor of slavery. Positioning the compromises as being purely ideological has been a vexing, and largely uninvestigated alibi. Slavery being legal during colonial times is the core predicate of America's historiography. However, slavery was never lawful during British rule—but it operated extrajudicially during the 17th and 18th centuries in the American colonies due to England's unwritten policy of salutary neglect. Then colonial slave practices were rendered inert by the Twelve Judge's decision in the *Somersett* case that slavery was not "allowed and approved by the laws of this Kingdom" and can only be legal by "positive law". All putative slaves and slave masters living in the American colonies legal status and legal rights were conclusively determined by the *Somersett* ruling. The resulting policies which could be perceived as complicity by the British government became irrelevant. The government officials were tantamount to unindicted co-conspirators and slave masters were criminals.

The slave masters in the American colonies, as Englishmen were faced with a binary choice and elected an alibi that has endured for many years. However, in the scheme of things... once the British formally repudiated slavery by freeing slaves in November 1775 and then the American colonies declared themselves independent of the British in July 1776—but formally adopted English law; the alibi became feckless and hollow.

A generation ago former-Vice President Hubert H. Humphrey reflected upon how the passage of time—overlooked facts, unearthed evidence, or renewed objective scrutiny can, and must change common knowledge regarding historical events, observing:

> "Today we know that World War II began not in 1939 or 1941 but in the 1920's and 1930's when those who should have known better...

persuaded themselves that they were not their brother's keeper."

Similarly, now we know slavery was a criminal practice during colonial times, and black people were placed *below* the rule of law to preserve the Union.

In *The Atlantic* in 2014, Ta-Nehisi Coates wrote an essay titled *The Case for Reparation*, [135] positing that "To celebrate freedom and democracy while forgetting American's origins in a slavery economy was patriotism *a la carte*" … "If Thomas Jefferson's genius matters, then so does his taking of Sally Hemings' body. If George Washington crossing the Delaware matters, so must his ruthless pursuit of the runagate Oney Judge." Such is the case, as Thomas Jefferson was a U. S. Envoy and Minister to France when he brought a fourteen-year old Sally Hemings to Paris, France in 1787. Jefferson was forty-four, and while in Paris, he repeatedly raped this young black child. The truth about slavery's origins in the U. S. makes Jefferson's taking of Hemings' body extremely important since she was born a free English person in Virginia in 1773—under the rule of law. Hemings was not Jefferson's slave; she was a free Englishperson and Anglo-American law proves it.

Historians have promoted the narrative that slavery was a lawfully authorized practice during colonial times. This was not true. They claimed slavery in the U. S. was a British inheritance, when in fact, slavery was not inherited from the British and it was never "allowed and approved" by English law and all black people born within the American colonies in the year 1773 had British subjecthood, by virtue of the Twelve Judges' ruling in the *Somersett* case of that prior year. The Mansfieldian Moment of him adjourning the habeas case in May 1772 and then submitting the question of Virginia's slave laws legality to the Twelve Judges for adjudication, rather than him making a ruling, made it a solemn decision. [136] Certainly, the ruling that slavery was not "allowed and approved by the laws of this Kingdom" and can only be lawful by virtue of "positive law" controlled the colony of Virginia; under the colonial charter. Slavery was repugnant to English common law and Virginia's hereditary slave laws did not have the assent of either King James I who died in 1625, King Charles I, who reigned 1625 until his execution in 1649 or his heir, King Charles II, who reigned started in 1661 *after* a suspense of the monarchy and his exile or any succeeding monarch thru King George III. The colonial charter's repugnancy provision and the bicameral legislative structure made this the case and thus, the *Somersett* decision was a dispositive ruling upon the issue of slave practices in Virginia. They have airbrushed America's true slave history to sustain the legacy of flawed men.

Blithely, historians have accepted America's heroes claim that they *legally* owned black citizens under English rule, and that it would have been wrong, unfair to deprive them of property, if enslaved black people were freed. This is the parallelism of U. S. history which Coates openly questioned. America's history is tethered to slavery's misanthrope legacy—they are mirror images. One cannot be hoisted high for genius, while misanthrope deeds are buried. This is America's dilemma.

The practice of colonial slavery was a product of colonial corruption, and at all times relevant was an extra-legal (criminal) practice that could not, did not confer unto Jefferson or Washington legal ownership of either woman. Such was the reason Jefferson, and others slaveholding Americans supported Jefferson's proposed legislation before the First Congress to supplant English law with Roman law in 1776. The bill not passing had consequences and *Somersett* rendered all hereditary slavery laws void and the continued practice became *per se* criminal in 1772. Thus, as of 1773, when Hemings and Judge were born——Virginia's hereditary slave law faced three jurisdictional hurdles; (1) overturning the Twelve Judges' ruling in the *Somersett* case that slavery was not "allowed and approved by the laws of this Kingdom"; (2) establishment of positive law legalizing slavery and (3) establishment of positive law changing the patrilineal descent system to a matrilineal of *partus sequitur ventrem*. Any one of these three jurisdictional hurdles were destructive to even the suggestion that either woman was a slave under English law.

Factually, the *Somersett* decision rendered Virginia's hereditary slave laws null and void. Hemings was born in Virginia in 1773 to Betty Hemings——a biracial slave woman. Hemings' father was John Wayles and Jefferson knew him to be a free born white Englishman, as he was his son-in-law. Jefferson married Wayles' daughter Martha Wayles Skelton Jefferson in 1772 and thus Hemings was Jefferson's sister-in-law. *Somersett* was the rule of law in 1773 and English law was *partus sequitur patrem* and Hemings had British subjecthood at birth——by virtue of John Wayles' status as a free Englishman.

History supports, in the early days of the Virginia colony, mixed-race children of black mothers, and a white planter inherited the father's condition of servitude under English common law, as in the case of Elizabeth Key in 1656. Key was the illegitimate daughter of a white planter father. She prevailed in a freedom lawsuit based upon *partus sequitur patrem*—winning her freedom and her child. [137]

The *Somersett* ruling in 1772 reinstated the controlling precedent of the *Key* case. The ruling in the *Key* case had motivated Virginia's House of Burgesses to enact a law that child's status as free or bond (slave) was to follow the mother's status—contrary to England common law of *partus sequitur patrem*. The reinstatement of the *Key* precedent occurred since Virginia's legislative assembly had not lawfully decriminalized kidnapping; did not legalize slavery and did not change the controlling patrilineal descent system, and in all instances did not enact positive law by securing the King's assent. *Key* was controlling precedent when Hemings was born in 1773; firstly: Virginia's legislative assembly did not lawfully enact its hereditary slave law of *partus sequitur ventrem* in 1662 and secondly, even if it did, England's Twelve Judges ruled slavery was unconstitutional throughout the Kingdom in the *Somersett* case in 1772 and it was immediately, the law of the land. Hemings had English subjecthood by birth in Virginia in 1773 because her father was a white Englishman, as well as her mother was born in colonial America and the colony of Virginia could not substantiate that its slave practice constituted "positive law".

Key was controlling precedent in 1773 and Jefferson had famously stated "ignorance of the law is no excuse in any country. If it were the laws would lose their effect, because it can always be pretended". Jefferson knew—ignorance of the law was no excuse for violating it and it is probative, if not conclusive that Jefferson knew Hemings' father to be a white Englishman and that Virginia's governor, Lord Dunmore had liberated Virginia's slaves in November 1775 and in authoring the Declaration of Independence the first three grievances lodged against King George III relates to His Majesty's withholding of his assent to colonial laws, and if a careful student bridged back it would reveal that this grievance also attached to Virginia's hereditary slave laws. And while the ratification of the federal constitution in 1789 deprived black citizens of life, liberty, and property—it violated English law. These federal laws purported to elevate slave owning Americans *above*, while institutionally placing black people *below* the rule of law. But as the rule of law stood resolute, this made Jefferson's taking of Hemings' body a big deal, and a criminal wrong since while in France, Hemings became pregnant with Jefferson's child, and had six more of his children over the years—while living at Monticello.

It is equally illustrative of who Jefferson was that he allowed and exploited the condemnation of his own children as slaves—in derogation of natural law, as well as man's law. Jefferson's actions are condemnatory when one considers the fact that he knew England's patrilineal descent system of *partum sequitur patrem* made Hemings a free-born Englishwoman—under the rule of law. Thus, Jefferson's children with Hemings were not slaves.

Few can really claim—that a fourteen-year old child being taken overseas, and then submitting to the sexual advances of a powerful, older man, having been swept away to Paris under false pretense can be deemed consensual... even by 18th century norms. English laws protected young girls. [138] Doubtlessly, the taking of Hemings' body does matter—but any recrimination of Jefferson, with respect to his actions turns upon whether Hemings was a free-born English citizen or a slave. Pursuant to the *Stapylton* precedent the legal burden to prove ownership of Hemings was placed upon Jefferson and his alone. English common law was *partus sequitur patrem* in 1773 and slavery was not "allowed and approved by the laws in this Kingdom" in 1773, and as a matter of law, the *Somersett* decision had already overturned *partus sequitur ventrem,* as Virginia's legislative assembly had not bothered to secure the King's assent to this hereditary slave law.

While the imperialistic British directed its colonial rule of law officials to not apply the precedential consequence of *Somersett*, no third party in the Kingdom was inoculated from its legal consequence, and as a legislator, lawyer, and an officer of the English court, Jefferson was bound by the rule of law. He could not claim ownership of Hemings who was born in Virginia post-*Somersett* that rendered all colonial slave laws null and void. No one living in colonial America had the legal right, privilege, or status to sell an English child to Jefferson, and it cannot be chalked up to being a reflection of the times, especially since Virginia's colonial governor, Lord Dunmore liberated slaves exercising *executive* powers of His Majesty King George III in November 1775 and the First Congress adopted English law when Hemings was three years old. Further, Jefferson participated in the treaty negotiations with England that resulted in the Treaty of Paris of 1783 that warranted liberty for Hemings and he certainly, knew that England had claimed such people as its citizens when he took this fourteen-year old girl to

Paris. Jefferson did not and could not prove legal ownership of this Afro-Briton child named Sally Hemings *circa* 1787; but he did not care. Lord Mansfield's ruling in the *Stapylton* case was controlling precedent.

George Washington's pursuit of Judge matters in the same way as Hemings, as the *Somersett* decision rendered Virginia's hereditary slave laws null and void. Judge was born in Virginia and her father Andrew Judge was a white Englishman, and her mother Betty was a bi-racial woman "owned" by Washington's wife, Martha. Andrew was a tailor working as an indentured servant at Mount Vernon. Washington knew Judge to be a white Englishman. The claim that Judge was a free born English citizen is moored to the uncontroverted fact that this woman—like Hemings was born in Virginia in 1773—*after* the *Somersett* decision, and this woman's father—like Hemings was a white Englishman living in Virginia. Virginia's colonial charter bound colonial citizens to the *Key* case. England's common law of *partus sequitur patrem* controlled—not—Virginia's hereditary slave law of *partus sequitur ventrem* because it was repugnant to English common law and England's patrilineal descent system was not lawfully changed by "positive law". Judge was a free-born English subject, as a matter of law.

It is a dispositive fact that both Hemings and Judge were born in Virginia in 1773 during colonial times—the year *after* the historic *Somersett* decision struck down Virginia's extrajudicial hereditary slave law. In addition to ruling slavery was not "allowed and approved by the laws in this Kingdom", England's high court ruled slavery could only be legal in the Kingdom by "positive law". This announced a kingdom-wide standard that slave laws had to meet to be lawful. Such being the case, Virginia's putative colonial laws faltered as a matter of law, as the bicameral legislative structure required the King's assent—but the King had never agreed to enact slave laws, or to change the patrilineal descent system to a matrilineal one. Then Virginia's highest-ranking rule of law official, Lord Dunmore liberated black people suffering as slaves in November 1775 and Congress adopted English law—thus it toppled all putative ownership claims, as Lord Mansfield's holding in the *Stapylton* case held that "being black will not prove property".

The delegates to the federal constitutional convention had no power to enact an *ex post facto* law to disfranchise Hemings or Judge of birthright

British citizenship, or to enact a bill of attainder to enslave them. The enslavement of Hemings and Judge were in derogation of the rule of law. Jefferson and Washington could not rely upon the Framers' putative legal authority over these English subjects to enslave them due to the Treaty of Paris of 1783. Jefferson and Washington proceeded at their own legal peril, and such is the reason why a *locus classicus* on the origins of slavery is doubly important.

The First Congress bound Jefferson, and Washington to the *Key* decision. Thus, in treating these Englishwomen like slaves—each man was treating a legally free person, as if she was his property. This was criminal behavior. Furthermore, subsequent to the *Somersett* decision, no legislative assembly enacted a law legalizing slavery, and none ever created a class of person known as "slave" during colonial times. Virginia remained legally bound by colonial charter to English law to *partus sequitur patrem*. Thus, Hemings and Judge were not slaves and were entitled to liberty pursuant to the Treaty of Paris of 1783.

The existence of mixed-raced children like Hemings and Judge's mothers were threats to the very existence of the slave-based colonial community; but highly valued as slaves. Their treatment as slaves to America's patriots, although free-born Englishmen under English law, and their entitlement to be "set at liberty" *per* Treaty of Paris of 1783 should disabuse the entire notion that Jefferson and Washington lorded over legal slaves, inherited from England. Nonetheless—admirers of Jefferson and Washington will still give them free passes, classifying them as enlightened slave masters who treated their black slaves well, and sought to emancipate some. They will then quickly point out that Washington was a hero of the American Revolution, and for his part, was a greatly compassionate slave master, who did not break-up families, and emancipated them in his will. As Washington explained:

> "To sell overplus, I cannot, because I am principled against this kind of traffic in the human species. To hire them out is almost as bad because they could not be disposed of in families to any advantage, and to disperse [break up] the families I have an oversion."

Hemings and Judge's lives as slaves in the U. S. matters and are perfect allegories of the larger question concerning restitution for U. S. slavery. The dispositive arbiter has always been English law: *partum sequitur patrem* and Virginia's colonial assembly's failure to adhere to the bicameral legislative system——a check and balance to the power of colonial legislatures. Without the King's assent such colonial laws were nugatory. Thus, Virginia's 1662 law of *partus sequitur ventrem* was not a lawfully promulgated colonial law.

It was while each man was the head rule of law official in the U. S. that Jefferson exerted ownership of Sally Hemings——fathered children with this free black woman and Washington claimed ownership of Oney Judge——then relentlessly pursued her throughout America. However, pursuant to the rule of law, as Hemings and Judge were free-born English citizens born *after Somersett*——liberty was guaranteed by the Treaty of Paris of 1783, neither woman should have suffered as a slave. Doubtlessly, as the U. S. formally adopted English law after the Declaration of Independence and agreed to "set at liberty" *per* the Treaty of Paris of 1783, such people were legally free people and if not, why not? The enslavement of Hemings and Judge were searing affronts to the rule of law, and to republican ideals upon which the U. S. was founded and for which, so many had given their lives.

This observation was made as early as 1845, in a book titled *The Unconstitutionality of Slavery* by Lysander Spooner where he wrote:

"A man's natural rights are his own, against the whole world; and any infringement of them is equally a crime, whether committed by one man, or by millions; whether committed by one man, calling himself a robber, (or by any other name indicating his true character) or by millions, calling themselves a government."

The liberal, individual rights-focused nature of the Enlightenment has been viewed, as the main historical impetus behind the American Revolution. Tirelessly, they railed against excesses of England's tyranny, and divine rule. They portrayed England's King George III as a new Caesar, when Parliament passed revenue bills, such as the Stamp Act. They did so knowing slavery was a criminal scheme, and all presumptions of English law were in favor of liberty. Some abolitionists defended the founding generation against British instigated claims that the civil war was hypocritical, and profane, as they sought freedom for themselves, but slavery for blacks who were equal in legal status and condition, under English law. Such a defense of the founding generation was misplaced since the Twelve Judges in the *Somersett* case ruled slavery was not "allowed and approved by the laws in this Kingdom" and could only be lawful by virtue of "positive law" in 1772, and the U. S. agreed to free all English citizens in the Treaty of Paris of 1783.

Historians will forever point to the fact that the Constitution was ratified by the thirteen states in 1789, and has been amended twenty-six times, with the first ten amendments, the Bill of Rights, dealing with individual rights and protections against the national government. The Civil War Amendments that "abolished" slavery, gave blacks suffering as slaves, U. S. citizenship and the right to vote are the thirteenth, fourteenth, and fifteenth amendments. However, it officiated over Jim Crow laws and institutionalized racial repression. And although the Constitution may not have been a proslavery compact, the lack of federal oversight (enforcement) and an ethos of hooliganism euphemistically called a "compromise" and corruption at the federal and state levels of government made it feckless. Such is the legacy of slavery here in America. Slavery existed and expanded extrajudicially and restorative justice for slavery it is not moored to intent, rather, to the legal effect of the founding generation's failure to honor the Treaty of Paris of 1783. Treaty terms should have been honored——but British-styled tyranny allowed slavery to become endemic throughout America when our rule of law officials succumbed to mob rule and they compromised.

Slavery within the American colonies operated extrajudicially and it was a criminal enterprise. King

George III's attempt to tighten his imperial authority after a long period of salutary neglect was called "tyranny" by scofflaw colonists and an English civil war erupted within the North American colonies. The end of salutary neglect and the fate of British citizens by birth——who suffered under a species of tyranny were melded, once the Twelve-Judges' decision in the *Somersett* case declared slavery was unconstitutional throughout the Kingdom and could only be lawful by way of positive law; a process of adhering to the bicameral legislative structure that had been long abandoned by the colonists.

The British abolished the slave during colonial times... but the master remained and only by bridging back to the arrival of the first nineteen Africans in Virginia in 1619 and by analyzing the jurisdictional shortcomings in promulgated slave laws can restorative justice be accomplished here in the U. S., as black people living within the former American colonies were criminally robbed of their legal, and natural rights at the dawn of this country——in derogation of an international treaty. The systemic disfranchisement and exploitation of 500,000 black people, who held dual British-U. S. citizenship in violation of the Treaty of Paris of 1783, and the ferocious institutionalization of racial-based laws and practices of suppression against them and their progeny weaponized the U. S. to establish a system of government that has seen thirteen Atlantic states transform into a world-class powerful nation that spans from sea to shining sea. [139]

Colonial slavery was an extrajudicial institution because the practice violated English common law. During the period of salutary neglect by the British, colony governments created a new species of tyranny; hereditary slavery. These colonial slave practices thrived due to graft and corruption—but were struck down by England's Twelve Judges' determination in the *Somersett* case that ruled slavery was not allowed and approved by the laws of this Kingdom. Lord Dunmore abolished slavery in November 1775, however, the slave masters reinvented themselves. The resulting civil war was resolved by treaty and although the treaty did provide for the release of all British citizens, the U. S. enslaved 500,000 black Englishmen and then exploited them as America's slavery pool, without affording them due process that was authorized under law. The assault upon the rule of law occurred in plain sight and certainly, the master has sculpted America's historiography and have not been called out, least held to account. This enslavement of British subjects was a violation of the Treaty of Paris of 1783—an international wrong.

Acknowledgments

This book could not have happened without my Dream Team of friends and family. Dr. James Brewer Stewart, History Professor Emeritus at Macalester College, St. Paul, Minnesota and founder, Historians Against Slavery... I don't even know if I have the words to describe how essential my reconnection with you have been to this project. You created the time to take a good hard look at the first draft. The critique that it is a call for first principles, a reconceptualization of U. S. citizenship and urges a transformation of the American political culture that can lead to social justice were inspiring words. Thank you. Calvin Simmons, you heard me and then stepped in and took that insatiable intellectual curiosity of yours and transformed it into spirited discussions, insights and valued perspectives. Thank you. Finally, to my family—Drew you've been amazing. I am proud of you. Gina, you've been my rock throughout this journey. Thank you.

Bibliography

Adams, Russell L. *Great Negroes Past and Present*, Afro-Am Publishing Co., (1963)

Allen, Theodore W. *The Invention of the White Race: Racial Oppression and Social Control*, New Expanded Edition, VersoBooks (2012)

Althusser, Louis. *Politic and History: Montesquieu, Rousseau, Marx, Ben Brewster* (trans.) London, VersoBooks (2007)

Anderson, Fred and Andrew Cayton. *The Dominion of War: Empire and Liberty in North America, 1500 – 2000*, New York: Viking Penguin (2005)

Armitage, David. *The Declaration of Independence: A Global History*, Cambridge, Massachusetts: Harvard University Press (2007)

Ashcraft, Richard. *Revolutionary Politics and Locke's Two Treaties of Government*, Princeton University Press, Princeton (1988)

Auden, W. H. and Louis Kronenberger. *The Viking Book of Aphorisms*, New York: Viking Press (1966)

Bailyn, Bernard . *The Ideological Origins of the American Revolution*, Cambridge: Belknap of Harvard U. P. (1992)

Banks, Taunya Lovell. *Dangerous Women: Elizabeth Key's Freedom Suit – Subjecthood and Racialized Identity in Seventeen Century Colonial Virginia*, Digital Commons Law, University of Maryland Law School (April 2009)

Barro, Robert J. Determinants of Economic Growth: A Cross Country Empirical Study (Cambridge, Massachusetts, MIT Press (1997)

Bell, Derrick. *Race, Racism and American Law*. Boston, M.A. Little, Brown & Co. Law Book Div. (1992)

Bennett, Lerone, Jr. *The Shaping of Black America*, New York: Penguin (1993)

Bennet, Lerone, Jr. *Before the Mayflower: A History of the American Negro in America 1619-1964*. Chicago, Il. Johnson Publishing Co. (1966)

Berlin, Ira. *Many Thousands Gone: The First Two Centuries of Slavery in North America*, Cambridge, Mass.: Harvard University Press (1998)

Blackburn, Robin. *The Making of New World Slavery: From the Baroque to the Modern 1492-1800*, London, New York: Versobooks (1997)

Blight, David W. *A Slave No More: Two Men Who Escaped to Freedom, Including Their Own Narratives of Emancipation*, Boston, Mass.: Houghton Mifflin, (2007)

Blumrosen, Alfred W. and Ruth G. Blumrosen, *Slave Nation: How Slavery United the Colonies & Sparked the*

American Revolution, Naperville, Illinois: Sourcebooks, Inc. (2005)

Bogus, Carl T. *The Hidden History of the Second Amendment*, 31 U.C. Davis Law Review (1998)

Brewster, Holly. *By Birth or Consent*, UNC Press: Chapel Hill (2007)

Bristow, Peggy. *We're Rooted Here and They Can't Pull Us Up: Essays in African Canadian Women's History*, University of Toronto Press (1994)

Brookhiser, Richard. *Founding Father: Rediscovering George Washington*, New York: Free Press (1996)

Browne, G. P. *CARLETON, GUY, 1st Baron DORCHESTER* in Dictionary of Canadian Biography, vol 5, University of Toronto/Universite' Laval (2003).

Burstein, Andrew. *America's Jubilee: How in 1826 a Generation Remembered Fifty Years of Independence*, New York: Knopf (2001)

Carpenter, A. H. *Naturalization in England and the American Colonies*, The American Historical Review, American Historical Association (1904)

Catteral, Helen Tunnicliff. *Judicial Cases Concerning American Slavery and the Negro, Vol. I: Cases from the Courts of England, Virginia, West Virginia, and Kentucky, Washington, D.C.*: Carnegie Institution of Washington (1926)

Christian, Charles M. *Black Saga: The African American Experience: A Chronology*, Washington, D.C.: Civitas (1999)

Churchill, Ward. *Fantasies of the Master Race*, Monroe, ME: Common Courage Press (1992)

Davis, David Brion. *Inhuman Bondage: The Rise and Fall of Slavery in the New World*, New York: Oxford University Press (2006)

Davis, Kenneth C. *A Nation Rising: Untold Tales of Flawed Founders, Fallen Heroes, and Forgotten Fighters from America's Hidden History*, Harper-Collins Publishers (2010)

Day, Thomas. *Fragment of an original letter on the Slavery of the Negroes*, written the year 1776, London: Printed for John Stockdale (1784), Boston Re-printed by Garrison & Knapp, at the office of *"The Liberator"* (1831), p. 10 Retrieved 2014-02-26: "If there be an object truly ridiculous in nature, it is an American patriot, signing resolutions of independency with one hand, and with the other brandishing a whip over his affrighted slaves."

de Bracton, Henry. *Of the Laws and Customs of England*, 2 tans. Samuel E. Thorne, Cambridge, MA: Harvard University Press, Belknap Press (1968)

Dicey, A. V. *Introduction to the Law of the Constitution*: 1885 http://www.constitution. org.cmt/avd/lawcon.htm

Doe, Norman. *Fundamental Authority in Late Medieval English Law*, Cambridge: Cambridge University Press (1990)

Douglass, Frederick. *Autobiographies (Narratives of the Life of Frederick Douglass, an American Slave; My Bondage and My Freedom; Life and Times of Frederick Douglass)*, New York: Library of America (1994)

Ellis, Joseph J. *American Sphinx: The Character of Thomas Jefferson*, New York: Knopf (1997)

Fehrenbacher, Don F. *The Slaveholding Republic: An Account of the United States Government's Relation in Slavery*, ed. Ward M. McAfee, New York: Oxford University Press (2001)

Felton, Howard W. *Mumbet*, New York: Dodd, Meade & Co. (1970)

Finkelman, Paul. *Emancipation and Reconstruction: Vol. 3. Race, Law and American History 1700-1990.* New York, N.Y. Garland Pub. (1992)

Fitzpatrick, John C. Editor. *The Writings of George Washington from the Original Manuscript Sources 1745-1799, Vol. 26, 1January 1783 – 10 June 1783.* Washington D. C.: United States Government Printing Office

Fogel, Robert and Stanley Engerman, *Time on the Cross: The Economics of American Negro Slavery*, New York: W.W. Norton and Company (1974)

Forner, Eric. *Give me Liberty: An American History*, Volume I, New York: W. W. Norton & Co. (2006)

Franklin, John Hope and Alfred A. Moss, Jr. *From Slavery to Freedom: A History of African Americans*, 8th ed. New York: Knopf (2009)

Genovese, Eugene D. *Roll Jordan, Roll: The World the Slaves Made*, New York: Random House (1974)

Gipson, Lawrence Henry. *The Coming of the Revolution 1763-1775*, in Henry Steel Commager and Richard B. Morris, eds., *The New American Nation Series* (New York: Harper & Row, Torchbook University Library (1954)

Goodell, William Rev. *Slavery and Anti-Slavery: A History of the Great Struggle in Both Hemispheres*, New York: William Harned Pub. (1852)

Gordon-Reed, Annette. *Thomas Jefferson and Sally Hemings: An American Controversy*, Charlottesville: University Press of Virginia (1997)

Hadden, Sally E. *Slave Patrols: Law and Violence in Virginia and the Carolinas*, Harvard University Press (2003)

Harper, Douglass. *Emancipation in Massachusetts, Slavery in the North*, Retrieved 2010-05-22.

Hayek, Friedrich. Law. *Legislation and Liberty*, Volume 3: The Political Order of a Free People (1973)

Hayek, Friedrich. *The Constitution of Liberty* (Definitive ed.), Chicago: University of Chicago Press, ISBN 978-0-226-31539-3 (2011)

Hayek, Friedrich. *The Road to Serfdom,* Chicago: University of Chicago Press (1994)

Historical Demographics, Economic and Social Data: The United States 1790-1970: Historical Statistics of the United States, ICPSR Study

Hoffman, Ronald and Peter J. Albert. *Peace and the Peacemakers: The Treaty of 1783*, University of Virginia Press (1981)

Holdsworth, William. *History of English Law,* Brown, Little, Brown & Co. (1909)

Hoyt, Edward A. *Naturalization Under the American Colonies: Signs of a New Community*, Political Science Quarterly, Academy of Political Science (1952)

Ignatief, Michael. *American Exceptionalism and Human Rights*, Princeton University Press (2005)

Isenbberg, Nancy. *Fallen Founder: The Life of Aaron Burr*, New York: Viking (2007)

Jasanoff, Maya. *Liberty's Exiles: American Loyalists in the Revolutionary World*, New York: Alfred A. Knopf (2011)

Johansen, Robert Walter. *Manifest Destiny and Empire: American Antebellum Expansionism*, Texas A & M (1997)

Journals of the Continental Congress, Library of Congress

Kaplan, Sidney. *The Domestic Insurrections of the Declaration of Independence*, Journal of Negro History (PDF) Vol, 61, No. 3 (July 1976)

Kidd, Thomas. God of Liberty: *A Religious History of the American Revolution*, New York: Basic Books (2010)

Ketcham, Ralph. *James Madison: A Biography*, Macmillan (1971)

Kettner, James H. *The Development of American Citizenship, 1608-1870*, University of North Carolina Press (1978)

Koh, Harold. *American Exceptionalism and Human Rights*, Princeton University Press, (2005)

Kohlmetz, Ernest. *Encyclopedia of American History*, Guilford, CT: Dushkin Publishing, (1973)

Kolchin, Peter. *American Slavery: 1619 to 1877*, New York: Hill and Wang (1994)

Kulikoff, Allan. *Tobacco and Slaves: The Development of Southern Cultures in the Chesapeake, 1680 – 1800*, Chapel Hill and London: University of North Carolina Press (1986)

Lawrence, William Bench. *In Elements of International Law: 2nd annotated ed.*, London: S. Low (1863)

Lepore, Jill. *New York Burning: Liberty, Slavery and Conspiracy in Eighteenth Century Manhattan*, New York: Knopf (2005)

Levy, Leonard W. and Kenneth L. Karst. *Encyclopedia of the American Constitution*, Macmillan (1987)

Locke, John. *Second Treatise of Government*, ed. C. B. Macpherson, Hackett Publishing Co., Inc. (1980)

Lovejoy, Paul E. *Transformation of Slavery: A History of Slavery in Africa*, London Cambridge University Press (2012)

Lusane, Clarence. *Black History in the White House*, San Francisco: City Lights Books, (2011)

Maier, Pauline. *American Scripture: Making the Declaration of Independence*, New York: Knopf (1997)

Main, Jackson Turner. *The Social Structure of Revolutionary America*, Princeton, N. J.: Princeton University Press (1965)

McPherson, James. *Abraham Lincoln and the Second American Revolution*, New York: Oxford University Press (1991)

Meltzer, Milton. *Slavery: A World History*, Da Capo Press: New York (1971)

Meyer, Reinhold. *Classica Americana: The Greek and Roman Heritage in the United States,* Detroit: Wayne State U. P. (1984)

Middlekauff, Robert. *Glorious Cause: The American Revolution, 1763-1789*, Oxford University Press (2005)

Miller, John C. *Crisis in Freedom: The Alien and Sedition Acts*, New York: Little, Brown and Company (1951)

Morgan, Edmund S. *American Slavery, American Freedom: The Ordeal of Colonial Virginia*, W.W. Norton & Company, Inc. New York (1975)

Namier, Lewis B. *King George III: A Study in Personality; in Personality and Power*, London: Hamish Hamilton (1955)

Nash, Gary B. *The Unknown American Revolution: The Unruly Birth of Democracy and the Struggle to Create America*, Penguin Random House (2006)

New Catholic Encyclopedia, Vol, 13 (New York: McGraw-Hill Book Co. (1967)

Nicolay, John G. & John Hay, eds., *Complete Works of Abraham Lincoln*, Vol II (New York: Francis D. Tandy Co., 1894 and 1905)

Paine, Thomas. (January 14, 1776). *Common Sense: Paine Collected Writings*, The Library of America, ISBN 978-1-4286-2200-5

Pangle, Thomas. *Montesquieu's Philosophy of Liberalism: A Commentary on The Spirit of the Laws*, Chicago: University of Chicago Press (1973)

Paterson, Thomas, Garry J. Clifford, Shane J. Maddox. *American Foreign Relations: A History to 1920*, Wadsworth Publishing (2009)

Pease, Donald E. *The New American Exceptionalism*, University of Minnesota Press, (2009)

Presser, Stephen B. *Book Review*, 14 Const. Comment, 229 (1997)

Poser, Norman. *Lord Mansfield, Justice in the Age of Reason*, (McGill-Queen's University Press, Canada (2013)

Quarles, Benjamin. *The Negro in the Making of America*, New York: Macmillan (1987)

Rahe, Paul. *Montesquieu and the Logic of Liberty*, New Haven: Yale University Press (2009)

Rediker, Marcus. *The Slave Ship: A Human History*, New York: Viking (2007)

Reid, John Phillip. *Constitutional History of the American Revolution: The Authority of Rights*, University of Wisconsin Press (1986)

Reinstein, Robert J. *Completing the Constitution: The Declaration of Independence, Bill of Rights and Fourteenth Amendment*, 66 Temple L. Rev. 361, 362-363 (1993)

Risch, Erna. *Encouragement of Immigration: As Revealed in Colonial Legislation*, The Virginia Magazine of History and Biography, Virginia Historical Society (1937)

Russell, Conrad. *The Origins of the English Civil War*, Macmillan, ISBN 0333124006 (1973)

Rutherfurd, Edward. *London: The Novel*, The Ballantine Publishing Group (1997)

Shientaig, Bernard L. *Lord Mansfield Revisited: A Modern Assessment*, 10 Fordham L. Rev. 345 (1941)

Smith, Page. *A New Age Now Begins: A People's History of the American Revolution,* (New   York: Penguin Books, (1976)

Smith, Thomas W. *The Slave in Canada"* Collections of the Nova Scotia Historical Society, X (1896-98)

Stampp, Kenneth M. *The Peculiar Institution: Slavery in the Ante-Bellum South*, New York: Vintage (1984)

Stannard, David E. *American Holocaust: The Conquest of the New World*, New York: Oxford University Press (1992)

Stein, Peter. *The Classical and Influence of the Roman Civil Law: Historical Essays*, London: The Hambledon Press (1988)

Szatmary, David P. *Shay's Rebellion: The Making of an Agrarian Insurrection*, University of Massachusetts Press (1980)

Tocqueville, Alexis de. *Democracy in America*, Trans. George Lawrence, New York: Perennial (1988)

Toppin, Edgar A. *A Biographical History of Blacks in America since 1528*, New York: David McKay Company, Inc. (1971)

Trevelyan, George O. *George III and Charles Fox: The Concluding Part of the American Revolution*, Longmans, Green (1912)

Van Buskirk, Judith L. *Generous Enemies: Patriots and Loyalists in the Revolutionary*, New York (Philadelphia University of Pennsylvania Press) (2002)

Wiecek, William M. *Somerset: Lord Mansfield and the Legitimacy of Slavery in the Anglo-American World*, University of Chicago Law Review, Vol. 42, No. 1 (Autumn 1976)

Williams, Eric. *Capitalism & Slavery with a New Introduction* Colin A. Palmer. Chapel Hill & London: The University of North Carolina Press (1994)

Willis, Garry. *A Necessary Evil: A History of American Distrust of Government*, Simon & Schuster, (1999)

Wilson, James Grant. *Dunmore John Murray, Appleton's' Cyclopedia of American Biography*, New York (1900)

Wilson, Theodore Brantner. *The Black Codes of the South*, University of Alabama Press (1965)

Wise, S. M. *Though the Heavens May Fall: The Landmark Trial that Led to the End of Human Slavery*, Cambridge, Mass. (2005)

Wood, Gordon S. *The Creation of the American Republic, 1776-1787*, University of North Carolina Press (1969)

Wood, William J. *The Illegal Beginning of American Negro Slavery*, 56 American Bar Association Journal (#1) (Jan. 1970).

Woolhouse, Roger. *Locke: A Biography*, Cambridge University Press, Cambridge (2007)

Wright, Gavin. *Slavery and American Economic Development*, Baton Rouge, Louisiana: Louisiana State University (2006)

Yaffe, Gideon. *Liberty Worth the Name: Locke on Free Agency*, Princeton University Press: Princeton (2000)

End Notes

[1] Francis Hargrave, *An Argument in the Case of James Somersett, a Negro, Lately Determined by the Court of King's Bench: wherein it is attempted to demonstrate the present unlawfulness of Domestic slavery in England. To Which is Prefixed, a State of the Case. By Mr. Hargrave, one of the counsel for the Negro* (London and Boston, reprinted by E. Russell, 1774; William M. Wiecek, "*Somerset Lord Mansfield and the Legitimacy of Slavery in the Anglo-American World*," University of Chicago Law Review 42(1974), 86-146; Steven Wise, *Though the Heavens May Fall: The Landmark Case that Led to the End of Human Slavery*, Cambridge: Perseus/Da Capo Press (2005).

[2] Charles Stewart's names is also reported as being spelled "Steuart"; Somersett's place of origin is reported Africa, Jamaica and Virginia.

[3] The Court of King's Bench jurisdiction was "to correct all crimes and misdemeanours that amounted to a breach of the peace, the King being then plaintiff, for such were in derogation of the *Jura regalia*; and to take cognizance of everything not parceled out to the other courts"; A. T. Carter, *A History of English Legal Institutions*, Butterworth (1910).

[4] English justices delivered their rulings orally and legal historian William M. Wiecek in his article titled *Somerset: Lord Mansfield and the Legitimacy of Slavery in the Anglo-American World* made the observation that "whether their words survived depended on the accident of whether a lawyer or other person was present to take notes. Somerset was preserved in this way".

[5] It was reprinted in Granville Sharp, *The Just Limitation of Slavery, in the Laws of God, Compared with the Unbounded Claims of the African Traders and British American*

Slaveholders, app 8 (1776), quoted in pertinent part throughout.

[6] Francis Hargrave, *An Argument in the Case of James Somersett, a Negro, Lately Determined by the Court of King's Bench: Wherein it is Attempted to Demonstrate the Present Unlawfulness of Domestic Slavery in England* (London: F. Hargrave, 1772), 4-11.

[7] *Luke v. Lyde*, 2 Burr. 882, 97 ER 614 (1759).

[8] The phrase "Mansfieldian Moment" is taken from David Waldstreicher, *Slavery's Constitution: From Revolution to Ratification* (New York; Hill and Wang, 2009).

[9] The practice of reserving cases for twelve-judge deliberation began in the 18th century, but only a handful appeared before the 1770s, all with Mansfield. Prior to the late 18th century, there was no regular printed record of the twelve-judge procedure. Occasional twelve-judges cases turned up in the nominative reports, and trial records in a few seminal cases printed in pamphlet form.

[10] James Oldham, *New Light on Mansfield and Slavery*, Journal of British Studies, 27 (Jan. 1988).

[11] This interpretation is supported by William M. Wiecek, "*Somerset Case*". It is referenced in the treatise, *Encyclopedia of the American Constitution* by legal scholars Leonard W. Levy and Kenneth L. Karst, eds. New York: Macmillan Reference USA 2000, Vol. 5, pp 2452-2452, where they concluded the *Somersett* decision impacted America "because the precedent had become part of American common law." The *Somersett* ruling was a unanimous repudiation of slave practices, by England's Twelve Judges and colonial slave laws were nullified.

[12] Matthew Mason, *Slavery and Politics in the Early American Republic* (Chapel Hill, N.C.: University of North Carolina Press, 2006) & *North American Calm, West Indian*

Storm: The Constitutional Politics and Legacy of the Somerset Decision, Brigham Young University, p. 3.

[13] James Oldham, *Informal Law-Making in England by the Twelve Judges in the Late 18th and Early 19th Centuries*, 27 Law & History Review (2005).

[14] *Murry v. Eyton and Price*, 2 Show. K.B. 104, 89 ER 823 (1680) (the cause "adjourned into the Exchequer Chamber, *proper difficultatem,* before all the twelve judges."). Once a case is decided by the Twelve Judges, as was the custom—one of the judges announces the opinion. Lord Mansfield did just that.

[15] *Calvin's Case*, 7 Co. Rep. 1a, 77 ER 377 (1608).

[16] *Tonson v. Collins*, 1 Bl. W. 301, 96 ER 169 (1761).

[17] *Millar v. Taylor*, 4 Burr. 2303, 2327, 98 ER 201 (1769).

[18] Matthew Mason, *North American Calm, West Indian Storm: The Constitutional Politics and Legacy of the Somerset Decision*, Brigham Young University, p. 4.

[19] The Kingdom of Great Britain comprised the dominions, colonies, protectorates, mandates and other territories ruled or then administered by King George III in 1772.

[20] Mason, *North American Calm, West Indian Storm: The Constitutional Politics and Legacy of the Somerset Decision*, p. 5.

[21] James Oldham, *English Common Law in the Age of Mansfield* (2004) discusses civil litigation and how judges could follow the well-established method of taking the verdict subject to a legal question being resolved by the twelve-judges procedure and he reported the question and circumstances of the case to the full court sitting the next term. Such was exactly what Mansfield stated that he was doing at the May 14, 1772 hearing.

[22] One example of criminal law was *In re Rudd*, 1 Leach 115, 168 ER 160 (Old Bailey 1775) (the twelve judges fully

considered and finally settled, how far, under what circumstances an accomplice to a crime ought to be entitled to favor and mercy.).

[23] Matthew Mason, *North American Calm, West Indian Storm: The Constitutional Politics and Legacy of the Somerset Decision*, Brigham Young University, p. 8.

[24] James Oldham, *Informal Law-Making in England by the Twelve Judges in the Late 18th and Early 19th Centuries*, 27 Law & History Rev. (2011) Scholarship @ GEORGETOWN LAW When a legal question arose about which the trial judges were doubtful, the most sensible course was to reserve the question for discussion with brother judges at the next opportunity, perhaps at the gathering of all of the judges on the first day of the following term.

[25] The Declaratory Act was passed along with the repeal of the Stamp Act in March 1766 to assert Parliament's authority to rule over the American colonies.

[26] *James Somersett v. Charles Stewart*, Lofft 1; 20 Howell's State Trials 1; 98 Eng. Rep 499 (King's Bench, June 1772). Matthew Mason observed in his article, p. 4 *North American Calm, West Indian Storm: The Constitutional Politics and Legacy of the Somerset Decision* observed that Lord Chief Justice Mansfield "Then on 22 June, after hearing more arguments and then deliberating over a recess he ruled on **behalf of the four-judge court** that Steuart had no right to compel Somerset out of England into colonial slavery, and that Somerset should go free". It was actually a twelve-judge court—not four.

[27] William W. Wiecek, *The Sources of Antislavery Constitutionalism in America, 1760-1848* (Ithaca, N.Y. Cornell University Press, 1977), 7-8, 20-51, quotations on 21.

[28] *Black History in the White House*, San Francisco: City Lights Books (2011).
[29] *Cundy v. Lindsay*, 3 App Cas 459 (1878) discussing the legal concept of void *ab initio* under English law.
[30] Under English law, slavery came to be construed as an event that never, in the contemplation of the law occurred and there's no logical, legal reason to abolish slavery—an act, condition and practice which is disallowed and disapproved in the first instance by a court with proper jurisdiction.
[31] *New Catholic Encyclopedia*, Vol. 13, New York: McGraw-Hill Book Co., (1967).
[32] *Matter of Cartwright*, 11 Elizabeth; 2 Rushworth's Coll 468 (1569).
[33] *Shanley v. Hervey*, 2 Eden 126 (Chancery, March 1762).
[34] *Smith v. Brown and Cooper*, 2 Ld Raym 1274; 2 Salk 666; 91 Eng Rep 566 (1765).
[35] Slavery was based upon assaultive, criminal behavior as the early American Supreme Court, in the case of *The Antelope*, 23 U. S. (10 Wheat) 66 (18 Mar 1825) found "[T]hat it [slavery] is contrary to the law of nature will scarcely be denied. That every-man has a natural right to the fruits of his own labor, is generally admitted: and that no other person can rightfully deprive him of those fruits, and appropriate them against his will, seems to be the necessary result of this admission".
[36] Taunya Lovell Banks, *Dangerous Women: Elizabeth Key's Freedom Suit – Subjecthood and Racialized Identity in Seventeen Century Colonial Virginia*, Digital Commons Law, University of Maryland Law School (April 2009).
[37] *The Antelope*, 23 U S (10 Wheat) 66, 120; 6 L Ed 268, 281 (18 March 1825).

[38] Patricia Bradley, *Slavery, Propaganda, and the American Revolution*, (Jackson: University Press of Mississippi, 1998).

[39] David Waldstreicher, *Slavery's Constitution: From Revolution to Ratification*, supra. p. 38-40.

[40] Goodell, *Slavery and Anti-Slavery* (New York: William Harned, 1852) at 49-51 that "there neither then was, nor ever had been any legal slavery in England".

[41] The case of *Lewis, a Negro, v. Stapylton, His Master* (1771), MS, New York Historical Society. Legal historians have observed that Mansfield could have used the Twelve Judges procedure in the *Stapylton* case. Instead, he unsuccessfully sought to dissuade the defendant from using the legality of slavery as the fulcrum of his defense.

[42] *Smith v. Gould*, 2 Ld. Raym. 1274-75; 92 Eng. Rep. 499 Q.B. 1706).

[43] "The citizens are the authors of law, and therefore its owners, regardless of who actually drafts the provisions, because the law derives its authority from the consent of the public, expressed through the democratic process," citing *BOCA v. Code Technology, Inc.*, 628 F2d 730, 734 (CA 1. 1980); *State of Georgia v. The Harrison Company*, 548 F.Supp. 110, 114 (DND Ga.ATL Div. 1982).

[44] *Wheaton v. Peters*, 33 U. S. 591; 8 Peters, 8 L.Ed 1055 (1834).

[45] Fred Anderson & Andrew Cayton. *The Dominion of War: Empire and Liberty in North America, 1500-2000*, New York: Viking Penguin (2005).

[46] John C. Fitzpatrick, ed., *The Writings of George Washington from the Original Manuscript Sources 1745-1799*, Volume 26, January 1, 1783 – June 10, 1783 (Washington, DC: Government Printing Office, 1938), 402-405. Proclamations promising freedom to blacks

issued by Lord Dunmore in November 1775; by General Clinton in June 1779 and by General Leslie in June 1782.

[47] In this Court of King's Bench case, tried before Lord Mansfield the defendant Stapylton was charged after attempting to forcibly deport his purported slave, Thomas Lewis, who claimed himself to be a freeman. Stapylton's defense rested on the basis that as Lewis was his claimed slave, his actions were lawful. During the proceedings, Mansfield was unsuccessful in his attempt to dissuade the defense counsel on his stated legal point. He was forced to direct the jury that they should assume Lewis was a free man, unless Stapylton was able to prove otherwise. He further directed the jury that unless they found that Stapylton was the legal owner of Lewis "you will find the Defendant guilty." Lewis was permitted to testify. Stapylton was found guilty. However, in summing up, Mansfield was careful to state "whether they [slave owners] have this kind of property in England has never been solemnly determined".

[48] Fitzpatrick, *The Writings of George Washington,* 26:401-402.

[49] In *Thames Ditton* a black woman by the name of Charlotte Howe had been brought to England as a slave by one Captain Howe. After Captain Howe died Charlotte sought poor relief from the Parish of Thames Ditton. He ruled that Charlotte was not entitled to relief under Poor Laws because relief was dependent on having been "hired", and this did not relate to slaves.

[50] *Smith v. Gould,* 2 Ld. Raym. 1274, 1274-75; 92 Eng. Rep. 338 (Q.B. 1706).

[51] George A. Bonner, *The History of the Court of King's Bench,* Journal of the Law Society's School of Law, The Law Society. 11 (1933) observed that the King's Bench main jurisdiction was over "pleas of the crown; cases

which involved the King in some way"... "With the exception of revenue matters, which were handled by the Exchequer of Please, the King's Bench held exclusive jurisdiction over these case"., p. 6.

[52] Adrian Briggs, *The Conflict of Law*, (second ed.) Oxford University Press (2008) observing that conflict of laws concerns relations across different jurisdictions between litigants; their legal obligations and the appropriate forum and procedure for resolving disputes between them.

[53] D. Schaffter, *The Bicameral System in Practice*, (1929).

[54] Edlie L. Wong, *Neither Fugitive nor Free: Atlantic Slavery, Freedom Suits, and the Legal Culture of Travel* (New York: New York University Press, 2009).

[55] Ruth Paley, *After Somerset: Mansfield, Slavery and the Law in England, 1772-1830*, in Norma Landau, ed., *Law, Crime and English Society, 1660-1830* (Cambridge: Cambridge University Press, 2002), p. 165-84.

[56] David Brion Davis, *The Problem of Slavery in the Age of Revolution, 1770-1823* (Ithaca, N.Y.: Cornell University Press, 1975, p. 231, 470.

[57] Walter Bagehot, The English Constitution in Norman St. John-Stevas, ed., *The Collected Works of Walter Bagehot*, London, The Economist, vol. 5, pp/ 273-274.

[58] General Leslie to Francis Marion, April 4, 1782, Robert Wilson Gibbes, *Documentary History of the American Revolution: 1781-1782* (D. Appleton & Co.: New York, 1857), p. 153.

[59] Glenn G. Lammi and James Chang, *Michigan High Court Ruling Offers Positive Guidance on Challenges to Tort Reform Laws*, Washington Legal Foundation, ISSN 1056-3059 (Dec. 17, 2004).

[60] They were noted in two separate registries labeled *Book of Negroes*: England's *Book of Negroes* is held in its

National Archives in London, England, and the United States' version is preserved in the National Archives and Records Administration in Washington D.C. These registries legitimize the international controversy concerning the 500,000 black citizens—who the U. S. made slaves.

[61] *Smith v. Brown and Cooper*, 2 Ld Rayn 1274; 2 Salk 666; 91 Eng Rpt 566 (1765).

[62] The U. S. position is analogous to that of a petulant teenager who a parent had entrusted their home and the care and custody of younger siblings to, while they enjoyed a short vacation. The teenager did not honor any of the rules and the household suffered. However, the teenager is barely admonished when the parent returns home, however, the next time he leaves, he brings into the household an older—no nonsense cousin and installs him as warden and babysitter over the teenager. This, at its core was the consequence of the British abandonment of the unwritten policy of salutary neglect.

[63] Robert J. Reinstein in *Completing the Constitution: The Declaration of Independence, Bill of Rights and Fourteen Amendment*, 66 Temple L. Rev. 361 (1993).

[64] Pauline Maier, *American Scripture: Making The Declaration of Independence* 186 (1998).

[65] Paul D. Carrington, *Remembering Jefferson*, 2 William & Mary BILL OF RTS. J. 455, 463 (1993).

[66] Steven M. Wise, *Though the Heavens May Fall: The Landmark Trial That Led to the End of Human Slavery* (Cambridge, Mass.: DaCapo Press, 2005).

[67] *The Anti-Slavery Examiner,* American Anti-Slavery Society (1838).

[68] Under English common law, as soon as a negro arrived on English soil he was free. *Matter of Cartwright*, 11

Elizabeth; 2 Rushworth's Coll. 468 (1569) held "England was too pure an air for slaves to breathe in".

[69] England's King Charles I presided over the British Kingdom from March 27, 1625 until his execution on January 30, 1749. Then the monarchy was suspended until Charles II became King in 1661 and he agreed to honor the Petition of Right and accept a limited income.

[70] *Ashby v. White*, 92 ER 126; 2 Ld Raym 938 (K. B. 1703).

[71] For a long time in colonial America, the first blacks were called Blackamoors, Moors, Negers and Negars. Theodore W. Allen—in his seminal two-volume study titled, *The Invention of the White Race* posits that England invented the "white race" as a ruling class policy to define and implement racial proscriptions against free people of African descent in colonial America.

[72] Lewis Tappan, *Address to Non-Slaveholders of the South: On the Social and Political Evils of Slavery* (New York: S. W. Benedict, 1843), p. 36.

[73] Donald von Drehle, *The Civil War, 1861-2011, The Way We Weren't,* (Time, 18 April 2011, p. 40.

[74] The extant court documents reporting Elizabeth Key's case are reprinted in THE OLD DOMINION IN THE SEVENTEETH CENTURY: A DOCUMENTARY HISTORY OF VIRGINIA, 1606-1689 165-69 (Warren M. Billings ed, 1975).

[75] David Waldstreicher, *Slavery's Constitution: From Revolution to Ratification* (New York: Hill and Wang: 2009), p. 21-56.

[76] Matthew Mason, *North American Calm, West Indian Storm: The Constitutional Politics and Legacy of the Somerset Decision*, Brigham Young University.

[77] George William Van Cleve, *A Slaveholder's Union: Slavery, Politics, and the Constitution in the Early American*

Republic (Chicago and London: University of Chicago Press, 2010), p. 17-18.

[78] Samuel Martin, Sr., *A Short Treatise on the Slavery of Negroes in the British Colonies*, (Antigua: Robert Mearns, 1775).

[79] David Brion Davis, *The Problem of Slavery in the Age of Revolution, 1770-1823*, (Ithaca, N.Y.: Cornell University Press, 1975).

[80] According to historians Murray Newton Rothbard and Leonard P. G. Liggio, *Conceived in Liberty*, Vol. 1, Arlington Publishers House (1975) that the policy had "... allowed the representative colonial assemblies to wrest effective power from royally appointed governors by wielding the power of the purse over colonial taxes and appropriations, notably including the governor's own salaries. Thus, from 1720 through the 1750s, the American colonies were virtually *de facto* independent of British imperial control, an independence bolstered by libertarian spirit and ideology eagerly imbibed from the radical libertarian English writers and journalists of the period."

[81] English aristocracy had long provided royal patronage to slavery, through the establishment of the Company of Royal Adventurers Trading to Africa, which after five years, the company was recapitalized and incorporated into the Royal African Company (RAC) in 1663. The RAC was headed by the Duke of York, and members of the royal family were prominent investors. During the early 1770s... fifteen lord mayors, twenty-five sheriffs, and thirty-eight aldermen were also shareholders in the RAC; and it was estimated that when the founding generation declared themselves independent in July 1776, forty members of the British parliament were making money from slave investments.

82 David Waldstreicher, *Runaway America: Benjamin Franklin, Slavery, and the American Revolution* (New York: Hill and Wang, 2004).

83 Maya Jasanoff, *Liberty's Exiles: American Loyalists in the Revolutionary World* (New York: Alfred A. Knopf) pp. 85-91 (2011).

84 G. P. Browne, *CARLETON, GUY, 1st Baron DORCHESTER* in Dictionary of Canadian Biography, vol 5, University of Toronto/Universite' Laval (2003).

85 The historian Judith L. Van Buskirk in her book *Generous Enemies: Patriots and Loyalists in the Revolutionary, New York* (Philadelphia University of Pennsylvania Press) (2002) have applauded Carleton's "principled defense of the black loyalists," but all historians have overlooked the obvious corollary point: if Carleton was right, what about the 500,000 black people who became America's slaves? This was the actual origins of U. S. slavery.

86 *The Black Loyalist Directory: African Americans in Exile After the American Revolution*, edited by Graham Russell Hodges, Susan Hawkes Cook and Alan Edward Brown, William and Mary Quarterly, 1996, Third Series, Vol. 53, No. 4 (2011).

87 *Wheaton v. Peters*, 33 U S 591, 602; 8 Peters, 8 L Ed 1055, 1059 (1834).

88 *Ware v. Hylton*, 3 U.S. (3 Dall.) 199 (1796).

89 In the Smithsonian Magazine's article of November 30, 2017 *Five Things to Know About Queen Charlotte* the writer Tatiana Walk-Morris states that the late 18th century royal Queen Sophia Charlotte of Mecklenburg-Strelitz as being England's first biracial queen and was the lawful wife of King George III.

90 The U. S. adopted English law after America's Declaration of Independence in 1776. Then the country

organized under Articles of Confederation, which was formally adopted by all States on February 2, 1781. Pursuant to the Articles of Confederation—it granted unto the U. S. Congress assembled "the sole and exclusive right and power to determine peace and war... to enter into treaties and alliances, with some provisos; to establish rules for deciding all cases of captures or prizes on land or water".

[91] *e.g. Winchendon v. Hatfield*, 4 Mass 123 (1808); *Commonwealth v. Aves*, 35 Mass (18 Pick) 193, 209 (27 Aug 1836). And in the book *Slavery and Anti-Slavery*, William Goodall observed that the former colonies, now states, all wrote and ratified their Constitutions with bills of rights, using Declaration of Independence styled wording, all redundantly banning slavery. This too disrupted the practice, as "customs and usages do not define or create law... but should [must] be controlled by it".

[92] Howard W. Felton, *Mumbet*, New York: Dodd, Meade & Co. (1970).

[93] Relying upon Anglo jurisprudence, *Royal Bank of Canada v. Newell*, 147 D.L.R. (4th) 268 (N.S.C.A.), in which a woman forged her husband's signature on forty checks, totaling $58,000. To protect her from prosecution, her husband signed a letter of intent prepared by the bank in which he agreed to assume "all liability and responsibility" for the forged checks. However, the agreement was unenforceable, and was struck down by the courts, because of its essential goal, which was to "stifle a criminal prosecution". Because of the contract's illegality, and as a result voided status, the bank was forced to return the payments made by the husband.

[94] See William M. Wiecek, *Somerset's Case, Encyclopedia of the American Constitution*, Leonard W. Levy and Kenneth L. Karst.

[95] Carleton and Washington's agreement and the nations separate registries of black people who Carleton ferried out of the U. S. in November 1783——the *Books of Negroes* are probative. And in Thomas W. Smith's book *The Slave in Canada*, Collection of the Nova Scotia Historical Society he explained circumstances surrounding Washington's agreement to refer this treaty dispute to Congress for resolution.

[96] Benjamin Quarles, *The Negro in the American Revolution* (Chapel Hill: NC: University of North Carolina Press, 1961), p. 167-171.

[97] *William Stephens Smith to Washington, May 30, 1783,"* Founders Online, National Archives. httpp://founders/archives.gov/documents/Washington/99-01-02-11449.

[98] Bob Ruppert, *How Article 7 Freed 3000 Slaves: Politics During the War (1775-1783)*, Journal of the American Revolution, August 4, 2016.

[99] G. P. Browne, *CARLETON, GUY, 1st Baron DORCHESTER* in Dictionary of Canadian Biography, vol. 5, University of Toronto/Universite' Laval (2003).

[100] *Jones v. Ypsilanti*, 26 Mich App 574; 182 NW 2d 795 (1970).

[101] Edmund S. Morgan, *American Slavery, American Freedom: The Ordeal of Colonial Virginia*, W.W. Norton & Company, Inc., New York (1975).

[102] George William Van Cleve, *Somerset's Case and Its Antecedents in Imperial Perspective*, Law and History Review (Fall 2006), p. 603-606.

[103] The term salutary neglect had long remained unnamed until Edmund Burke addressed the British Parliament on March 22, 1775 and he stated "wise and salutary neglect" were the prime factor in the booming commercial success of the country's North American holdings.

[104] *James Somerset v. Charles Stewart*, Lofft I, 18-19, 98 Eng. Rep. 499, 509-510 (King's Bench, June 1772).

[105] *Matter of Cartwright*, 11 Elizabeth; 2 Rushworth's Voll 468 (1569).

[106] William W. Wiecek, *The Sources of Antislavery Constitutionalism in America, 1760-1848* (Ithaca, N.Y.: Cornell University Press, 1977), 7-8, 20-51, quotation on 21. For other discussions on this phenomenon, see Jerome Nedelhaft, "The Somersett Case and Slavery: Myth, Reality and Repercussions," *Journal of Negro History* 51 (July 1966): 193-208 and Adam Hochschild, *Bury the Chains: Prophets and Rebels in the Fight to Free an Empire's Slaves* (New York: Houghton, Mifflin, 2005), 50-51.

[107] Quoted in Jack P. Greene, *Peripheries and Center: Constitutional Development in the Extended Politics of the British Empire and United States, 1607-1788* (Athens: University of Georgia Press, 1986), 101.

[108] And in the book *The Illegal Beginning of American Negro Slavery*, the writer William J. Wood makes the observations that the mandate was to follow "the common law and the equity thereof". Slavery was forbidden within the American colonies, and the early colonial American rule of law officials revered English law.

[109] *Shanley v. Harvey*, 2 Eden 126 (Chancery, March 1762) ("As soon as a man puts foot on English ground, he is free").

[110] Courts have ruled that the Declaration of Independence abolished slavery. *Commonwealth v. Aves*, 35 Mass (18 Pick) 193, 209 (27 Aug 1836); *Winchendon v. Hatfield*, 4 Mass 123 (1808) and *Littleton v. Tuttle*, 2 Dane Abr. 413 (1796).

[111] *Jones v. Ypsilanti*, 26 Mich App 574; 182 N.W. 2d 795 (1970) ruled lawmakers are "presumed to have

knowledge of judicial construction of existing constitutional provisions".

[112] The public both owns and is presumed to know the law and court precedents, e.g. *Wheaton v. Peters*, 33 U S 591; 8 Peters, 8 L Ed 1055 (1834); *Davidson v. Wheelock*, 27 F 61 (CCD Minn 1866); and *Howell v. Miller*, 91 F 129 (CA 6, 1898).

[113] *Talbot v. Seaman*, 5 U. S. (1 Cranch) 1, 35; 5 L.Ed (1801).

[114] *Town of Pawlet v. Daniel Clark, et al.*, 13 U. S. (9 Cr) 292, 332-333; 3 L Ed. 735, 749-750 (10 Mar 1815).

[115] *Matter of Cartwright*, 11 Elizabeth; 2 Rushworth's Coll 468 (1569) ruled that slavery was unconstitutional under common law; the act of restraining a person was a crime.

[116] *Jones v. Ypsilanti*, 26 Mich App 574; 182 N W 2d 795 (1970).

[117] Lawmakers were presumed to have knowledge of judicial construction of existing constitutional provisions. See *Jones v. Ypsilanti*, 26 Mich App 574; 182 N.W. 2d 795 (1970).

[118] G. P. Browne, CARLETON, GUY, 1st Baron DORCHESTER in Dictionary of Canadian Biography, vol 5, University of Toronto/Universite' Laval (2003).

[119] Kenneth M. Stampp, *The Peculiar Institution: Slavery in the Ante-Bellum South* (New York: Random House Vintage Books, 1984).

[120] John G. Nicolay & John Hay, eds., *Complete Works of Abraham Lincoln*, Vol II (New York: Francis D. Tandy Co., 1894 and 1905).

[121] *U. S. v. Alexander*, 69 U. S. (2 Wallace) 404; 17 L. Ed 915 (10 March 1865).

[122] *McElvain v. Mudd*, 44 Ala 48; 4 Am Rep 106 (Jan 1870) (Dissent by J Peters ¶23) discussing Thirteenth Amendment abolishing slavery stating it is "not the language of repeal; it does not acknowledge that slavery

ever rested upon statute law, or upon right; but it denies its authority [no] longer to exist".

[123] *Biafore v. Baker*, 119 Mich App 667, 326 N W 2d.598, (1982); *The T. J. Hooper*, 60 F2d 737, 740 (CA 2 1932).

[124] *Marbury v. Madison*, 5 U. S. (2 Cranch) 137, 174, 176; 2 LE 60 (1803) ruling that "All laws which are repugnant to the Constitution are null and void".

[125] Stephen B. Presser, *Book Review*, 14 Const. Comment., 229 (1997).

[126] Robert J. Reinstein, *Completing the Constitution: The Declaration of Independence, Bill of Rights and Fourteenth Amendment*, 66 Temple L. Rev. 361, 362-363 (1993).

[127] In the year 1867 in *Cummings v. Missouri* and *Ex parte Garland* the Supreme Court—by way of Chief Justice Salmon P. Chase condemned bills of attainder and ex post facto laws the passage of post-American Civil War loyalty-test oaths—which were designed to keep Confederate sympathizers from practicing certain professions. Chief Justice Chase, in a court whose majority narrowly construed the postwar Thirteenth and Fourteenth Amendments to the Constitution, he tried to protect the rights of black Americans from infringement by state action.

[128] *Josephine, a slave v. State of Mississippi*, 39 Miss (10 Geo; 19 Miss Annot Ed) 613, 647 (Oct 1861).

[129] *Casey v. Piphus*, 545 F2d 30 (CA 7, Ill, 1977) rev'd and remanded 435 U S 247; 98 S Ct 1042; 55 L Ed 252 (1978) damages for procedural due process violation is an "absolute" constitutional right.

[130] *In re African-American Descendants Litigation*, 304 F. Supp. 2d 1027 (N.D.Ill.2004). This was a lawsuit brought by descendants of slaves seeking relief from private

corporations who had allegedly profited from the institution of slavery. The federal judge rejected the case citing three procedural points: standing, the statute of limitations and political question doctrine.

[131] For the chattel principle as central to the definition of slavery, see Moses J. Finley, *Ancient Slavery and Modern Ideology*, (New York: Viking Press, 1980): Claude Meillasoux, *The Anthropology of Slavery: The Womb of Iron and Gold* (Chicago: University of Chicago Press (1991) and David Brion Davis, *Inhuman Bondage: The Rise and Fall of Slavery in the New World*, (New York: Oxford University Press, 2006).

[132] *Shanley v. Harvey*, 2 Eden 126 (Chancery, March 1762) ruling that "As soon as a man puts foot on English ground, he is free".

[133] Lysander Spooner, *Unconstitutionality of Slavery*, Boston: Bela Marsh (1845).

[134] William M. Wiecek, *Somerset's Case, Encyclopedia of the American Constitution*, Leonard W. Levy and Kenneth L. Karst, eds.

[135] Ta-Nehisi Coates, *The Case for Reparation*, The Atlantic (2014). Coates grappled with the rationalization for slavery and their persistence in twentieth-century policies like Jim Crow and redlining. He argues for renumeration for the economic impact on African-Americans denied the ability to accumulate wealth or social status for generations.

[136] William Holdsworth, *History of English Law*, 12; 146 (reprint 1966). Holdsworth stated, that "A [Twelve Judges] decided case makes law for future cases and will bind all inferior courts, and generally courts of co-ordinate jurisdiction."

[137] Taunya Lovell Banks. *Dangerous Women: Elizabeth Key's Freedom Suit – Subjecthood and Racialized Identity in*

Seventeen Century Colonial Virginia, Digital Commons Law, University of Maryland Law School (April 2009).

[138] An example is *R. v. Alexander*, 1 Leach 63, 168 E.R. 134 (Old Bailey 1767). The defendant was a negro servant who was convicted of perjury for falsely swearing in Doctors' Commons that his fiancée was 21 when she was only 16. The evidence corroborated that defendant Joseph Alexander had been accepted in the house of Mr. Nesbit as an instructor for Mr. Nesbit's daughter, Charlotte. Joseph was to teach Charlotte the French language and "other fashionable accomplishments, of which the prisoner was perfect master." Over time, Joseph obtained Charlotte's consent to marry, and this led to the license and his false oath. Joseph as found guilty and committed to Newgate prison, where he died. Obviously, even 16 years old, a female was protected by English law.

[139] The nature of civil government, and of civil law, as defined by English common law repudiated the legalization of slavery. Founder James Madison made the observations that "[T]o secure man's inalienable rights, governments are instituted among men" and consequently, they can have no lawful authority to violate the rights which they exist only to protect".

Made in the USA
Monee, IL
05 February 2020